WHEN A LOVED ONE IS ILL

WHEN A LOVED ONE IS ILL

How to Take Better Care
of Your Loved One,
Your Family, *and* Yourself

by
Leonard Felder, Ph.D.

NAL BOOKS
NEW AMERICAN LIBRARY
A DIVISION OF PENGUIN BOOKS USA INC., NEW YORK
PUBLISHED IN CANADA BY
PENGUIN BOOKS CANADA LIMITED, MARKHAM, ONTARIO

for Martin and Ena Felder,
who have given a lot of love to their children

PUBLISHER'S NOTE

The ideas, procedures, and suggestions contained in this book are not intended as a substitute for consulting with your physician. All matters regarding your health require medical supervision.

Published simultaneously in Canada by Penguin Books Canada Limited

Acknowledgment

When Bad Things Happen to Good People. Copyright © 1981 by Harold S. Kushner. Schocken Books, New York.

 NAL BOOKS TRADEMARK REG. U.S. PAT. OFF. AND FOREIGN COUNTRIES
REGISTERED TRADEMARK—MARCA REGISTRADA
HECHO EN DRESDEN, TN, U.S.A.

SIGNET, SIGNET CLASSIC, MENTOR, ONYX, PLUME, MERIDIAN
and NAL BOOKS are published *in the United States* by New American Library,
a division of Penguin Books USA Inc.,
1633 Broadway, New York, New York 10019,
in Canada by Penguin Books Canada Limited,
2801 John Street, Markham, Ontario L3R 1B4

Library of Congress Cataloging-in-Publication Data

Felder, Leonard.
    When a loved one is ill: how to take better care of your loved
one, your family, and yourself / by Leonard Felder.
        p.   cm.
    ISBN 0-453-00712-0
    1. Critically ill—Family relationships. 2. Terminally ill—
Family relationships. 3. Interpersonal relationships. I. Title.
R726.8.F46   1990
616'.0019—dc20   89-13179
                                                        CIP

Designed by Leonard Telesca

First Printing, February, 1990

1 2 3 4 5 6 7 8 9

PRINTED IN THE UNITED STATES OF AMERICA

Acknowledgments

This book tells the stories of many courageous people who helped an ailing or disabled loved one. I wish to thank the many clients, relatives, teachers, friends, and groups who shared their experiences with me. They include Lucky Altman, The American Association of Retired Persons, The American Society on Aging, Felice Apodaca, Rachel Friedman Ballon, Teri Bernstein, Harold Bloomfield, Adelaide Bry, Catherine Coulson, Jenny Davidow, Susan Dempsey, Angela and Jeff Dondanville, Greg Edmondson, Glen Effertz, Ted Falcon, Christa Festini, Frank and Kathy Fochetta, Lillian Freeman, Melinda Garcia, Carol Ginsburg, Marilyn Graves, Dennis Hicks, Jennifer Jensen, Elisabeth Kübler-Ross, Harold Kushner, Arlene Levin, Bret Lyon, Alice March, The National Alliance for the Mentally Ill, Laura Pawlowski, Helene Pine, Glen Poling, Rhoda Pregerson, Peter Reiss, Barbara Rotman, Janet Ruckert, The Self-Help Clearinghouse, Cheryl Sindell Heller, Marc Sirinsky, Phyllis Solow, Leonora Sommers, Neil and Bernice Van Steenbergen, Sonya and M. Robert Syme, Sirah Vettese, Linda Waddington, and Barbara Waxman.

Special thanks go to my family members, who were extremely helpful in making this book possible. They include Martin and Ena Felder, June and William Schorin, Janice and Craig Ruff, Edward Rothenberg, Gerry Felder, Nellie Kolb, Jeffrey Schorin, Ruth Wilstein, Ron and Colleen Wilstein, David Bayer, Kate Pintz, Andrea Bayer, and Mary Ellen Samuels.

More than anyone else, my wife, Linda Schorin, provided a wealth of ideas and creative suggestions for this book. Her knowledge, love, and encouragement on this and other projects have made a tremendous difference.

Finally, I want to thank my editor, Michaela Hamilton, and my agents, Maureen and Eric Lasher. They believed in this book from the start and helped in numerous ways. It has meant a lot to me to have an editor and agents who felt personally committed to this subject and to the need to assist family members and friends who want to come through for their loved ones.

A Note to the Reader

To protect confidentiality, the names and identifying details in the case histories reported within this book have been changed.

Anyone who has a history of psychiatric disorder, who feels emotionally unstable, or who is taking major tranquilizers or antidepressant medication should not do the exercises in this book without first consulting a qualified mental health professional.

Contents

CHAPTER ONE

The Author's Story

It began with her annual visit to the doctor. "Nothing to worry about—just a checkup," my mom assured me.

I was ten years old. My mother and my best friend Steve's mother both went for breast examinations on the same day. Steve's mom had a lump in her breast which turned out to be benign. My mother's lump was malignant.

Mom was going to lose her breast. What a strange notion for this ten-year-old boy to comprehend. I was at that awkward prepubescent age when my friends and I would giggle and blush if someone uttered the magic word "breasts." Yet suddenly I entered a world of mastectomies, chemotherapy, radiation treatments, and hospitalizations. The cancer seemed to be contained at first, but then it spread.

One afternoon we were alone in the kitchen and my mother turned to me with tears in her eyes as she asked, "Do you think I'll ever be healthy again?"

I didn't know what to say. I was an *A* student, but there were no courses in school on "How to Talk to a Family Member Who's Seriously Ill."

1

For the next four years, I tried to be there for my mom. If she was moody or upset, I assumed there must be something I should be doing to remedy her discomfort. But it's so hard to witness a loved one in pain. No matter how much I tried to help, a voice in the back of my mind said, "You should be doing more."

I had trouble sleeping at night and couldn't concentrate on my schoolwork during the day. I felt guilty about doing anything that might be considered selfish. My father, my sister, and I became worn out physically and emotionally. Even though we wanted to be optimistic, we found ourselves frustrated that all our efforts weren't making my mother well. We each did our best to pretend we were fine, yet her illness was taking a toll on all of us.

The Oxygen Mask

I've often wondered why it is that we neglect to take good care of ourselves when we're attempting to be there for someone who's ailing or disabled. Why do we let ourselves get burned out just when someone needs us the most?

This situation reminds me of the oxygen masks on an airplane. When you are about to take off on a commercial jet, the flight attendant instructs the passengers that in the event of an emergency you must put the oxygen mask over your own face before trying to help the person next to you. Although your first reaction might be to take care of your loved ones, if you're not breathing and healthy, you will be of little use to anyone around you.

On an airplane, it's not selfish to put the oxygen mask over your own face before attempting to help others. In fact, it's essential if you are to be helpful at all.

Yet when a loved one is ailing or disabled, it's hard to think of your own needs. It's more common to ignore your own health and pretend you're OK even when you're not.

Unresolved Questions

Back in 1964, the recovery rate from breast cancer was much lower than it is today. My father, my sister, and I tried to keep my mother alive until the cancer survival rates were higher. But that was not to be. At the age of forty-six, my mother lost her life.

After this four-year ordeal, I felt confused and exhausted. I wondered if I could have done a better job of helping my mother cope with her pain. I thought about what I might have said differently when she asked for my emotional support. Could I have been more honest? Did I miss some key opportunities to really talk about what was going on? I also wondered if I could have taken better care of myself, not getting so run down while taking care of my mom. Was there a way, I wondered, for family members to stay healthy while giving better care to the person who's ailing?

Learning from First-Hand Experience

Unfortunately (or fortunately—I'm not sure which), I have had several additional chances to learn how to take good care of myself while taking better care of an ailing loved one. I've had to discover through trial and error how to navigate these turbulent emotional tides.

Almost ten years ago, I was asked to coauthor a book with Adelaide Bry, a therapist and writer who lived courageously with cancer throughout our working together. During our writing sessions, Adelaide described to me with incredible honesty how it feels to live close to the edge, forced by a prolonged illness to rely on others.

In several conversations that I will never forget, Adelaide told me what an ailing person wants from those who care for her, explaining what made her feel smothered and overprotected as well as what made her feel guilty about placing too much burden on her loved ones.

From Adelaide's courageous battle with cancer, I gained

a wealth of information about how to be a healthy caregiver. She taught me specific ways to regain a sense of balance and keep from burning out, and how to be helpful while respecting a loved one's dignity and right to privacy. Many of her insights and guidelines have helped me as I have counseled people who are caregivers; they have also helped me to write this book.

The Ups and Downs of Long-Term Ailments

I have spent the past nine years learning how to respond better to the needs of a close family member who has been diagnosed with schizophrenia. Even though I learned a lot of textbook information about mental illness during my doctoral training in psychology, it wasn't until a troubled family member was part of my daily life that I truly began to appreciate the complexities of helping someone with a chronic ailment.

Every week, as I spend time with this individual I learn something new about what it means to be a caregiver and a friend. It's only through first-hand experience, I've found, that you can understand the daily ups and downs of long-term care.

You Are Not Alone

When I look back at the four years I watched my mother battle cancer, I remember feeling so incompetent. Yet over the years my own experiences as well as the insights of those I have counseled and interviewed have taught me exactly what's involved in taking excellent care of a loved one without neglecting the emotional needs of your family or yourself.

Although it's normal to feel alone when you're a caregiver, in fact you are in plenty of company. Most of us don't realize that:

- There are over sixty million Americans who are currently faced with the illness or disability of a loved one.
- On any given day, one out of every four American workers has the added job of responding to the needs of an ailing parent, child, sibling, lover, spouse, or friend.
- One out of every four families has a close relative who has been disabled, physically ill, or mentally ill for more than six months.
- Every year the number of support groups, seminars, and organizations to help families assist their ailing relatives is increasing.

I have collected personal stories of dozens of women and men who have been successful in taking good care of themselves even as they took excellent care of their loved one. Their accomplishments at times of crisis are inspiring. More importantly, their insights, techniques, and resources are included here to help guide you through.

Every Family Member is Affected

A relative's prolonged illness or disability has a powerful impact on each family member. Even the silent members of your family who seem to be "handling it so well" might be suffering inside and holding in feelings that can erupt later in unfortunate health problems.

Quite often other family members are silent about the stress they undergo when a loved one is ill. This is especially true in dysfunctional families—those in which there is alcoholism, drug abuse, emotional abuse, or an unwillingness to discuss feelings openly and honestly. If the people in your family have trouble expressing their emotions to begin with, the illness of a close relative can make them even more secretive.

When relatives are facing an illness or disability, there is usually one member who tends to be "the rescuer"—the person who, trying to take care of everyone else, becomes burned out. If that lonely rescuer role has fallen into your lap, you may find yourself at risk of becoming physically or emotionally drained.

Sharing the Work

Taking care of others is an important human activity that hasn't been shared equally by men and women in our society. Research shows that more than seventy percent of the people who shoulder most of the caregiving tasks are women. Just as women have been traditionally underpaid and undcracknowledged for homemaker tasks, so have they been undervalued for caregiving tasks.

My personal goal for this book is not only to help female caregivers who have been taken for granted much too long, but also to show compassionate males how to excel at a job that is the responsibility of both women *and* men. There is a tremendous dignity in helping someone who needs you. Whether it's your child, parent, sibling, spouse, lover, or friend, being of service is one of the most meaningful human challenges.

My hope is that in the coming years people will value caregivers more highly and understand more deeply the stresses they suffer and the courage they display. I'm not going to hold my breath waiting for our society to pay higher salaries to caregivers than it pays to "socially important" jobs like corporate takeover specialists or weapons designers. But I foresee a time when caregiving becomes a more respected priority in our personal and political values.

As the French essayist Montaigne once said, "To storm a beach, conduct an embassy, govern a people—these are brilliant actions; however, to deal gently and justly with one's family and oneself—that is something rarer, more difficult and less noticed in the world."

What to Expect from This Book

Whether you are male or female, the responsibility of helping a loved one who's ailing or disabled is a challenging job. Even if you now feel inadequate to deal with the many difficulties that have entered your daily life, be aware that you can become more adept at responding to the needs of your loved ones. And you have the capability of becoming more effective at addressing your own legitimate needs and feelings.

In the chapters that follow, you will be taken on a journey that can bring you some relief. You will be introduced to people who have walked a similar path to the one you are on now. How did they resolve the emotional and financial issues that you currently face? How did they make sure they weren't swept away by the responsibility of caring for someone in need? How did they manage to successfully come through for the ailing or disabled person?

I won't promise any easy answers, but I believe that by learning from the experiences of others, we each can become more adept at dealing with this important challenge.

You have to make the fundamental choice on how to respond to your loved one's situation. Taking care of someone who needs your support can be a burden or a tremendous gift. It can make you put up walls and hide from the responsibility, or it can make you courageous and strong.

My hope is that this book will help you turn this crisis into one of the most meaningful and loving times of your life. If you truly care about the person who is ill or disabled, you owe it to both of you to discover how to meet this challenge.

CHAPTER TWO

"But How are *You* Holding Up?"

If someone you love is ailing or disabled, you probably can appreciate what happened to Eleanor, a forty-eight-year-old woman with three grown children and a job in advertising. Eleanor's husband, Gordon, recently was diagnosed with a serious illness and is undergoing treatments at home. During a hectic week of juggling her double responsibilities of working full time and caring for her husband, Eleanor arrived at her office on a Friday morning. Here she describes what happened:

> As I walked in the door at work, the receptionist said "Good morning," and asked, "How's your husband feeling?"
>
> I appreciated her concern and told her he's in some pain but we're hoping for the best.
>
> Then at the Friday morning department meeting, my boss asked, "How's Gordon?" I said he was doing OK under the circumstances.
>
> At lunch, my closest friend from the office stopped

eating right in the middle of her tuna salad sandwich. She leaned forward with a great deal of concern in her expression. I thought she was going to tell me she was having an affair or something like that. But instead she asked, "Really, tell me the honest truth. How *is* Gordon?"

When I left work at five-thirty and stopped by the cleaners, the man behind the counter asked, "How's Gordon holding up?"

Then at the supermarket, I ran into an old neighbor of ours and she wanted to know, "Is Gordon OK? I heard he wasn't doing so well."

As soon as I got home and walked in the door, the phone rang. It was my mother-in-law calling to ask, "Is Gordon all right? Did he get enough sleep last night? What did the doctors say?"

I didn't realize how much this was beginning to affect me until my youngest daughter, Jenny, called and asked, "How is everything?" I began to tell her about how Gordon was when Jenny stopped me and said, "Mom, relax, we'll talk about Dad in a second. But first, how are *you* holding up?"

That question caught me by surprise.

I started to say, "Don't worry about me. I'm fine." But there were tears in my eyes. Jenny was the first person in weeks who noticed that I was hurting, too. It made me cry to have someone ask, "But how are *you* holding up?"

First Reactions

When someone you care about has been diagnosed with a serious condition, it might seem at first that you are an outside observer and that only the person with the ailment is going through major changes. All the attention is focused on your loved one and your own issues and problems seem minor by comparison.

However, the illness or disability of someone you love is a

powerful force that dramatically affects your own life as well. Plans are put on hold. People treat you differently. Small problems of daily living feel like more crises to deal with. Important decisions have to be made. Expectations of the future are suddenly altered. Even your notion of who you are, or what your priorities are, may be thrown into turmoil.

For most of us, the first reaction is shock and disbelief. Which of these examples from people I've counseled sound familiar to you?

When the phone rang and I got the bad news, I couldn't take it in. He looks great, so how was I supposed to accept this ominous-sounding diagnosis?

We were stunned when the doctor said she might need to come in for more tests. This was *not* supposed to happen. We had plans for a trip that we'd been anticipating for months. Suddenly all of our plans were put on hold.

What upsets me is not just that my child is ill. Children are always coming down with one thing or another. What frightens me is that with this kind of illness, he may never become the person he could have been.

I always thought my partner would grow old gracefully. It never occurred to me that he would suffer like this or become so dependent and unable to care for himself.

Going to the hospital each day has become a ritual and I've adjusted to it. But what I haven't adjusted to yet is that the whole world looks different to me now. I used to be the kind of person who could put things aside and sleep peacefully at night no matter what. Now I wake up night after night with so much on my mind. Decisions. Feelings. Questions. I seem to be questioning everything now.

Something Has Jolted Your World

For the past eleven years I've lived in California and had my first experiences with earthquakes. While some people take these rumblings and shakings in stride, my background in Michigan, Ohio, Pennsylvania, and New York didn't prepare me to be jolted out of bed at five in the morning. I never thought I'd see furniture doing the cha-cha while bowls rattled on shelves because the earth had indigestion. Even the noisiest New York subways never made me feel as uneasy as I've felt during an earthquake, with the floor under my feet literally bouncing and swaying.

The shakiness of an earthquake has always reminded me of the feelings of disorientation I've experienced when someone close to me was seriously ill. It's as though the ground that seemed so secure a minute ago has suddenly moved in an unexpected direction and is no longer trustworthy. And you can't predict when the next aftershock or piece of bad news will shake you up again. You're never quite the same when your world is jolted—by an earthquake or by the illness of someone you love. Even if you're the kind of person who can take most things in stride, the thought of a loved one in discomfort can throw you off balance in several ways.

Assessing the Situation

Immediately after a major earthquake it's customary to check and see what areas of your home and community have shifted or fallen out of place. Government workers flying in helicopters check the dams, reservoirs, and freeway bridges to make sure they aren't cracking or collapsing. Owners of homes and apartment buildings check their water heaters for gas leaks caused by the quake. Most people inspect their offices and living spaces to see if there are cracks in the ceiling, books needing to be reshelved or picture frames to be straightened.

When your life gets shaken up by the serious illness of a loved one, there is a similar need to take note of certain key changes. Remember, the ailment or disability is not only affecting your family member—it also has a profound impact on every person in the family, including yourself.

What are some of the areas of your life that have shifted or fallen out of place because of an illness in the family:

- Have you cut yourself off from some of your closest friends because of the family crisis?
- Are there splits and tensions emerging between certain family members who are doing most of the caregiving tasks and those who aren't helping out at all?
- Are you noticing major shifts and interruptions in your daily schedule as a result of someone you love needing help with errands, appointments, and frequent dilemmas?
- Are there stresses between you and the person who's ailing or disabled?
- Are you finding it difficult to relax and unwind at the end of each busy day?

You Need Sustenance

If you recognized yourself in one or more of these stressful changes, I want to welcome you to the club. Millions of people who are concerned about someone in need go through these aftershocks on a daily basis. The good news is that there are many proven ways to reduce these stresses so you can take better care of your loved one, your family, and yourself. The bad news is that these challenges are not likely to disappear overnight. It will take time and persistence. Even though we might wish everything could quickly go back to the way it was before, it's more productive to face the fact that your world has been altered somewhat by the ailment of someone who's important to you.

Unfortunately, most people react to the illness of a loved one as if it were a fifty-yard dash, when in fact it's more like a marathon. You need to pace yourself and get sustenance or you will collapse long before the finish line. You need to look closely at the support and nourishment you will require to stay healthy for your loved one's benefit over the long haul.

Here's a case that illustrates what I mean by pacing yourself:

I recently counseled Barbara, a woman in her fifty's who was beginning to grow weary because of the pressures of taking care of her ailing mother. Every single day Barbara was faced with a different crisis or a difficult decision. On Monday her mother suffered a bad fall and needed to see the doctor. On Tuesday there was an argument with the housekeeper whom Barbara's mother had been complaining about for weeks.

On Wednesday Barbara was hurt when her mother stared directly at her and called her by her younger sister's name. As Barbara admitted, "No matter how much I do for my mother and how little my sister helps out, I know my sister will still be her favorite."

On Thursday there was a fight with the insurance company that was refusing to cover certain bills from the most recent hospitalization. On Friday Barbara received a long-distance phone call that her daughter's engagement had broken off for the second time. Just an average week in the life of a caregiver.

When Barbara and I talked about how she could cope better with these and other stresses, we came up with several specific ideas that could not only improve her own well-being but also enhance her mother's quality of life.

But then I asked Barbara a question she wasn't expecting, "When was the last time you had a good laugh?" Barbara looked at me as though I were kidding. When I let her know I was serious, she thought for a moment and replied, "It's been a long time."

Like most dutiful daughters, Barbara had become so accustomed to the daily crisis of caregiving that she had forgotten how to enjoy herself. She felt she no longer had time for movies or walks by the water or a relaxing lunch with a close friend. Prior to her mother's illness, Barbara was a healthy and energetic person who had several good friends. Now she was aging quickly herself and had drifted away from most of her closest companions.

I urged Barbara to schedule a day off for herself. At first she resisted, saying, "I can't. My mother needs me."

But as we talked, Barbara began to remember how much she used to enjoy spending a relaxing Saturday or Sunday afternoon with her long-time friend Paula. Ever since high school they had been able to make each other laugh. No matter what crisis either friend was going through with men or jobs, children or finances, they could always get together and wind up laughing heartily about some small thing.

I told Barbara to try not to think of time off as something selfish or self-indulgent, but as a break that would not only benefit her *but also her mother*. I pointed out that unless she finds a way to relax and unwind, she'll soon become impatient and less effective in caring for her mother's needs.

The next Saturday, Barbara spent four hours relaxing with Paula. They caught up on each other's lives and they laughed a lot. Paula even presented Barbara with an exquisite bowl of chicken soup—caregivers need chicken soup too!

Those four hours of sustenance didn't solve all the problems Barbara was facing. *But it was a start.* It replenished Barbara's internal resources, giving her the strength to keep going.

So let me ask you the question: "How are *you* holding up?"

If it's been too long since you were able to laugh, to relax with a friend, to spend quiet moments in a natural setting, or to have someone lovingly prepare a bowl of soup for *you,* now is your chance to stop being a martyr. Who can you call right now to schedule a few hours replenishing your strength and maybe even having a good time? If the first person you call is unavailable, don't give up. Who is your second choice for someone whose support can help renew your energies? Who is your third choice? Make sure you don't give up until you find someone who can join you in a few hours of sustenance and renewal.

What is Success as a Caregiver?

There's a tremendous satisfaction in knowing that you are giving from the heart to someone you love. As Emerson once said,

> To share often and much . . .
> to know even one life has breathed easier
> because you have lived.
> This is to have succeeded.

However, if you don't take better care of yourself you won't have that feeling of satisfaction. You will become overwhelmed and exhausted because of the demands in caring for someone who's ill. I can't force you to start looking for support and sustenance. But I can guarantee that your ailing loved one will benefit as you discover ways to regain your strength and renew your energies of love and care.

To continue to act like a martyr not only wears you down but hurts the person who needs you. Searching for a sense of balance is crucial if you want to successfully help another human being.

CHAPTER THREE

Rising to the Challenge

Imagine being hired for a job and then finding out that you've been hired not just for one job but five jobs at the same time.

That may sound strange, but in fact that's what you probably are experiencing on a daily basis in your role of helping someone who's ill or disabled.

Being a caregiver—someone who responds effectively to the needs of a family member or friend—isn't just one job. If you do it well, it usually entails at least five separate jobs, including networker, part-time nurse, motivational coach, errand runner, and spiritual counselor.

Let's look at these jobs one at a time to help you learn ways to become more skillful and effective at them.

Networker

One of the most valuable things you can do for a loved one who's ailing or disabled is to become a better information-seeker and expert-finder. Nearly every day a question will arise that requires your skill in finding the right people who can help your loved one. For example, you may need to improve your efficiency as a networker in order to locate the following:

- The right doctors, treatment programs, and physical therapists for a specific ailment
- The latest information on new medications, their side effects and potential benefits
- The right housekeeper or home-care nurse for your family member or friend
- The highest quality nursing home or board-and-care facility you can afford
- The best day-care facilities in your area
- The best support group and community resources that have experience with this particular ailment
- The most reliable rehabilitation specialists in your community
- The names and phone numbers of patients who have benefited from a specific treatment program
- Specialized equipment to help your loved one become more mobile and active
- An information hotline with knowledgeable people available to help you with specific questions

Believe it or not, you are only a few phone calls away from the most reliable answers to each of these pressing problems. However, many people have a tough time with the job of networker for a variety of reasons. See if any of these hesitations sound like you or someone you know:

- Some people are naturally shy or reserved. They find it difficult to be assertive on the telephone or to call up several strangers to ask for advice or referrals.
- Many people are easily frustrated and they give up when they encounter a rude or apathetic bureaucrat, or if the first several phone calls provide no new answers.

- Most families are secretive about an illness or disability and are reluctant to ask for help from people they don't know.
- Most people are too busy to spend a lot of time researching at great length for the right answers to a health-care problem. They would rather settle for whatever the first person they reach recommends, even if it's more costly or less effective than what they could find with additional phone calls.

Becoming a More Effective Networker

Over the past several years, I have spoken with hundreds of people who have an ailing or disabled loved one. Repeatedly I have seen that one of the fundamental differences between those caregivers who feel overwhelmed or helpless and those caregivers who take charge and get results has to do with learning to be a better networker.

Like most challenges in life, becoming a better networker has pluses and minuses. One of the pluses is that you don't need a graduate degree or a fancy certificate to become a better resource-finder for your loved one. Anyone can do it!

One of the minuses is that you may need to become as pushy as Woodward and Bernstein, the two reporters who unraveled the Watergate scandal. If you've ever read the book or seen the movie, *All the President's Men,* you'll recall that Bob Woodward and Carl Bernstein (played by Robert Redford and Dustin Hoffman in the movie version) refused to give up or stop searching for answers no matter what obstacles they encountered. People slammed doors in their faces. Sometimes it took ten or twenty phone calls to unravel an important piece of information. Often they had to keep asking the same questions until they found the person who could provide them with a crucial fact that opened up a whole new avenue. With stubborn perseverance, they eventually uncovered the secrets of the Watergate scandal and changed the course of history.

The next time you are looking for answers for your loved one and you hit some obstacles or delays, give yourself permission to be as pushy and persistent as Woodward and Bernstein. Even if you are a shy person or feel unfamiliar when networking on health issues the more you do it the easier it gets. Don't be afraid to make that first call. Don't give up until you find the facts or resources that can improve the quality of life for the person you care about. Even if it takes a dozen phone calls, you need the best answers and solutions that can be found at a reasonable cost.

But how do you locate the right people to call? Where can you learn about the most up-to-date information and resources? If you're new to networking health services, how do you get good at it quickly? And if you live far from your ailing family member or friend, how do you locate the best resources in his or her community?

Here are the steps taken by caregivers like yourself who learned quickly to find the best answers available to help their loved ones. See which of the following tasks you already are performing well and which steps you can take to become an even more efficient networker:

Call the information clearinghouses for this person's specific ailment or disability. If you look in Appendix B at the back of this book, you will find hotlines and referral services that specialize in all the major illnesses (AIDS, Alzheimer's, Asthma, Autism, Cancer, Cerebral Palsy, Childhood Disabilities, Cystic Fibrosis, Diabetes, Down's Syndrome, Epilepsy, Emphysema, Heart Disease, Hodgkins, Huntington's, Manic Depression, Multiple Sclerosis, Muscular Dystrophy, Myasthenia Gravis, Parkinson's, Schizophrenia, Spinal Cord Injuries, Strokes, and many others).

Even if your loved one has an *extremely rare* illness or disability, there are numbers to call in Appendix B to receive knowledgeable advice and specialized referrals to the resources that are most convenient for you and your loved one.

Ask the doctors, nurses, and case workers at your local

hospital or clinic about where you can find specialized re-sources to help your loved one. You will often be surprised at how much practical information you can receive by asking the people who specialize in a particular ailment.

Call your local service agencies. There are many such resources like the county health department, your area agency for the aging, the department of social services, Jewish Family Service, Catholic Social Services, or other denominational support organizations. You can ask your minister, priest, or rabbi for the agencies to call. Ask for information about where to find local answers to any of your pressing needs.

Send for and read the pamphlets, books, and guides listed in Appendix A at the back of this book. You can become far more knowledgeable and effective in helping your relative or friend if you stay informed and up-to-date. You can also pass these written materials along to other members of your family who may need some additional information to help them understand and appreciate the intricacies of your loved one's ailment.

Find a support group in your area. Support groups are extremely useful for people who are seeking reliable information and treatment programs for their loved one's condition. While many people shy away from anything called a "support group" because they mistakenly think it will be a therapy encounter group, in fact most support groups are networking opportunities to exchange valuable information about how to help an ailing relative or friend. People like you and me get together once a week or once a month to exchange problem-solving information for the caregiving challenges we have in common.

If no support group exists in your area, you may want to start one. For more information about how to locate an existing group or start a new one, see Appendix C.

"I No Longer Feel So Helpless"

As a counselor, one of the great satisfactions of my work comes from helping a caregiver make the transition from feeling powerless or overwhelmed to eventually becoming more empowered and effective. This transition often takes place once a person taps into a wealth of practical information and community resources. For example:

Donna is a fifty-nine-year-old woman who was filled with anxieties and legitimate concerns after her husband suffered a serious heart attack. According to Donna:

> I had so many uncertainties to deal with. Should my husband be back at work or will the stress worsen his condition? What are the right foods and exercises to lessen the risk of another heart attack? Should we avoid making love? Should we ride bicycles for recreation or is that too strenuous? Should we switch doctors? Are there special treatment and prevention programs that we can afford?
>
> For several weeks after my husband's heart attack, I felt as though no one was available to answer all my questions. Our doctor always seemed to be in a hurry and my friends kept giving me their unsubstantiated opinions about how to take care of a heart patient.
>
> But then I found out about a hotline for questions about heart ailments, and I also went to a support group meeting for relatives of heart patients. For the first time since my husband's illness, I no longer felt so helpless. With these phone referral services and support group meetings, no question was off-limits and no one criticized me for asking whatever was on my mind. Suddenly I had dozens of reliable people to call for answers to every difficult issue that came up.
>
> Instead of feeling uncertain and indecisive, I had tapped into an extensive network of specialists, clinics, experts on various medications, and information about day-to-

day patient care. While I still have some occasional worries about my husband's recovery, I at least know where to go for excellent advice and emotional support.

Guy, thirty-two, has a developmentally disabled younger brother named Brian. According to Guy:

For many years I was impatient with Brian. I couldn't really tell when he was playing for sympathy and being difficult on purpose, or when he actually couldn't control his actions because of his disability.

But I never wanted to ask anyone too many questions about Brian. I must have assumed that since he's my brother, I'm supposed to know automatically what's troubling him and what to do about it. I never wanted to let anyone know how uninformed and awkward I felt about helping my kid brother.

So I kept my questions to myself and began to avoid Brian and his problems. Then two years ago I finally agreed to make a phone call to one of the local social service agencies that work with people like Brian. I began asking questions and I also showed up for a support group meeting for relatives of the disabled.

I hadn't expected to find out that most of these family members had similar questions and feelings of awkwardness. I discovered I'm not the only one who pulled away from a disabled family member because of lack of understanding.

Most importantly, I learned what's possible and what's unlikely for helping Brian. I made contact with a number of experts and local resource people. Talking with them helped me learn how I can improve the quality of life for Brian in small but meaningful ways. I also learned about an excellent physical rehabilitation program in our community that is affordable and has helped Brian a great deal these past several months. I now feel a lot less impatient with the things Brian can't change and a lot more hopeful about the progress we're making to help him live a more satisfying life.

Caroline, forty-one, insists,

> I'm *not* the kind of person you would see enrolling in therapy or anything called "a support group." That's just not my style.

But three years ago when Caroline's daughter Stacy was diagnosed with schizophrenia, Caroline admits,

> I spent the first year blaming myself and feeling powerless to do very much to help Stacy. I assumed that schizophrenia must be our family's fault and I feared that there was little we could do to help Stacy. I also figured that I would have to deal with this on my own. I didn't want to talk about it with my friends or relatives. And my husband certainly didn't want to confront the reality of Stacy's condition.

For several months, Caroline was encouraged by one of Stacy's doctors to attend a support group meeting of family caregivers called The Alliance for the Mentally Ill (AMI). But according to Caroline,

> I just didn't want to go. I imagined a bunch of neurotic families sitting around and obsessing about their mentally ill relatives. I thought it would be embarrassing and demeaning to put myself into a situation like that.

When Caroline finally asked a friend to go with her to her first AMI meeting, she discovered something entirely different.

> This group of family members was quite intelligent and not all that neurotic. In fact, the meetings were filled with valuable information on the exact issues that I was finding difficult when dealing with Stacy.

The support group repeatedly came up with useful solutions to my toughest concerns—how to get a mentally ill person to take medications on time; how to find the best doctors and treatment programs; how to handle spending money, bus passes, and other problems of daily living; how to understand the mood swings and angry outbursts; what to do with suicidal threats or self-destructive behaviors; what things can be changed and what things need to be accepted; and how to find programs to help Stacy develop independent living skills and useful job skills.

What I thought was going to be a waste of my time turned into the most productive way of taking charge of a difficult situation. I found out to my surprise that doctors and theorists no longer believe mental illness is caused by the family. Stacy had a predisposition for schizophrenia and no one can tell exactly what causes that first break. But I now can stop blaming myself or feeling ashamed about my daughter's situation.

I'm also lucky that there are monthly group meetings not far from where I live. At each session, we put our experiences together and come up with creative ways to be more successful with our ailing loved ones. Every month there are new challenges and difficulties to resolve. But it's a relief to be able to brainstorm with caring individuals who are coping with similar situations.

Like Donna, Guy, and Caroline, all of us start out reluctant to ask for advice and assistance. Especially in our highly individualistic society, it's hard to admit out loud, "I need some support here. This is new for me."

Yet when you have unanswered questions and a strong desire to help a relative or friend, it's time to push through your hesitations and start making the phone calls that can get you in touch with valuable experts and helpful allies. *You don't have to solve all your loved one's concerns by yourself.* There are knowledgeable individuals and organizations who can help. Use the phone numbers and addresses in Appendix B and Appendix C to start becoming a more effective networker for your loved one. Not only will you be helping your loved one, you will be helping yourself as well.

Part-Time Nurse

Most people think you can simply send your ailing loved one to a hospital or clinic for treatment. In fact, most illnesses and disabilities involve a small percentage of time when health-care professionals are doing the work and a *huge* percentage of time when family and friends are performing the caregiving chores.

Yet unless you are a trained nurse, you will need a quick course in how to perform many of the complicated caregiving tasks that your relative or friend needs from you. The biggest mistake many people make is to pretend they know what they're doing. You can injure yourself and your loved one by attempting to perform delicate nursing maneuvers without proper instruction.

Here are several things you can do to become a better "part-time nurse," even if you've never been formally trained:

Call your local senior citizen centers and social service agencies. Find out if anyone is giving a brief course on how to take care of a dependent loved one. Many local centers give these courses several times a year for family caregivers with no previous training.

Talk to your favorite nurse practitioner or physical therapist. Find a few minutes to ask questions and get some practical advice, or take him or her out for lunch or coffee—away from the distraction of home or office. Ask this person to explain to you all the intricate details of how to help your loved one.

Find out all you can about how to lift and turn someone properly. This is essential to prevent injuring the other person or causing a spasm in your own back muscles. When you receive instruction in lifting and turning someone, make sure you have the opportunity to be the patient at least once during the demonstration. This will allow you to find out what it feels like to be lifted or turned improperly and will give you a better understanding of your loved one's needs.

Be sure to take a first-aid course on how to respond to various emergencies that can arise. If you know ahead of time what to do in case of a heart attack, choking, a bad fall, a convulsion, or other situations, you will be less anxious and more useful for your family member or friend. While most people would rather put their heads in the sand and pretend nothing like this could ever happen, I've seen many caregivers become more confident and helpful after taking a first-aid course. Even if they never needed to use the specific skills they learned in the course, the fact that they took it seems to make them feel less overwhelmed by the responsibility of taking care of someone else.

Receiving some instruction in a few of the specialized talents of a nurse can make a significant difference in the overall approach you take to caregiving. Instead of feeling like an awkward or useless onlooker, you will have a greater sense of your own ability to come through no matter what your loved one needs.

For example, Irene, fifty-three, has an elderly widowed father who used to be athletic and active in many business and recreational pursuits. But in the last four years he has had several illnesses and recently was diagnosed with Alzheimer's Disease. According to Irene:

> The toughest job for me was making the adjustment from seeing my dad as a strong, two-hundred-pound man to appreciating how vulnerable and dependent he has become. His memory is no longer sharp and he sometimes doesn't have the strength to dress himself or brush his own teeth.
>
> At first I tried to do everything to take care of him, even though I have no experience as a nurse or a home-care aide. But after taking a brief course at a local

seniors center, I realized I was making a lot of unnecessary mistakes.

Now I know how to lift him without straining my back or possibly causing him to be injured. I found out some innovative ways to make it easier for him to bathe himself, brush his own teeth, and get some exercise each day.

I also discovered how to work more successfully with a home-care nurse. While we can't afford one seven days a week, I've figured out how to get the most benefit from the person who comes in to help us out two days a week.

I wouldn't say that taking care of an Alzheimer's patient is easy, but I would estimate that it's become 40 percent easier since I got some instruction on how to do it more intelligently. What I don't understand is why I waited more than two years before admitting that I needed some help to do a better job for my father.

If your role as a caregiver includes the responsibility of performing various physical chores and nursing skills, please don't assume you're supposed to know it all automatically. Nurses, home-care aides, and physical therapists are highly trained people and they've learned how to do various procedures with less strain on themselves and the patient. Your job as a family member or friend is to learn whatever you can about how to perform these intricate procedures more intelligently. Make sure you take advantage of whatever courses, workshops, or personalized instruction you can find in your community.

Motivational Coach

Another important job that nearly every caregiver does from time to time is that of the "Motivational Coach." This job entails:

- Helping your loved one stick with the treatment or recovery steps that have been prescribed by a doctor or other health professional.

- Knowing what to do and what not to do when the ailing person ignores the doctor's advice or abandons the treatment program.
- Helping your family member or friend have a positive attitude and work toward realistic goals.
- Assisting your loved one in taking good care of himself or herself *without* the two of you nagging each other or becoming adversaries.

Becoming a more successful motivational coach for your family member or friend is no simple task. There are plenty of obstacles you will encounter along the way. For instance:

If your loved one tended to be stubborn or to rebel against your advice on important matters *prior* to the illness or disability, then you can expect he or she will continue to be stubborn and resist your advice and suggestions now as well.

Also, some people have trouble admitting that the ailment is real or that progress is possible. In these cases, you can expect some resistance to whatever positive suggestions you make.

Finally, if you tend to be impatient, you may find yourself battling your loved one overtly or in subtle ways. For example, if you and this individual have different styles of making decisions—if one of you makes decisions quickly and the other likes to move slowly and cautiously—there may be a battle over whose way is best. You may feel strongly that there's one right way to respond to a crisis, while your relative or friend feels just as strongly about a different approach.

Looking at your own situation for a moment, what have been some of the motivational issues so far? Has it been difficult to help your family member or friend follow medical advice? Has your loved one resisted certain constructive steps you wanted to pursue? Have you felt impatient or judgmental at times because this person has ignored your good advice? Have there been times when you felt you were battling each other and you wished you could be partners on the same side of the battle?

The key to being a more successful motivational coach is not to fight about whose way is right or who's in control. Becoming adversaries and battling one another only makes matters worse. It's more productive and a lot more sensible to remain allies with your ailing loved one as you face these difficult challenges. Even if you disagree about specific steps or if one of you feels stubborn, you still need to remember that you're in this together. You both want what's best for your relative or friend, even if you hold different opinions about what that might be.

Here are some ways to remain allies rather than adversaries as you motivate your loved one to take reasonable steps toward improvement:

Find out why this person is afraid or reluctant to take the next constructive step forward. Instead of judging or criticizing your loved one, take a moment to patiently ask this person, "What do you anticipate will happen if you take the next step? What can I do to make it feel safer and less threatening?" Having empathy is a lot more productive than becoming impatient or judgmental.

Recognize that your job is to love this person whether or not he or she abides by your way of doing things. You can give advice and make suggestions, but at a certain point you need to let go and accept the fact that you can't control another individual. Respect that this is an autonomous person who will do what he or she wants whether you like it or not.

Don't take it personally if your loved one listens to other people instead of you. It's a simple fact of life that we often resist the advice of those who are closest to us, even if it's good advice. If a parent suggests something constructive to a child, the child often will do the opposite just to assert her or his independence. If a spouse or lover recommends something to the partner, quite often the partner will resist the advice until an outside authority—a doctor, nurse, pamphlet, book, or article—confirms the same advice.

Instead of feeling personally disrespected when your relative or friend ignores your good advice, recognize that rebelliousness and independence are important parts of what make human beings tick. If you take it personally and say, "But why are you listening to this doctor's advice when I've been telling you the same thing for months?" you miss the point of what's important. Your loved one has probably heard your advice and resisted it a bit because you two are so close to one another. But when he or she heard it again from an outside source it made more sense. Be grateful that your family member or friend is taking a positive step forward and accept the fact that it had to come from someone other than you.

Don't expect your loved one to be rational all the time. Especially when an illness or disability occurs, we human beings have a variety of defense mechanisms and hesitations that come into play. As Elisabeth Kubler-Ross pointed out in her best-selling books on coping with serious illnesses, there are several stages that usually take place before we accept and deal rationally with painful news. These stages include denial and isolation, anger, bargaining, depression, and acceptance. If you want to be a successful motivational coach, then you need to recognize these stages in your loved one and appreciate that all individuals move through these stages at their own rate. You may want to read some of the books listed in Appendix A or talk to a counselor, nurse, or social worker about the stages of acceptance that both patients and relatives tend to go through because we are human.

"I Can't Control His/Her Every Move"

Here is an example that illustrates the difficulties of the job of motivational coach and suggests some ways to do it more effectively:

Julia is a fifty-three-year-old woman whose husband Anthony has a severe respiratory illness that requires a strict regimen of medications, treatments, and stress reduction in order to stabilize or improve.

The problem for Julia was that Anthony stubbornly refused to stick to the doctor's orders. Sometimes he forgot to take his medications. Occasionally he wouldn't show up for treatments. Some days he would say he didn't feel like using his respirator to clear his clogged lung passages. Frequently he would allow his stresses at work to pile up, which often led to another setback that put him back in intensive care.

At first Julia tried to be patient and let Anthony do things his own way. But after her husband had two more flare-ups and hospitalizations, her impatience and irritation began to increase. For several months, Julia hounded Anthony and tried to make sure he kept up with his medications and treatments.

Julia discovered, however, that Anthony was going out of his way to resist her suggestions. The more she demanded that he take better care of himself, the more he rebelled and found ways to avoid his medications and physical therapy appointments.

Eventually their marriage became a power struggle, with Julia picking at Anthony with sarcastic remarks about his stubbornness and Anthony irritating Julia in his silent but revengeful way. For instance, if Julia spent several days trying to arrange an appointment with a specialist, Anthony would come up with a last-minute excuse for canceling it. If Julia took steps to improve Anthony's diet and avoid foods that aggravated his respiratory condition, Anthony found a way to eat the forbidden foods when he was on his own at work.

When Julia and I spoke about her battles with Anthony, she admitted: "I'm furious at him for being so stubborn. But more than that, I'm terrified that he's going to die unless he starts following the treatment program more conscientiously."

Like many caregivers, Julia was caught in a bind. The

more she tried to help her husband, the more he resisted her and even went so far as to jeopardize his own health. Was there a way of motivating and helping Anthony without making matters worse?

To be a successful motivational coach for someone who's ailing or disabled, you have to learn when to push and when to relax. There's a middle ground between doing too little and doing too much to help someone. To find that middle ground, Julia needed to begin by working on her own impatience and tendency to be judgmental.

I urged Julia to talk with Anthony about when she could help him and when she should back off. I also suggested that she talk with a few nurses and caseworkers at the clinic where Anthony received his treatments. In those conversations, Julia discovered that Anthony wasn't the only patient who occasionally rebelled against the strict regimens of treatment. Nor was he the only patient who sometimes fell into denial and acted against his own best interests in order to maintain a sense of independence. As one nurse told Julia,

> These patients hate the feeling of constriction that they have to endure every single day because of the respiratory illness. The last thing they need is more constriction because of well-intentioned but overly critical loved ones.

When Julia talked about this issue with Anthony, he reinforced what the nurse had said. Anthony admitted,

> Sometimes I feel so much pressure to get better that I begin to tighten up from all the advice and rules I have to follow. I know you care about me, but when you give me too much advice all I can think about is pulling back and doing things my own way.

Instead of judging Anthony or seeing him as a rebellious adversary, Julia gradually began to understand the reasons for his self-defeating behaviors. As she explained,

I can understand his desire to have some control, even if it's a negative kind of control. I don't like it and I wish he could be more sensible and follow the doctor's guidelines. But I do appreciate that he's human and I need to focus on what works, not on what I happen to believe is "the right way."

The next step for Julia and for anyone else who wants to be a successful motivational coach was to start catching herself every time she began to react with impatience, sarcasm, or too much advice. I urged her to take a ten-minute break whenever she noticed herself hounding or battling Anthony. During those ten minutes, Julia could write in her journal, meditate, take a relaxing walk, have a soothing shower or bath, or call a good friend to release her frustrations about Anthony. The important goal is to take charge of one's own impatience rather than trying, ineffectively, to change your loved one.

Using these techniques, Julia achieved noticeable results.

The more I take time to relax and not panic when Anthony is stubborn, the easier it is to encourage him to get back on the program. I realized that what he really wants from me is not to hound him or attack him with advice that makes me sound like a nagging parent.

What he really needs from me is love and steady support. That means if I bring him printed material and medical pamphlets, I need to let him read the material at his own pace and make up his own mind. I can take him to experts and provide him with good alternatives, but in the final analysis it's his body and his life.

What I've discovered is that if I'm calm and level-headed, he will eventually listen when I give him suggestions or remind him that it's time to take his treatments. But if I'm the least bit impatient or judgmental, he feels it and he resists me like a rebellious teenager. I can't control his every move, but I can control how I treat him. And I've found that the less controlling I am toward him, the more cooperative he is. Instead of being adversaries, we can go back to being partners in coping with this illness.

If you too have been feeling impatient or irritated with a loved one who sometimes acts in a stubborn or self-defeating way, now might be a good time to break the pattern. Instead of hounding this person into further resistance, try something new. Start to work on your own feelings of panic and impatience. Begin to recognize that you can't control your loved one, but you can control your own reactions and responses. You can offer your help and advice, but you must recognize that you can't force someone to take it.

One additional step that can help you become a more effective motivational coach is to keep in mind the famous prayer of Reinhold Niebuhr:

> God give us grace to accept with serenity the things that cannot be changed, courage to change the things which should be changed, and the wisdom to distinguish the one from the other.

I recommend that you write these words on a notecard and carry them in your wallet or purse. You can't imagine how often you will benefit from reading this prayer in the middle of a stressful situation when you and your loved one are seeing things differently. By repeating these words, you will be reminded that your job as caregiver is to do the best you can without blaming yourself or the ailing person for being human. The best motivational coach is someone who doesn't waste time and energy battling over things that cannot be changed, but focuses patiently and persistently on those things that can be improved.

Starting today, make sure you improve your effectiveness as a motivational coach by asking: What makes my loved one tick? What does this person need in order to feel supported and encouraged? What does this person not need so as not to feel pressured or trapped? What does he or she usually require before taking a risky step forward? What specific things can I help to change, and what specific things do I need to accept that cannot be changed?

The Errand Runner

This job may seem like the most trivial, but it can often be the most grueling and the most crucial.

Nearly every day there are errands to run, chores to perform, and transportation to provide that can add or subtract from your loved one's quality of life. Each individual chore may seem small by itself, but if you add them all together you will see how important and time-consuming the "Errand Runner" job can be.

For example, look at your own life these past few weeks. Is there one person who's been doing an inordinate amount of errand running and other tasks to help an ailing family member or friend?

How many times have you or this person driven in traffic to take your loved one to an appointment or to pick up an essential item?

How many times have you or this person run errands for the ailing individual and found that the errand took longer or was more complicated than you anticipated?

On how many occasions have you thought it was time to relax, but then realized there were one or two more errands to run?

If you live a great distance from an ailing loved one, do you sometimes worry about who will do the transporting, who will pick up various items, and who will perform important chores for your family member or friend? Long-distance caregiving is especially challenging because you can't be there to personally make sure each important task gets done correctly.

Whether you live near or far from a loved one who needs assistance, errand running is one of the prime causes of burnout and unnecessary worries. More people become anxious and emotionally drained by the demands of all these errands and daily chores than by any other of the five caregiving jobs. But, once again, there are alternatives that can both help your ailing loved one and protect you from exhaustion or anxiety.

Here are some practical suggestions to help you succeed at the errand runner job more intelligently and creatively. See which of these strategies you already are using and which new ones might lighten your load substantially:

Find out about transportation services near your loved one that could free up some of your time. In many communities, there are fully equipped vans that provide free or low-cost rides for ailing or disabled individuals. Most people don't use these services because they don't know about them or they're reluctant to try anything new. But if you call a local seniors center or social services agency and ask them, "Are there any high-quality ride services in this area?," you might be surprised at what you've been missing.

For example, near where I live in Santa Monica, there are excellent ride services available at no charge for the elderly and the disabled. Just one phone call can arrange a courteous ride to and from a doctor's appointment or another important outing. Rather than being the chauffeur all of the time, start using the local resources and focus your time and energy on other important tasks. You can always drive your family member or friend to appointments where your support and love are needed. But when your personal attention isn't necessary, make sure you find out about other alternatives.

Start using the meal delivery services in your area. Many

communities have a "Meals on Wheels" or other food services program for shut-ins and dependent relatives. Even if
you enjoy cooking on most days or if your loved one prefers
your special style of cooking, you can still use these free or
low-cost meal delivery services a few days a week to
lighten your load. By calling local agencies, your county
social services department, or your area agency on aging, you
will discover some excellent ways to have hot meals brought
to your family member or friend as often as you both feel is
convenient.

Find out if a local pharmacist delivers free of charge. Many
caregivers waste a lot of time and energy driving to the drug
store and waiting in line for prescriptions. In most areas,
you can order free delivery of medications and anything else
carried by a pharmacy. So instead of having one more
unnecessary errand, you can simply make a phone call.

*Start assigning errands to relatives, neighbors, and friends
who might be able to help out.* Even though many caregivers
are too proud or too shy to ask others for help, there is a lot
to be said for delegating errands you don't need to run
personally. Starting today, begin to see yourself not as someone who has to do every single chore on your own, but
rather as a "caregiving executive" who has the right to ask
others to pitch in with their support.

Is there another relative or friend who lives nearby? Even
if this person has been reluctant to help out in the past, are
there some specific errands and chores that you could get
this individual to do reliably?

Is there a local social service agency, church, or synagogue that can provide free volunteers to run errands? Quite
often there are volunteer programs that can arrange for a
responsible adult to stop by, assist in household chores,
help with carpooling and rides, or run a few errands. You
simply have to call around until you find some volunteers
who can help out with specific tasks. If no volunteer program exists in your area, then brainstorm with a social

services agency or religious institution about possibly starting one.

Are there some local undergraduate or graduate school
students who might be able to do an internship by helping
your ailing or disabled loved one? You can set up this kind
of internship or assistance by calling some local professors
of gerontology, social work, mental health, psychology,
nursing, or psychiatry. Ask these professors if they have
any reliable students who might want to volunteer or work
for a low wage to help your loved one with day-to-day
chores and necessities. I have seen some creative uses of
student volunteers. In between their classes and studies,
some mature students are able to devote between five to
twenty-five hours a week to working as caregiving assis-
tants, which can dramatically reduce your errand runner
responsibilities.

Some of the most competent and effective caregivers are
those who use the most creativity when handling errands
and other chores. For example, Marcella is a forty-four-year-
old woman in Chicago who has a full-time job and three
children to care for. In addition, she has elderly parents in
Florida who frequently need her advice and assistance.

Seven months ago, Marcella's seventy-seven-year-old
mother suffered a painful and debilitating stroke. Unfortunately, Marcella's eighty-two-year-old father hasn't responded
very well to his wife's illness. According to Marcella,

> I think my father's waiting for Mom to get better and
> start taking care of him again. So he still hasn't learned
> how to cook very much more than toast and tea. He still
> won't clean up around the house. I guess if I want my
> mom to recover from her stroke, I've got to find some
> affordable ways not only to get help for her but also to
> take care of my father.

For several weeks, Marcella felt overwhelmed by the difficult task of trying to arrange things for two people she

cares about who live over a thousand miles away. She recalls,

> I couldn't figure out how to find assistance for them in Florida when I'm working full time and raising a family in Chicago. I spoke to several friends and coworkers, but most of them just nodded sympathetically and said, "We're so sorry, Marcella. That's a tough one."

Then Marcella began making phone calls to various social service agencies and religious leaders in the community where her parents live. Within a few weeks she was able to arrange the following:

- Free transportation for her mother to all of her doctor's appointments and physical therapy sessions.
- A "Meals-on-Wheels" program five days a week so her mother could relax and not have to cook.
- A series of volunteers from a local religious institution that agreed to come by twice a week to clean the house, go shopping for groceries, and run other errands.
- A helpful neighbor who agreed to look in on Marcella's parents every few days to see if they needed anything.
- A graduate student in social work from a nearby college who was interested in doing an internship that involved helping Marcella's parents with various daily chores, medical problems, and practical details like helping them fill out insurance forms.

Marcella discovered:

> I had always assumed that my parents were on their own and that if they couldn't take care of each other they were in deep trouble, or else I was going to have to quit my job and move down there to take care of things. But I've learned instead that there are some creative ways I

can arrange to help my parents cope. It's not easy trying to reach people or interview them long-distance. But with persistence and a lot of help from agencies near where they live, I got the job done. Thank goodness my parents are doing a little better now, and I know they're not alone any longer.

While not every long-distance caregiving problem gets resolved as successfully as Marcella's did, there are probably a lot more options available for your loved one than you previously imagined. Even though our society has a long way to go in order to provide adequate resources for those who are ill or disabled, there are still a variety of helpful people and programs that can be found in most communities. Your job as caregiver is to locate these reliable errand-running sources and, most importantly, don't be shy when asking for help.

Spiritual Counselor

Finally, we come to one of the most fascinating and challenging aspects of helping someone cope with a serious illness or disability. Even if you don't consider yourself a very religious person, there is a strong possibility that in the next few weeks or months you will be asked by someone in your family to address various religious and spiritual questions. You may even have spiritual questions of your own.

For instance, here are three people like yourself who suddenly found themselves in the role of "Spiritual Counselor," even though they had little if any previous training:

Phyllis, fifty-seven, grew up in a somewhat dogmatic religious family and stopped practicing any form of religion when at eighteen she went away to college. She admits:

Religious and spiritual questions were not very important for me until recently when my husband became seriously ill.

One night we were up late and the conversation sur-
prisingly turned to subjects we had never really talked
about before: "Did I believe in God?" "Did I think there
is an afterlife?" "Why would God allow so many good
people to suffer for no apparent reason?" "Do our lives
have a deeper sense of meaning and purpose?"

I felt unprepared and uncomfortable talking about
these questions with my husband. He really needed
someone to share his concerns about these important
issues. But I found it hard even to discuss things like
God or an afterlife because of how much I resented
having religion shoved down my throat when I was growing up.

I wish I weren't so skeptical and turned off to the
whole subject of religion. I wish I had done some more
reading or given more thought to these issues so I could
be a better partner to my husband right now. I guess it's
not too late, but it's hard to be a spiritual counselor when
I'm so put off by the whole subject.

Andrew, thirty-two, has a different experience with religion. He explains:

I've always gone to services and been active in my
congregation. But my belief in God has been pretty luke-
warm. In fact, I've been a little jealous of relatives and
friends who seem to be able to handle life's hardships a
lot better because they trust so strongly in a loving sense
of God.

Last year Andrew's nine-year-old son was diagnosed with
cancer and has been asking his father a lot of questions
about why God would allow something like this to happen.
Like many parents, Andrew has felt uncomfortable with the
role of spiritual counselor. Describing his reaction to his
son's questions, he says:

On the one hand, I don't want to be a hypocrite and pretend I have complete faith in God. I don't want to lie to my son or pretend I have all this figured out perfectly. But at the same time, I don't want my son to get the impression that I'm a nonbeliever or that he shouldn't be able to have complete faith in a caring God who can offer him strength.

It's so hard to sort out exactly what I feel about God and religion, especially when I'm feeling a bit angry with God for letting this happen to my son. And it's even harder to know what to say to my son who's seriously ill and looking for answers.

Doreen, forty-one, had always been a strongly religious person who felt a close connection to God. Then six months ago, Doreen's best friend Vicki was hit by a drunk driver and paralyzed from the waist down. According to Doreen:

Seeing Vicki's life fall apart so suddenly has really shaken me up. I started questioning things I'd always held onto with complete certainty. I began to wonder if there really is a God and if there's a deeper purpose for the things that happen to us.

I realized that I wouldn't know what to say to Vicki if she asked me for my views about God or the reason for her tragedy. I don't know what I believe anymore.

I'm not comfortable living in a world with no God or no meaning. Yet at the same time, I don't know if I can ever go back to that same secure sense of an all-powerful father figure that I believed in since childhood.

In your own life recently, have spiritual or religious questions felt more pressing because of the ailment of a loved one? Have you been asked by anyone in your family to talk about the deeper meaning of why good people suffer? Have you felt uncertain when a loved one asks, "Why is this happening to us?" Or have you sensed a struggle in your own psyche between the part of you that wants to believe in God and the part of you that is afraid God won't respond to your prayers?

To deal with these important questions and to be available to your loved one who may need some spiritual counseling, there are four specific steps you can take:

Step 1: Recognize that you don't have to figure out the entire meaning of life by tomorrow afternoon.

Don't feel guilty or embarrassed by the fact that you don't have clear-cut answers to these spiritual questions. For many centuries, philosophers and theologians have struggled with the challenging issues of "Why do good people suffer painful tragedies?" and "Why do terrible things happen to people we love?" Even if you were fully trained as a priest, minister, or rabbi, you still might feel unsure of what to say to a loved one in pain.

Your job as a temporary spiritual counselor is not necessarily to have all the answers, but to be able to listen empathetically to your loved one's questions and concerns. What you say to your family member or friend might be less important than how well you help this person find his or her own answers.

For example, Marge is a college professor who has never been very religious. Recently, Marge's best friend Yolanda was seriously ill and asking Marge about whether God is listening. Like many nonreligious people, Marge wasn't sure how to be a useful spiritual counselor for her best friend. She explains:

> At first I felt uncomfortable when Yolanda wanted to talk about her faith in God and whether spirituality could help in a situation like this. But then I realized that it's not important whether or not I'm a practicing religious person. What's important is that I care about Yolanda

and I respect her beliefs, whether I agree with them 100 percent or not.

Ironically, I became a little more curious about spirituality from watching how much strength Yolanda received as a result of her stubborn faith in an infinite spirit that helps her carry on. I still don't know for sure if God is real, but I know that Yolanda's faith helped her recover. In addition to the medications and the therapies, Yolanda's belief that God is with her gave her the courage to hang in there and eventually get better. I'm glad I supported her need to believe in something and I'm grateful she's still alive.

Like Marge, you may feel awkward when you discover a loved one has beliefs that are substantially different from your own. Yet your role as a spiritual counselor is not to debate or judge your friend's beliefs, but to support his or her unique search for spiritual strength.

Step 2: Look at this crisis as an opportunity to become more openminded and curious about spiritual possibilities, even if you've been skeptical in the past.

Whether your faith in a higher being was strong or weak previously, you must admit it certainly is being tested now. In order to be valuable to your loved one and your other family members as a spiritual counselor, you may need to look deeply at your own ambivalent feelings about religion and spirituality. Many people feel betrayed by God or religion when a loved one is suffering. They blame God for causing the illness and are reluctant to believe too strongly for fear that no one is listening.

I know these feelings quite well, because at the age of fourteen I prayed each night for my mother to recover from cancer. I pleaded with God to help her get better. And when she kept getting worse, I blamed God. I was angry that my prayers weren't making her healthy again, and that I couldn't sense any response from God. Yet the God I was praying to and blaming was a childlike image of an all-powerful old man with whiskers.

In the years since then, I have searched for a deeper sense of God and spirituality. Through reading many helpful books, attending numerous lectures, studying with various teachers, and searching deeply in my own heart, I eventually came to terms with my relationship to God. It took a while, but I gradually regained a sense of closeness with God and let go of my bitterness over my mother's death.

If you currently feel angry with or cut off from God, or if you simply feel in need of a renewed sense of strength, I invite you to set aside some time each week to do some searching of your own. I urge you to become curious about reconnecting with a spirituality that is meaningful and helpful to you during this difficult time. I can't tell you what to believe or how to practice your beliefs. But I hope you find a way to let go of your anger toward God or whatever else you blame for your loved one's ailment, and to start searching for a way to connect with a source of energy that is beyond our narrow selves.

Step 3: Don't be afraid to ask for help in resolving your spiritual or religious questions.

Talking to a supportive pastoral counselor, priest, minister, or rabbi is one way to start coming to terms with your mixed feelings about God or spirituality. In addition, one of the books that helped me to develop an adult sense of God, and that I recommend to anyone who is coping with the illness of a loved one, is Harold Kushner's *When Bad Things Happen to Good People*.

In this fascinating book, God is discussed not as a judgmental parent or an angry source of fear and guilt, but rather as a comforting source of strength and support who inspires the best in us to come out. Harold Kushner was trained as a religious counselor. But when his three-year-old son Aaron was diagnosed with a rare illness called progeria, which led to the child's rapid aging and death at the age of fourteen, his faith in God was tested.

In *When Bad Things Happen to Good People,* Harold Kushner came to terms with his son's terminal illness and found a renewed sense of faith and purpose. There are several passages from the book that I've discussed with many people who were feeling confused or angry about their own spirituality as a result of the ailment or disability of a loved one. Please read these passages and give them some thought. You may also want to share these with your family member or friend if this person needs some spiritual support. (I will be quoting Harold Kushner's words directly and he has used the male pronoun "He" to describe God. If you prefer, replace the "He" with "He or She" or with your own idea of a genderless infinite being.

> I believe in God. But I do not believe the same things about Him that I did years ago, when I was growing up or when I was a theological student. I recognize His limitations. He is limited in what He can do by laws of nature and by the evolution of human nature and human moral freedom. I no longer hold God responsible for illnesses, accidents, and natural disasters . . . I can worship a God who hates suffering but cannot eliminate it . . . Some years ago when the 'death of God' theology was a fad, I remember seeing a bumper sticker that read 'My God is not dead; sorry about yours.' I guess my bumper sticker reads 'My God is not cruel; sorry about yours.'
>
> God does not cause our misfortunes. Some are caused by bad luck, some are caused by bad people, and some are simply an inevitable consequence of our being human and being mortal, living in a world of inflexible natural laws. The painful things that happen to us are not punishments for our misbehavior, nor are they in any way part of some grand design on God's part. Because the tragedy is not God's will, we need not feel hurt or betrayed by

God when tragedy strikes. We can turn to Him for help in overcoming it, precisely because we can tell ourselves that God is as outraged by it as we are.

Does that mean that suffering has no meaning? . . . Let me suggest that the bad things that happen to us in our lives do not have a meaning when they happen to us. They do not happen for any good reason which would cause us to accept them willingly. But we can give them a meaning. We can redeem these tragedies from senselessness by imposing meaning on them. The question we should be asking is not, 'Why did this happen to me? What did I do to deserve this?' That is really an unanswerable, pointless question. A better question would be 'Now that this has happened to me, what am I going to do about it?'

How does God make a difference in our lives if He neither kills nor cures? God inspires people to help other people who have been hurt by life, and by helping them, they protect them from the danger of feeling alone, abandoned or judged. God, who neither causes nor prevents tragedies, helps by inspiring people to help. As a nineteenth-century Hasidic rabbi once put it, 'human beings are God's language.' God shows His opposition to cancer and birth defects, not by eliminating them or making them happen only to bad people (He can't do that), but by summoning forth friends and neighbors to ease the burden and to fill the emptiness . . . God may not prevent the calamity, but He gives us the strength and the perseverance to overcome it.

Step 4: Don't avoid spiritual topics, even if you sometimes feel awkward or uncomfortable with them.

It can be extremely helpful and intimate to talk about spiritual concerns with an ailing loved one. In some cases, your family member or friend will initiate the conversation and start asking his or her religious questions. Your job is to be open minded, empathetic, and nonjudgmental, even if your loved one's beliefs are quite different from your own.

In other cases, you may be the one to start a dialogue by mentioning your own spiritual feelings. For example, you might say to your loved one, "I've been praying for assistance," "I've been meditating on the image of healing," or "I feel we're not alone in working toward an improvement." Then ask your family member or friend if prayer or meditation have been helpful to him or her. The goal is not to pressure or judge your loved one, but to open up the possibility of a dialogue between the two of you.

Even though we live in a very materialistic and secular society, I have found that almost all human beings are searching for a deeper sense of spirituality, a deeper sense of meaning and purpose. Especially when a tragedy strikes, we need support from empathetic clergy, close friends, relatives, and helpful books to sort out how we feel about life's most essential questions.

Unfortunately, many people become argumentative and intolerant on the subject of religion. Devout atheists are sometimes intolerant of believers. Devout believers are sometimes intolerant of anyone who is less devout. People tend to get self-righteous, thinking there's only one way to be a spiritual person, when in fact our world is filled with both human and religious diversity. If you notice yourself arguing about spirituality instead of listening to your loved one's different but equally valid viewpoints, stop and ask yourself, "Why are we arguing about this? Why don't we just appreciate that we each have a different way of connecting with a higher source?"

The key to doing a good job as a spiritual counselor for your loved one is to be a good listener and provide safe opportunities for this person to talk about her or his deepest concerns. The more comfortable you become with your own spirituality, the more you will be able to help your loved one find his or her own sense of spiritual strength.

Instead of being reluctant to talk about these important questions, begin to see them as a chance to get closer to your family member or friend. You and your loved one may find a much-needed sense of inner peace from exploring your connection to a loving and infinite higher being.

CHAPTER FOUR

Staying Healthy: The One Thing Most Caregivers Are Too Busy to Do

My mother's mother was a grand woman. Standing less than five feet tall, she was a powerful matriarch who many of us looked up to. A fine blend of European immigrant and patriotic American, she worked long hours in a Tootsie Pop manufacturing plant in Brooklyn before moving to Detroit and marrying my grandfather.

My grandmother made you feel at home with her incredible cooking and her gleaming eyes. She never learned to drive a car, but she was modern enough to know the strengths and weaknesses of every baseball player on the Detroit Tigers. No matter how badly the Tigers were beaten by their opponents, my grandmother listened to their struggles with complete devotion.

Complete devotion was also the way she treated my ailing grandfather year after year. As his heart troubles, ulcers, and moodiness got worse, my grandmother did more and more things to take care of him.

When her own health began to suffer, she refused to slow down or take better care of herself. Pretty soon my grandmother was in severe pain from her arthritis, her own heart problems, and hardening of the arteries. Yet she refused to listen when anyone suggested she needed help in attending to the constant needs of her husband. She refused to take seriously the warnings of doctors and family members that her own health was at risk.

Like many women who are raised to believe that their primary purpose in life is to take care of others, my grandmother put her own health in jeopardy because she was too busy helping someone else. As her heart condition worsened and her arthritis became even more crippling, she continued to cook three meals a day, wash clothes, clean the house, and never take a break from my ailing grandfather.

Then one day almost sixteen years ago, I received a phone call that my grandmother had died. And I began to wonder, What if she had taken better care of herself?

Yes, it was a positive trait that she cared so much about my grandfather, but maybe she could have helped him and still done a better job of taking care of her own health. There's nothing wrong with being a good wife, a good husband, a loyal relative or friend to someone who's ailing. But when that caring is out of balance and the caregiver becomes seriously ill as a result, something is wrong.

If my grandmother had focused just a little more on her own needs, she could have been there for my grandfather a lot longer and suffered a lot less.

The Caregiver Burnout Syndrome

If your loved one has been ailing or seriously disabled for a long time, you need to be aware of something called "The Caregiver Burnout Syndrome." Only in the past few years have researchers discovered a widespread phenomenon that affects millions of women and men who are taking care of someone in their families.

See how many of the following symptoms characterize

your own health or that of someone else in your family who might be suffering this often-undetected syndrome.

Have you been:

- feeling tired and worn out day after day?
- having trouble falling asleep at night or waking up in the morning?
- losing interest in the hobbies, friendships, and outside activities you formerly enjoyed?
- taking your loved one's condition personally, believing that if you somehow did more your loved one would get better?
- becoming irritated at those who urge you to slow down or take a break?
- telling other people that you're feeling fine when you know it's not true?
- ignoring or failing to get adequate treatment for a nagging physical discomfort?
- refusing to slow down and rest when you have a cold, the flu, or a more serious ailment?
- fearing that your life will be empty if your loved one should pass away?
- feeling impatient and short-tempered with individuals in your everyday life?
- feeling numb or disconnected from your sense of purpose and direction?

If these symptoms sound familiar, don't panic. But you must face an important decision—you can either continue to wear yourself down and risk a serious illness yourself, or you can begin to find creative ways to take care of your loved one while also taking good care of yourself.

The Seductiveness of Being Needed

But first let's be realistic. You can't expect an overburdened caregiver to magically change his or her ways—that's almost as unlikely as asking a chronic smoker to stop smoking immediately or a chronic drinker to stop drinking overnight. Long-term habits don't change that easily.

If you want to help a person—including yourself—who tends to give until it hurts, you need to take into account some deep-seated reasons why most caregivers can't stop giving, even when they become ill themselves. Ignoring these underlying psychological factors is like trying to pull a tree out of the ground without taking into account the extensive roots that keep the tree firmly in place.

Most caregivers do not consciously choose to become burned out. It sort of creeps up on them slowly over a period of time. For example, I recently counseled Sean, a man in his forties who was taking care of his aging mother in addition to working full time and being the parent of a sometimes-difficult eleven-year-old from a previous marriage.

When Sean came down with a winter cold several months ago, he was too busy to do much about it. Continuing to work full time, run errands for his mother, and carpool his eleven-year-old child, Sean soon discovered his mild cold had turned into a serious one. But since he was still too busy to take time off, he continued to push himself just as hard. Within a few days, the cold had turned into bronchitis.

Ignoring the advice of his physician to rest in bed and stay out of drafty rooms, Sean kept plugging away at his various responsibilities. Within a few weeks, the bronchitis had turned into pneumonia and Sean spent a few hours running up an enormous bill at a local hospital emergency room.

At no time did Sean say to himself, "I am now consciously choosing to put my own health at risk because my job, my child, and my dependent mom are more important than I am." Rather, Sean had given in to the subtle seduction that has gripped so many of us at times like these. He felt good about being needed and couldn't imagine admitting to his boss, his child, or his mom that he had his own needs and limits as well.

When Did You Learn that Your Needs Don't Matter?

The bottom line for most caregivers is that they have been taught at some point in their lives that their needs are less important than the needs of others. Quite often this message of self-denial is absorbed in our minds whether we are aware of it or not.

For example, many people learn to deny themselves and only take care of others because of their family background. Maybe you had a troubled sibling or parent who needed a lot of attention and you grew up believing, "It's wrong to think of my own needs. I have to focus my attention on my troubled relative who needs so much more." You might even have a memory of a time when you felt "selfish" or "bad" because things were going well for you and at the same time your troubled sibling or parent was suffering. As a result, you may have made a subconscious decision that it's not permissible to think about your own needs when there's someone else who has problems so much more severe than your own.

Possibly you were given a lot of praise and encouragement whenever you took care of others, while you were scolded or criticized when you did things for yourself. In many families, the eldest children are raised to take care of their younger siblings and are harshly reprimanded if they don't do it. Or you may have found that your role in your family was to be the helper, the rescuer, or the one who never has problems.

Sex roles are also a major reason that many of us fall into the trap of denying ourselves when someone around us is in need. In many families, the women are taught to cater to the demands of others while the men are encouraged to break out of the nest and be independent. Is it any wonder that there are so many expectations placed on women to be the primary caregivers for ailing family members?

Even if the messages were never spoken out loud, we pick up subtle clues that we aren't supposed to take good care of ourselves when someone else is ailing or disabled. For instance, if a woman puts her own needs ahead of the needs of her family, she might be accused, verbally or silently, of being "unwomanly." In a similarly restrictive role, if a man is concerned with his own health rather than assuming the women in his life will take care of it for him, he might be accused of being "weak" or "unmanly." Neither men nor women in our society are encouraged to honor their own health and well-being during times of crisis.

It also might be the case that you have been told repeatedly that it's your job to give your all to a certain person if she or he should ever become ill, and that you have no choice in the matter. Maybe you were told numerous times by your parents that since they made sacrifices for you, they would be expecting sacrifices in return if they ever became ill. Or you may have an unspoken agreement with your spouse or lover that if one of you became ill the other would be there 100 percent with no questions asked.

While there's nothing wrong with people caring for each other, there's something dangerous about caregivers who do not feel they have the right to respect their own health needs. This tendency for self-denial is revealed in many of the things that are said by well-meaning family members who feel responsible for an ailing or disabled person. Do any of the following sound familiar to you?

- "I try not to think of myself. After all, so and so has it much worse than I do."
- "I don't want anyone to think of me as selfish."
- "This is no time for me to start worrying about my own problems. Not when there's so much to do."
- "I have to work this hard. I don't have a choice."

The fact of the matter is that you *do* have a choice, but it's not the choice most people believe it to be. Your decision is not between being selfish or being an all-giving saint. Your two options are:

1 to ignore and deny your personal health needs while you are taking care of someone else, *or*
2 to treat your personal health needs as an equally important factor while you are taking care of someone else.

Being good to yourself so that you will have more energy for helping others *is not selfish*. It's sensible!

Yet if you were raised to believe it's selfish or had to be good to yourself, then you will need to be persistent and creative in breaking this lifelong habit. Don't be surprised if feelings of guilt or confusion arise when you begin to pay attention to your own health needs. Like a smoker or a drinker who tries to break a chronic habit, changing will require patience and courage.

Now let's explore some ways to get out of the burnout trap. There are several creative methods that can help you balance your own health needs with the demands of your ailing relative or friend. The more you put these techniques to good use in your daily life, the more you and your loved one will benefit.

Finding Time to Relax In An Overfilled Schedule

Most people who are caring for an ailing loved one would like to relax and stay healthy if they could. But there are only twenty-four hours in a day, and the responsibilities of being a full-time or a part-time caregiver often make it seem there's no time left for your own needs.

Fortunately, there is an increasing number of facilities that provide "Respite Care," which is designed to help overstressed caregivers get the rest and relief they so desperately need. If you've never heard or partaken of respite care, don't think you are the only one. Most people who could benefit from this low-cost gem of an idea have either never been told about it or have failed to use it sufficiently. Respite care in the United States currently consists of:

• More than one thousand adult day-care centers where you can take your loved one for a day of supervised activities or a variety of speech, physical, or occupational therapies. In most cases, for a low or nonexistent fee, your family member gets transported to and from the day-care facility by an equipped van. Meals and counseling are often provided. And you get the day off to rest or take care of your own pressing needs.

• A variety of child day-care centers that are specifically developed for seriously disabled or mentally ill youngsters. Finding the right facility that suits your son or daughter is often a challenge. But once you find a competent day-care support team, you will be surprised at the relief you can experience.

• Numerous public and private health agencies and in-home nursing services that provide overnight, weekend, and vacation respite care for you and your loved one. While these services are more expensive, they allow you to take a night to catch up on sleep. Or they enable you to take a weekend or vacation every so often to reenergize yourself and maintain your health.

• Helpful friends, neighbors, students, or relatives who can come over and stay with your loved one for a short time each day or each week while you get a chance to relax, go shopping, or take care of your own needs.

The word *respite* is defined by Webster's dictionary as "an interval of rest or relief." Respite comes from the same Latin root as the word *respect* and there are two essential elements of respect involved whenever someone uses the many respite care options available in most communities. First, if you find and use a quality respite-care program at least one day a week, it means you respect yourself enough to take good care of your own health needs. Second, if you spend some time apart from your loved one at least once a week, it makes it easier to respect your family member or friend without building up resentments that are bound to arise from spending every waking hour together. Many arguments and frustrations would be reduced or eliminated if family members were more willing to use available respite-care services.

Here are a few brief examples of how respite care has been a lifesaver for others in a similar situation as your own:

Annette's husband had a debilitating stroke four years ago and now requires constant assistance in order to bathe, eat, and move around the house. While Annette at first felt reluctant about asking anyone for help, she eventually began taking her husband to an adult day-care center two days a week where he participates in a variety of educational and social activities.

Annette calls those days "my lifesavers." She explains:

> Those are the afternoons I catch up on sleep, take a walk in the park, go see friends, or simply go shopping. Sometimes I get to watch one of the shows I've taped on television or I catch up on paperwork.
>
> I used to get cranky and irritable spending every waking hour with my husband. It's not that I don't love him—he's the most special person in my life and always will be. But who can spend twenty-four hours a day, seven days a week jumping to the beck and call of someone whose needs never end? Maybe Mother Teresa, but not me.
>
> After I've had my day to do my own thing, I actually miss my husband and I'm glad to see him. I think I was reluctant at first because "adult day care" sounded rather demeaning and frivolous. But now I realize it not only has helped me keep my sanity, but it also has strengthened our marriage.

Howard and Julianne have a three-year-old daughter named Patty who has a serious developmental disability. For the first two years of Patty's life, Howard and Julianne felt they were living a nightmare. They recall:

> We made the mistake of trying to do everything on our own. We heard about day care and respite care and visiting nurses and weekend babysitting, but we viewed all that as 'luxuries' for other people, not for us.

Then Julianne came down with a gradually worsening case of chronic fatigue. Month after month, she grew increasingly tired and susceptible to colds, flus, and occasional insomnia.

Howard remembers:

> We had tried so hard to be stoics and insist we could do it all, but the fact is we're only human. We started getting information about what we could afford and pretty soon some ideas started to make sense.
>
> Now we have four days a week where Patty is taken care of by some excellent places we found through our support group. When we bring her home each night at five o'clock we're glad to see each other. Julianne and I also started taking at least one weekend off every month and two vacation weeks each year. We thought we couldn't afford it, but with the help of some local agencies we found a way to make it happen. There's still a lot to do to take care of Patty, but it no longer feels like such a painful burden.

Feeling guilty about not spending twenty-four hours a day, seven days a week with an ailing loved one might be harmful to you and the person you care about. Using a respite-care program to give both of you a break from each other makes you a more competent caregiver. Otherwise you are bound to become impatient, resentful, or burned out from never having any time for yourself.

You may be asking, "But how do I find the best available respite-care facilities that are affordable in my community?" Here are some ways to locate and evaluate the adult day-care or disabled child day-care facilities in your area:

- Call your city, county, or state health department, area agency on aging, or children's social services. Or call the Jewish Family Service, Catholic Social Services, or specific denomination social services program in your community. Ask them for a recommendation.
- Call the organizations in Appendix B that relate to your loved one's illness or disability, and ask them for a referral.
- Talk to your doctor, nurse, hospital social services caseworker, or a local nursing registry.
- Call the toll-free number (1-800-648-COPE) set up by The Brookdale Center for Aging at Hunter College in New York, which operates a national information clearinghouse for families looking for adult day-care referrals that meet quality standards.

Once you have the names and addresses of several day-care facilities, make sure you inspect or double-check the quality of the ones you select. You may need to ask members of your support group, as well as some local doctors, nurses, and caseworkers, if they have any positive or negative information about a specific day-care center.

After you have inspected or researched the quality of the respite-care facility, make sure you work with the professionals on staff to be certain that your loved one receives good treatment there. While most day-care programs are staffed by excellent professionals, you may need to keep your eyes open and visit from time to time to make sure your family member or friend receives the proper meals, medical attention, and special services that the facility has promised.

Making Sure You Have Healthy Outlets For Releasing Difficult Emotions

Anyone who tells you it's easy to deal with the reality of a loved one suffering a long-term illness is either naïve or lying. There are many levels of sadness and frustration that most caregivers experience. Left unacknowledged, these feelings can undermine your health and effectiveness.

If you are to remain free from serious illness and stay productive on a daily basis, you need to do something to begin releasing some of the sadness and frustration you've been forced to keep inside. Otherwise the feelings keep building up until you either become susceptible to physical illness or prone to emotional depressions.

The problem for many family members and friends of people with a long-term illness is that they are usually too busy to slow down and unravel their feelings. They might be afraid of falling apart if they let go of the flood of emotions they've been holding inside.

Is there a safe and manageable way to release some of the emotional pain you've been carrying ever since your loved one became ill or disabled? Here are several possibilities that have worked for many people going through a challenge similar to your own. Which of the following do you think would be the best ways of taking better care of your emotional needs?

Finding the Right Counselor for You.

Many people are reluctant to talk with a psychiatrist, psychotherapist, social worker, pastoral counselor, or support group because, they say, "If I seek help, that must mean there's something *wrong* with me." That's an incorrect notion that unfortunately causes many individuals to become seriously ill or depressed with no outlet for their emotions.

Talking with a counselor or therapist doesn't mean you're sick. Rather, it shows that you have the good sense to talk about your legitimate feelings of sadness and frustration, instead of keeping them inside, getting physically ill, or taking your frustrations out on your loved ones.

A counselor will also be a good listener and brainstorming partner in your life who can help you come up with creative ways to take better care of your loved one, your family, and yourself.

Finally, you will have someone in your life whom you don't need to impress. With a counselor, you don't have to put up a strong front or pretend you have it all handled. A good counselor seeks to understand what you're going through without judging you or expecting you to do anything to please him or her.

To find the right counselor, ask a few friends, doctors, and nurses whom they would recommend. Then see what the chemistry is like between you and the counselors you meet. There's no crime in talking with more than one therapist before you select the one you trust the most. Remember, the counselor is there to listen to your needs, not to impose his or her agendas on you.

Developing a Twice-a-Week Telephone Partner.

This is one of the least expensive and most effective techniques for releasing the sadness and frustration we all experience when a loved one is ailing or disabled. Find someone you trust—a friend, relative, coworker, or a member of your support group—who is willing to become a twice-a-week telephone partner. You might say, "I need someone I can talk with twice a week about what's been going on. And I'd be willing to listen to your problems and struggles as well."

Then set up the following guidelines with your twice-a-week telephone partner:

Make sure you don't just say you're calling to call each other twice a week. This technique works only if you actually *do* call.

During each phone call, set aside ten minutes per person.

For ten minutes, you get to talk without being interrupted. Then for ten minutes, the other person gets to describe his or her daily struggles without being interrupted. *Make sure you support each other as courageous people and don't bombard one another with advice or criticism.* Simply listening and understanding is more important than trying to fix everything or "make it all better."

Be careful that your phone relationship is balanced. If one of you tends to be in crisis or wants to talk more than the other, take extra steps to make sure you both eventually get equal time. Each of you deserves ten minutes of uninterrupted time at least twice a week no matter how serious or mundane your issues seem to be.

Don't just share your frustrations with each other. Be sure you also describe your own persistence, your triumphs, great and small, your healthy strategies, and your struggle to find meaning and purpose in all the chaos. These phone calls shouldn't become a drudgery or a burden. Rather, they ought to be welcome opportunities to get things safely off your chest and to re-energize for the challenges you face on a daily basis.

Writing in a Private Journal.

Your greatest companion and most reliable friend during hard times might be your personal journal. Many women and men find that by writing down their feelings, concerns, struggles, and fears in a private journal, they not only gain new insights into how to improve their situation but also discover a sense of inner peace.

When you describe a feeling of sadness or frustration honestly in your journal, it often causes the emotion to lighten up or disappear altogether. Sometimes it can take fifteen or thirty minutes of writing in your journal before you notice your spirits beginning to lift. But in most cases, you will discover a renewed sense of energy and courage after releasing your fears onto the pages of your journal.

There are several excellent books about how to keep a

private journal. They are listed in Appendix A. In addition, here are a few guidelines for using a personal journal to release your sadness and frustration:

Make sure no one reads your journal. That may mean getting a firm commitment from everyone who lives with you. Or it may mean hiding your journal notebooks under lock and key. This journal is for *your* health and emotional release. You will feel much less inhibited or judgmental of what you write if you know it won't be seen by anyone.

Begin each journal writing session by writing the words "Here and Now" on the blank page. Then describe honestly your exact feelings and concerns at that moment. If you become blocked at any point and nothing comes out, just relax quietly and keep writing "Here and Now" until you begin to regain a connection with what you are worrying about or desiring at this moment.

Don't censor or judge anything you write. Your journal thoughts and feelings *aren't supposed to be logical or realistic.* Whatever comes into your awareness is there for a healing reason. Just as dreams are a release for the subconscious each night, so is journal writing a method for letting go of whatever is stuck or uncomfortable in your psyche.

Writing in a journal during whatever alone-time you can arrange might comprise some of the most insightful and relaxing moments of your daily life. No matter how out of control things might seem when a loved one is ailing or disabled, sorting through your feelings in a private journal can help you gain new clarity and understanding.

Finding Safe Opportunities to Have a Good Cry.

This final technique for releasing sadness and frustration may seem strange at first. Yet it's worked effectively for many people who had been building up a backlog of sadness after months or years of being concerned about someone whose condition was not getting better.

Just like heavy rainfall clears the air and is followed by the sweet sounds of birds singing, so does a good cry bathe your insides with a healing release. Yet you might be saying, "I'm too busy to cry" or "I have to be strong—I can't let the tears come."

I understand how you feel. I've often been reluctant to cry, even when I had been building up sadness for months or years. Especially with my upbringing as a male, I was never encouraged to simply let the tears flow.

But in fact we all need to cry at times like these. Even if you have great hopes that your loved one will recover soon and be well again, there's still a buildup of sadness that needs to come out.

Where can you find a safe and comfortable opportunity to have a good cry? Here are some creative ways of releasing the deep sadness that can hamper your health and effectiveness as a caregiver.

See a movie that you know is good for three or more Kleenexes. I've laughed and cried several times in order to cleanse my insides during difficult times by seeing movies such as *West Side Story, The Color Purple, Terms of Endearment, Chariots of Fire, The Black Stallion, The Sound of Music,* or *Dr. Zhivago.* Even if your tears seem to be about Tony and Maria's love affair, in fact you are releasing many months of suppressed sadness about your loved one's condition. If your children need a good cry, I recommend renting a video of *E.T.* I've yet to meet a child *or* adult who didn't cry during the scenes when *E.T.* was taken away from his friend by the insensitive scientists.

Take a hot shower and let the tears flow. Quite often I've found that when I'm enormously upset about a family member or friend being ill, the privacy and hot water of a long shower allow my wails of sadness to come up and out in an uninhibited way.

Look at a photograph of the person you are sad about. Frequently your feelings of love and sadness will arise at the same time, permitting you to release many layers of pent-up emotion.

Take a long walk near a body of water. For some reason,

the sound and feel of the ocean, a lake, or a river stirs up the fluid emotions within us. I've had many good cries while sitting or walking close to an alive and flowing body of water.

After a healthy release of tears, you will probably feel re-energized and ready to begin again the important task of helping your family member or friend. Be careful, however, that you take a little extra time and precautions to make sure you're all right again after a good cry. Don't jump immediately into a strenuous activity, such as driving a car or operating a Cuisinart. It may take a few minutes of regaining your sense of balance before you're ready to resume your activities.

Crying is a healthy way of releasing the pain that any normal person in your situation would feel. Rather than walking around with a huge load of unexpressed sadness weighing you down, find a safe opportunity for letting go of a flood of tears at least once a week.

Some Creative Ways to Start Getting Enough Sleep

For many caregivers and family members of the ailing or disabled, the toughest health issue they face is how to get enough sleep. Possibly your loved one wakes you up several times a night needing your assistance. Maybe you tend to wake up at night on your own with unresolved worries racing across your mind. Or you find yourself unable to relax and fall asleep after a hectic day—the moment your head hits the pillow you start thinking about things that went wrong today or things you need to take care of tomorrow.

I remember during the final two years my mother was battling cancer, I spent many nights lying awake or watching television reruns until three, four, or five in the morning. Even when I felt exhausted, I couldn't seem to drift off to sleep. It didn't matter if I was watching the most boring program—my heavy eyelids still remained open a crack, and my mind wouldn't relax enough to allow me a good night's rest.

Since that time I've always been fascinated with the study of sleep and insomnia. I've learned that when humans are deprived of adequate sleep for extended periods of time, many related symptoms can occur:

- Your "biological clock," or circadian rhythm, gets thrown off and it becomes increasingly difficult to re-establish a regular cycle of sleep and wakefulness.
- You may become unusually moody, irritable, tearful, cranky, depressed, or unable to focus on your daily tasks.
- You can easily become addicted to sleep medications or need larger doses each night in order to fall asleep.
- You become more prone to hypertension, muscle aches, colds, flus, stomach troubles, or more serious physical problems.
- You might become increasingly anxious about sleep, so that the mere thought of trying to fall asleep causes your adrenaline to flow and makes it even harder to drift off to dreamland.

If you have had trouble recently falling asleep or staying asleep during the night, you are not the only one. Surveys reveal that more than thirty percent of adults in the United States describe themselves as having sleep problems, and between fifteen and twenty percent of those consider their problem serious and chronic.

In addition, there is convincing proof that emotionally upsetting events, such as the illness of a relative or friend, can easily disrupt your normal sleep patterns. So finding a way to get sufficient rest becomes increasingly important when a loved one is ailing.

However, I urge you not to overreact if your sleepless nights are few and far between. It's normal to lose sleep every so often when there are serious issues and changes going on in your life. Rather than assuming immediately that there's something terribly wrong with you, you might just accept that every few weeks you are bound to have a rough night or two.

I don't quite understand people who never lose *any* sleep, even when they are facing the most serious dilemmas. I remember a few years ago Nancy Reagan was quoted as saying that her husband, who was then president of the United States, never lost a bit of sleep over any crisis or problem. That worried me. I would like the chief executive to be a little more emotionally impacted by issues like hunger, homelessness, and the possibility of nuclear war.

So if you find yourself lying awake every so often because a loved one is hurting, don't jump to the conclusion there's something wrong with you. You might just be a caring and concerned human being whose normal sleep pattern will be re-established after a few days.

On the other hand, if your sleeplessness is persistent and chronic, or if it begins to hamper your effectiveness in your daily life, then you need to do something about it. There are a variety of techniques suggested by sleep experts. No simple insomnia technique seems to work for everyone. You may need to experiment patiently with several of the following options before you discover the right mix of sleep strategies for you. Here are several possibilities that have worked well for other people like yourself:

Avoid substances that promote insomnia. Studies have shown that stimulants such as caffeine or nicotine, which are found in most coffees, black teas, chocolate, cigarettes, caffeinated soft drinks, diet pills, appetite suppressants, and some hypertension remedies can interfere with normal sleep patterns. You may find that by avoiding caffeine, nicotine, and other stimulants in the evening, your sleep problem will lessen or disappear.

Watch out for the faulty advice that alcohol is a safe and effective sleep remedy. While some people do find that a little bit of alcohol can induce drowsiness and help them fall asleep in the short run, it has dangerous long-term effects. Dr. Jean Matheson of the Harvard University Sleep Disorder Center has found that even if alcohol works for a few days, it causes disrupted sleep later. In addition, the body will build up a tolerance to the alcohol and you may find yourself needing increasingly larger amounts in order to relax. This creates a vicious cycle—the more alcohol you require in order to induce drowsiness, the more your natural sleep mechanisms are thrown off. In most cases, alcohol gradually worsens a sleep problem rather than improving it.

Take steps to insure a quiet and uninterrupted night. Sometimes the problem is noise from outside sources and the remedy is a pair of inexpensive ear plugs. Most pharmacies carry several varieties—wax, foam, or plastic—and your task is to find out which ones feel more comfortable.

Or the problem might be that your spouse or lover snores, tosses and turns, or wakes up frequently during the night. You may need to try sleeping in separate beds or separate rooms for a while until you have regained your health, as well as your confidence that you can sleep soundly again. I agree that it's not very romantic to sleep in separate beds or separate rooms, but it's a lot more healthy and romantic than building up resentments that you're awake each night because of your loved one.

Another practical step you can take to reduce your sleep problem is to keep a tiny flashlight, a pen or pencil, and a notepad next to your bed so that you can jot down quick reminders of things which come into your awareness when you're trying to fall asleep. Instead of mulling over these concerns in bed, simply write them down quickly and trust that you'll deal with them tomorrow.

Finally, an additional step you can take to prevent waking up repeatedly during the night is to make sure you don't drink any fluids for three hours before bedtime. You'd be amazed at how many people fill their bladder each night with several glasses of juice or soda and then wonder why they keep getting up to stumble their way to the bathroom.

If you find yourself lying awake for a long time at night, get out of bed. Don't treat your bedroom as a stressful prison. Most sleep disorder experts agree that a key step in breaking an insomnia problem is to lie in bed *only when you are tired and resting comfortably.* Your bed should not be used for stressful tasks such as paying bills, catching up on work from the office, arguments, anxious phone calls, or difficult decisions, If you can't fall asleep and your mind is racing, most sleep researchers recommend that you get out of bed and do your worrying in another part of the house or apartment. When you've resolved the issues that kept you awake, or decide these concerns can wait until daylight, then you can return to bed and drift off to sleep.

You can easily learn to relax your body at night and improve your odds of falling asleep. If you feel tense while lying in bed, you might begin to unwind by intentionally tensing and then relaxing each muscle area of your body, one section at a time. Gently and patiently tense and then relax your toes, feet, ankles, calves, thighs, buttocks, pelvis, stomach, back, neck, shoulders, mouth, eyebrows, forehead, and face. Breathing slowly in and out, do this in a dreamy and patient manner—this is not an aerobics or pumping-iron exercise! Many people have found they can release tensions and become relaxed and drowsy in ten to twenty minutes when they do this exercise slowly and deliberately.

Read up on the latest findings in sleep research. There are several good books on sleep research and remedies for insomnia listed in Appendix A. Many of these books are available at most libraries or can be ordered through your local bookstore. They may provide you with helpful ideas to improve your ability to sleep. Or they may simply be scientific and boring enough to lull you to sleep if you read them late at night.

Make sure your evenings are a time for unwinding and becoming drowsy. Too many people engage in stressful activities and conversations right up to the moment when they get ready for bed. Is it any wonder they find it difficult to unwind once their head hits the pillow?

You can improve your chances for a good night's rest if you stop all stressful tasks and conversation topics two or three hours prior to your bedtime. Then listen to music, read a relaxing book, watch a nature video, or take a bubble bath prior to going to sleep. Your insomnia problem might be nothing more than your body saying, "Hey, I need a few hours to wind down at night." Ten minutes of quiet after a hectic day is *not* enough.

If your sleep problem continues despite all these efforts, it may be a symptom of a more serious medical condition. Quite often a chronic sleep disorder is your body's way of informing you that you need to see a doctor for a different health concern. For example, if you tend to sweat a lot during the night, or have muscle cramps or aches and pains in the middle of the night, these might be clues that a physical problem exists and should be treated as soon as possible. Your insomnia may be helping you to become aware of an undetected problem, for which you should consult your physician immediately.

Or if you tend to get up more than once a night to go to the bathroom, your sleep problem might be related to a bladder or prostate condition that needs to be checked out. Be sure to see your family physician so you can treat the problem or eliminate it as a possible concern.

If a sleep disorder continues for several weeks, you might consider seeing a specialist. There are numerous psychologists, medical doctors, and others who have worked with hundreds of patients, often with favorable results in resolving a sleep disorder. To obtain information about a specialist in your area, you can ask your family doctor or write for a list of sleep disorder clinics and physicians at: The Association of Sleep Disorder Centers, PO Box 2604, Del Mar, CA

92014, or The Association of Sleep Disorder Centers National Office, 604 2nd Street, SW, Rochester, MN 55902. You can also obtain a referral to a physician with expertise in sleep disorders by writing: The Academy of Sleep Disorders Medicine, Pennsylvania State University College of Medicine, Box 850, Drawer G, Hershey, PA 17033.

Alicia's case is a good example of how frustrating it can be to have a recurring sleep problem, and how relieving it can be to finally sleep soundly again.

When Alicia's husband Frank became seriously ill, Alicia began lying awake at night with worries and ideas of things she had to do the next day. Unable to fall asleep for what seemed to be an eternity, she actually slept an average of three hours a night. But she never felt rested after spending hours tossing and turning anxiously. According to Alicia, "The most frustrating part was that no matter how tired I was, my head would hit the pillow and my mind would start racing with things I needed to do or figure out."

For several weeks, she tried to ignore the problem, but her tiredness during the day made her realize she needed to do something to get more sleep at night. She tried some over-the-counter sleep medications, which helped her fall asleep but also made her drowsy the next day.

After Alicia talked with a sleep disorders expert, she began making some subtle but important changes in her nighttime activities. She recalls, "The first thing I did was to stop drinking coffee and soft drinks after six in the evening. Then I began to take two hours each night to unwind, write in my journal, or take a relaxing bath."

For several weeks, her insomnia came and went. She might have three or four good nights of sleep, but then her sleeplessness and anxiousness would return for several consecutive nights. (It's quite common, after a sleep problem improves slightly, to have occasional setbacks.)

During this time, Alicia began to use a relaxation technique taught to her by her sleep disorders counselor. She explains:

> I would begin by relaxing each muscle area of my body and that usually got me feeling physically relaxed. But since my mind would still be racing with ideas and worries, I started using the visualization technique I learned from my counselor. I would imagine myself walking along the beach, holding a series of brightly colored helium balloons. As I let go of the string of one floating balloon after another, I would feel my mind becoming less and less anxious. Finally, after releasing most of the balloons, I would drift off to sleep.

After several weeks of consciously employing this visualization exercise, Alicia began to relax and fall asleep easily on most nights. While not everyone has equally successful results from using various sleep-induction techniques, she was typical in needing a combination of strategies to resolve her insomnia problem.

If you or someone you know has been lying awake at night too often, make sure you do something constructive about it. You need rest and sleep in order to maintain your health. Begin today to experiment with some of the techniques listed above, or find the right books or experts who can help solve your problem.

Taking Charge of Your Own Health Before It's Too Late

Most of us would rather pretend that stresses in our lives aren't getting to us, even when we secretly know we're close to the breaking point. We let difficult situations pile up, insisting, "Don't worry about me. I can handle it. I'm fine." Then when the pile of stressful challenges gets too high, a small irritation comes along and the entire pile topples over.

For example, listen to Rebecca's story and see if it has some resemblance to your own:

Rebecca has an aging father whose condition recently worsened. She also has a thirty-year-old son who is mentally ill and has been having problems with some of the side effects of his medications. Rebecca also has a challenging job for a local social service agency, where she admits, "We're all good at taking care of other people, but we never seem to have any time to take care of ourselves." In addition, Rebecca's best friend is going through a bitter divorce, and Rebecca has been trying to help her cope with it.

Like many caring individuals, Rebecca takes care of her father, her son, her clients, and her best friend without hesitation. But a few weeks ago, with her stress levels piled dangerously high, Rebecca encountered one more smaller irritation that toppled her sense of balance. Her eight-year-old foreign car began stalling at red lights, sometimes in heavy traffic. When Rebecca took it in for an estimate, she was told it would cost over six hundred dollars to fix the problem.

That news pushed her over the edge. With tears in her eyes, Rebecca started arguing with the car mechanic. Her anger and frustration from several weeks of pushing herself too hard suddenly erupted in a most unusual setting—a car repair shop where no one was interested. Embarrassed that she had made a scene in front of a total stranger and several onlookers, Rebecca realized that letting things pile up is not the most effective strategy.

If you also tend to let the stresses in your life accumulate until one additional frustration pushes you over the edge, this might be a good time to explore some alternative ways of coping more effectively. Here are some options that you can use to make sure you don't blow up in front of a stranger, or explode on an innocent loved one.

Learn how to delegate more. Every successful executive knows the importance of assigning burdensome tasks to other people. Yet most caregivers think they have to do everything by themselves. For many of us, the problem is that we tend to be perfectionists—we can't let anyone help us out because we're afraid they won't do a good enough job.

Starting today, every time you are about to do some task that is time-consuming or unpleasant ask yourself:

"Is this the best use of my energy and efforts, or should I be delegating this job to someone else so I can focus on the things I absolutely need to do for my loved one, my family, and myself?"

"Is there some way I could give this task to a family member, friend, student, or local volunteer who would do it sufficiently?"

"Why am I being so stubborn and trying to do it all by myself? Maybe it's time to be sensible and let others pitch in."

Don't overload your daily list of "Things to Do." Murphy was right when he said that things can and do go wrong. But you can prepare ahead of time to be able to deal with unexpected stresses and delays. Rather than overscheduling each day and then feeling stressed, make sure you build in a thirty percent cushion for delays and problems.

That means giving yourself an extra fifteen minutes travel time so that traffic or delays won't make you anxious. It also means scheduling in an extra half hour before lunch, before dinner, and after dinner for unwinding and not rushing through meals. In addition, it helps to have an hour each day with nothing planned. It will either be filled by an unexpected task or simply be there as a time to relax.

When dealing with doctors, hospitals, agencies and bureaucracies, be prepared for delays. Most people get impatient and upset when they're put on hold or forced to wait in long lines. This can be especially frustrating when you've got a long list of things to do and you're trapped in some waiting room with nothing but *Field and Stream* or *Guns and Ammo* magazines lying around. Or you're trying to get information about a serious problem and they put you on hold with elevator music numbing your ear. Or the receptionist keeps saying, "I'll just be a moment," and she says it for over thirty minutes.

In order to stay sane and healthy in the middle of these delays, I recommend you always prepare ahead of time. Anticipate that a ten-minute wait will take twenty minutes. If you have three calls to make, don't allot two minutes to make them—give yourself fifteen minutes and be overjoyed if you finish faster.

I also make sure to take some busy-work or some pleasurable reading material with me whenever I go to any office or institution where they tend to make me wait. Rather than looking at the clock and fuming, I'd rather read a good book, write some letters, sort through my mail, or write in my journal.

Finally, if you find yourself waiting for extended amounts of time, don't forget to breathe and relax. Holding your breath in anger or anticipation is the surest way to drain your energy. I usually take a thermos of hot soup, tea, or cold water to relax and enjoy while I'm cooped up in some boring waiting room.

Make sure you maximize your time with friends and colleagues who are supportive and understanding, while you minimize your time with those who are insensitive or upsetting. Some of us pull away from all social activities when a loved one is ailing. I can understand the desire to protect yourself and avoid the repetitive questions of "How's so and so" or "Have you tried this new miracle cure—I read in the *National Enquirer* that it's amazing!"

At the same time, we all need friends and supporters during these stressful times. So I urge you to be honest with yourself and ask, "Are there people I've been keeping at a distance who might be understanding and encouraging right now?" Make sure you reach out to those friends, relatives,

and colleagues who want to help and be sure to instruct
them on what you need most from them.

Watch out for "mood foods" that can sap your energy.
Quite often when a loved one is ailing, we feel stressed and
in need of a boost to keep going. As a result, we become
attracted to certain foods and substances that give a temporary adrenaline rush which is often followed by a long bout
of sluggishness or depression.

Many researchers now recognize that certain foods and
substances have a strong affect on our moods and energy
levels. In order to avoid becoming sluggish or depressed
each day from the cravings that wreak havoc on your blood
chemistry, you may need to reduce or eliminate certain
things.

For example, what are the foods and substances (such as
sweets, greasy foods, burgers, cigarettes, drugs, or alcohol)
that you seem to crave during stressful times? You may
need to talk with a nutritionist who can help you discover
what mood foods and food allergies may be hampering your
effectiveness each day. Or read one of the books suggested
in Appendix A under "Staying Healthy."

*Don't let your home environment become rundown or
depressing.* When a family member is receiving home care
or hospital care, many people add to their feelings of discouragement by letting their home environment turn into a
disaster area. It can get quite depressing when your home
looks like a sick bay, when the kitchen counter has three-
day-old unwashed pans, or if you haven't opened the curtains and let in some sunlight for several days.

One of the challenges of taking good care of a loved one
who needs you is to simultaneously bring some rays of hope
into your physical environment. Make sure you open the
curtains and let in some sunshine. Buy yourself some flowers every few days to add some color and brightness to your
home. Have some good books, relaxing music, and tasty
food available so you can unwind in comfort. Hire someone
or ask a volunteer from a local service group to help clean

your home thoroughly every so often. Make sure you take a long walk or get some exercise as frequently as possible.

Build up your immune system. Whether your loved one's ailment is contagious or not, you are facing additional stresses on your immune system every day. In addition to the challenge of working as hard as you've been working, your immune system has to deal with an increasing amount of pollution and toxic substances in the air and water. This might be a good time to talk with a health practitioner about how to build up your immunity to colds, flus, infections, and viruses. The sooner you realize that you need to take extra good care of yourself when helping others, the better your chances of remaining healthy and productive.

"I Woke Up to the Fact That I'm Not Invincible"

Jackie's situation illustrates what happens to many of us when we are devoted to helping a family member or friend who's seriously ill:

A forty-two-year-old woman with her own business and three children from a previous marriage, Jackie found out seven months ago that her best friend Grace has cancer. According to Jackie, "It shocked me. Grace has always been so energetic and positive. I never thought I'd be visiting her in a hospital or seeing her looking so run down from all the chemotherapy."

For several months, Jackie did everything she could for Grace. Jackie made phone calls to find the right doctors and treatments. She made arrangements to carpool Grace's three children and make sure they were taken care of after school each day. Jackie also did her best to spend a few hours visiting Grace at least five days a week.

She recalls, "In between my kids, her kids, my work, and the rest of my life, I managed to be there for Grace as much as I could."

But then Jackie came down with what she thought at first

was the flu, and later found out was mononucleosis. She explains, "That was an even bigger shock. I felt miserable and run down one week after another with no sign of it letting up. Lying in bed with almost no strength to do anything for anyone, including myself, I woke up to the fact that I'm not invincible."

Like many of us, Jackie had ignored her own health needs until her body rebelled with a powerful reaction. Gradually over a period of several months, Jackie recovered. But she regretted the fact that during several weeks of being out of commission because of her own ailment she had been forced to stop helping and visiting Grace.

When Jackie slowly began to resume her normal activities, she faced a crucial decision. She says, "I had started working hard again at my business and doing things for my children. If I went right back to helping Grace and her kids as much as before, I would probably get sick again. Yet I couldn't just walk away from a friend in need."

Rather than doing everything or doing nothing for Grace, Jackie discovered a middle ground. Like many healthy caregivers, she realized that there are saner ways to take care of someone in need than overdoing it and becoming ill in the process. Specifically, Jackie was able to assist Grace and her children by using the following guidelines:

She delegated more. Instead of being a perfectionist and doing everything herself, Jackie became more creative. She hired a college student at minimum wage to run many of the errands and do most of the carpooling she had formerly done herself. She encouraged Grace's eldest child to take more responsibility for her younger siblings. Jackie also began using a local community agency and referral service whenever she was trying to track down some information or alternatives for Grace. Instead of making twenty phone calls, Jackie discovered that by tapping into the community agencies she could get the best information with only two or three phone calls.

She started scheduling in time for her own rest and relaxation. Rather than filling her organizer notebook list of "Things to Do" up to the limit each day, Jackie made sure there was a cushion built in for delays, problems, and time to unwind. Instead of racing frantically to an overfilled schedule, she set less stressful goals she could easily achieve. As Jackie discovered, "I can get the same amount done with a lot less burnout if I schedule sensibly and don't push myself harder than I can be pushed."

She began working with an expert at preventing stress-related illnesses. By changing her diet slightly and taking some preventive remedies prescribed by her health practitioner, Jackie not only continued to recover from her mononucleosis but also reduced her chances of getting another immune system disorder.

She started treating herself with more gentleness and support. Whereas before she never had the time or inclination to do so, now Jackie began taking long walks and relaxing baths at least three times a week. She started letting more sunlight into her apartment and buying inexpensive but colorful flowers once a week to boost her own spirits. She also set aside time each day for connecting with her spirituality, something she had been too busy to do in the past.

As Jackie explains:

For so much of my life I was run by this nagging voice in the back of my head that kept insisting, "You're not doing enough! You're not doing enough!" But now I'm starting to listen to my body a lot more. It needs tender loving care and I'm the only one who can provide that. Even though I always feared that if I took better care of myself it would mean I'd become selfish or self-indulgent, I've discovered that's not the case. Right now I'm accomplishing just as much at work and I'm able to be there for Grace and her kids. The only difference is that this time I also take good care of my own health.

As Jackie and many other caregivers have discovered, there's no point in becoming physically ill or emotionally wiped out in order to prove how devoted you are to the person you're caring for. Even if you've never believed it before, you *can* take good care of yourself while you are taking good care of someone who's ailing or disabled. It may require some extra creativity and common sense, but it can be done.

Whenever you notice that you're pushing yourself harder than is reasonable, take a moment to catch yourself and remember you do have a choice. Even if considering your own needs right now is an unfamiliar task, it's important you do so to remain healthy and available for your loved one.

CHAPTER FIVE

Getting Closer: What to Say and How to Listen to Someone Who's Ill

In addition to trying to help your loved one's medical situation, there is another important role you can play—helping this person feel loved and cared for during this challenging period.

That's easier said than done. Quite often the interpersonal situation is almost as complex as the medical situation.

For example, Eileen is a fifty-six-year-old journalist who travels to a nursing home five days a week to visit her elderly mom. According to Eileen:

> I rush through traffic to get there and feel badly if I miss a visit, but once I'm with my mother I never know what to say.
>
> I make small-talk. My mom complains about the food. I sit there. She sits there. She gives me advice about how to run my life. I give her advice about how to run her life. I look at my watch. She asks me to stay longer. I argue and get defensive. She argues and gets defensive.
>
> We love each other, but we really don't know how to

82

talk to one another. Is this how it's supposed to be between mothers and daughters who've known each other for a lifetime?

Deniece, forty-two, has an older brother named Howard whom she hasn't seen for five years. Deniece explains:

Even when we were kids, Howard and I fought a lot. But I think we loved each other despite it all. Then five years ago, we stopped talking to one another after an incident at my dad's funeral. Howard was drinking as usual and he just couldn't stop saying things that he knew would hurt me. So I've kept my distance ever since.

Three weeks ago, Deniece learned that Howard has cancer of the liver. Now she has to decide what to do about their estranged relationship. She admits:

I know I want to see him and talk with him while there's still time. But I don't know what I'll say.

Do I unload all the anger I've kept inside or should I keep it to myself? Should I let him know how much he's hurt me, or do I have to smile and pretend he's an angel?

Carl is a thirty-eight-year-old accountant whose son Bruce has a developmental disability. According to Carl:

I want my son Bruce to know how much I love him and want to help him, but sometimes I worry about being too overprotective. He has certain disabilities, but in other ways he's a regular thirteen-year-old.

Sometimes my wife and I treat Bruce as more dependent and helpless than he actually is. He never says anything to protest, but I get the feeling he knows that we're pitying him. And that's not right. We should love him, but not pity him.

Rachel is a sixty-seven-year-old mother of four whose husband Tom is seriously ill. She admits:

Even though we've been together for more than forty years, I feel like a stranger sometimes with my husband. The illness has changed him in so many ways. Sometimes I look into his face and I get tears in my eyes wishing that I could have the old Tom back, the strong and patient man I've known for so long.

But instead I spend day after day with a man who is not the same as he once was. Physically he's changed a lot since the illness took hold. His personality is different. Sometimes I wonder if I'll be able to accept him the way he is now, or if I'll just keep missing the way he used to be.

Are You as Close as You'd Like to Be?

Like the four examples described above, each of us has moments of feeling emotionally cut off from our ill family member or friend. At the same time, we all have memories of truly connecting with this person or wanting to find a way to get past the obstacles and be closer again.

In some cases, the emotional distance with a loved one began a long time ago. In other cases, the illness or disability has made a close relationship become more strained.

Regardless of when you first noticed the distance between the two of you, now is a good time to see what can be done about it—not only for your own sake but also for the person who needs your love and affection now more than ever.

Ask yourself honestly:

- Do you find it difficult to talk with your loved one who is ailing or disabled?
- Are you nervous about saying the "wrong" thing or bringing up topics that always seem to make things tense between you?

- Is it hard for you to relax or be yourself when you are with this person?
- Are you carrying some unfinished business from the past that gets in the way?
- Has something changed since your loved one became ill, and you don't know how to restore the closeness and good communication that was once there?
- Is he or she more distant and hard to connect with?
- Are you somewhat more distant because you're not sure of what to do?

If you answered yes to one or more of the above questions, don't feel you are the only one who's facing some roadblocks with a loved one. Each of us has to be honest with ourselves about what's working and what's not working in our relationship with a family member or friend who's ill. However, once you recognize that a problem exists and that something is keeping you emotionally cut off from each other, then you can begin to address the issue and make some progress.

Developing Some Essential Skills

To break the isolation and get closer to your loved one, you may need to take a careful look at the way you listen and communicate with this person. Although we usually take these things for granted, listening and communicating are vitally important abilities, especially when you're trying to reach out to someone who's ailing.

Many people underestimate the need to work on their own skills at listening and communicating. Yet most career diplomats, family mediators, counselors, nurses, social workers, and therapists go to school for several years to learn to become better listeners and communicators. Many corporate executives, medical professionals, police officers, and teachers pay hundreds of dollars to learn to improve their listening and communication skills. These are highly valued talents that can be improved if you seriously want to learn how to get closer to the people you deal with every day.

However, most of us are reluctant to improve the way we talk with and listen to our loved one who's ill. Some of the resistances I hear quite often are:

> I'm too set in my ways to look at how to improve the way I talk with her.
> He is too stubborn to change. Why should I be the one who always has to make the first move?
> We go back a long way and I don't think our relationship has much chance of improving any longer.
> The problem is not that I don't know what to say to him. The problem is that he refuses to listen to me.
> We used to get along just fine, but the illness has made it impossible to communicate.

While it's true that your loved one's ailment can be an obstacle to communication, I'm willing to bet there's still a way to get closer in spite of it. Most people incorrectly assume that the communication problem with a loved one can't improve unless the other person changes. My advice is, "You should live so long," because the odds are your relative or friend is not going to change or initiate the improvements. *You* have to take the first step, even if you've done it before.

The opportunity to improve the closeness has a lot more to do with your own willingness to refine your communication skills. There are specific things you can do to bridge the communication obstacles even if your loved one doesn't change one bit.

When People Fail to Connect

No matter how difficult it seems right now, reaching out to your loved one will be worth the effort. I can say this with some certainty because of my own experiences, both as a family member and as a counselor.

Since the publication of *Making Peace With Your Parents* in 1983, I have given dozens of talks on "Making Peace Within Your Family" to groups throughout the United States and Canada. At nearly every lecture, I meet someone who painfully tells me about a loved one—a parent, child, sibling, spouse or friend—who unfortunately died before their relationship was healed. In almost every instance, there were some powerful reasons for the obstacles in their relationship, yet there was still so much love and caring that was never expressed.

I have often thought that one of the great tragedies in life is when people who care about one another can't seem to talk to each other or be genuine when they're together. Please don't let that happen to you and your loved one.

Guidelines for Getting Closer

Here are a number of "Do's and Don'ts" that can help you begin to break through some of the obstacles and unfinished business that stand between you and your family member or friend. By using these communication guidelines, I hope you will be able to say, "This time I really felt good about spending time with my loved one. This time we finally connected on a deeper level."

Even if you and this person have been unable or unwilling to connect for a long time, there is hope. The next time you are with this individual, you can improve the closeness if you keep the following guidelines in mind:

Don't Treat Your Loved One Like a "Sick Person."

Quite often the emotional distance begins as soon as we stop viewing our loved one as a whole person and start seeing him or her as a "sick person." It's not something we do consciously. In fact, you probably never intended to start treating your loved one any differently because of the illness. Yet here are some subtle clues that you might be viewing your family member or friend as less than a whole person. Be honest with yourself as you take note of whether you or anyone else in your family have been doing the following:

- Have you noticed that sometimes people talk about your loved one as if he or she isn't in the room, when in fact this person is sitting right there?
- Have you seen your loved one interrupted and spoken for more often than usual because other people assume the ill person can't speak for himself or herself?
- Are people treating this individual as more helpless and dependent than is actually the case? Have you or others stepped in and done things for this person that he or she would rather have done independently?
- Are you aware that a lot more is going on in this person's life than just the illness or disability? Have people started focusing only on what's going wrong and lost sight of the human being who still has preferences, opinions, feelings, and other passionate interests?

If you or someone you know has been unintentionally treating your loved one as a helpless person rather than as a complete human being who happens to be physically or mentally challenged, the point is not to feel guilty about it but rather to stop doing it.

Yet that's easier said than done. It's a natural tendency to want to jump in and do everything for someone you care about who is ailing or whose abilities have been diminished somewhat. That can be harmful, however, if you begin doing things that this person can and should be doing with minimal assistance.

If you have often played the "rescuer" role in your family or love relationships, it's not going to be easy to break the habit now. But that's the challenge of being a compassionate family member or friend. You must identify what activities your loved one needs you to help with, and what things he or she can do that must not be taken away by an overzealous rescuer.

Here's an illustration of what I mean by not "rescuing too much" or treating your loved one as less than a person. See if this incident is similar to anything that's been going on in your family.

I recently had lunch with a forty-two-year-old man named Oscar, who has cerebral palsy, and his caregiving mother, whose name is Carla.

Although Oscar spoke slowly and with some difficulty as a result of his cerebral palsy, I could understand 90 percent of what he was saying and felt pretty comfortable asking him to repeat the few things I didn't understand. What made me uncomfortable was seeing Carla treating this forty-two-year-old intelligent person as an infant.

She frequently interrupted his sentences, spoke as though he weren't sitting right there, and repeated things for him that didn't need to be repeated. She seemed impatient and embarrassed when he occasionally had trouble eating or if he fidgeted in his wheelchair. Even though Oscar was quite capable of having a meaningful conversation about a variety of topics, Carla kept apologizing for him and focusing only on his shortcomings. She was so intent on "helping" Oscar that she actually was hindering his efforts to do things his own way.

In Carla's defense, I realize she has spent many years taking care of Oscar through good times and bad. She's probably learned to be apologetic for Oscar because we live in a fairly intolerant society. Carla has not only had to adjust to Oscar's physical challenges but also to the judgments and insensitivies of her friends, relatives, and community.

Yet at some point, Carla and the rest of us need to begin working on our own sense of discomfort and embarrassment with our loved one's condition. Until we start recognizing that our ailing family members have strengths and capabilities, we will lose sight of their humanity and only see their weaknesses.

Sometimes the hardest thing for us to do as loved ones is to just listen and accept what's going on—to stop giving advice or trying to fix everything. We shouldn't trample over our loved ones' independence and self-respect by trying to help them at times when they don't need help.

If you want to be closer to someone who's ill, it's essential that you relate to this person as a human being who struggles as we do, and not as a lesser being who has no rights. You may need to look below the surface and tune into the soul of the person who is crying to be heard.

Here's a poem that illustrates the importance of listening better to our loved ones who need support, and avoiding overadvising or overassisting them. You may want to share this poem with others in your life who have good intentions but who sometimes forget to just listen.

Please Listen

When I ask you to listen to me
and you start giving advice,
you have not done what I asked
nor heard what I need.

When I ask you to listen to me
and you begin to tell me why I shouldn't feel that way,
you are trampling on my feelings.

When I ask you to listen to me
and you feel you have to *do* something to solve my problems,
you have failed me—strange as that may seem.

Listen, please!
All I asked was that you listen.
Not talk nor "do"—just *hear me*.
Advice is cheap. A quarter gets both "Dear Abby" and
astrological forecasts in the same newspaper.
That I can do for myself. I'm not helpless.
Maybe discouraged and faltering—but not helpless.

When you do something for me *that I can and need to do for myself*,
you contribute to me seeming fearful and weak.

But when you accept as a simple fact that I do feel what I feel, no matter how seemingly irrational, then I can quit trying to convince you and can get about to understanding what's behind what I am saying and doing—to what I am feeling.

When that's clear, chances are so will the answers be, and I won't need any advice. (Or then, I'll be able to hear it!).

Perhaps that's why, for some people, prayer works, because God is mute, and doesn't give advice or try to fix what we must take care of ourselves.

So, please listen and just hear me.

And if you want to talk, let's plan for your turn, and I promise I'll listen to you.

−Anonymous

Even if it's been difficult to listen and not jump in with advice or assistance these past few weeks and months, you can begin today to turn over a new leaf. The next time you are with your ailing family member or friend, keep these things in mind:

- If you notice yourself giving advice rather than listening to what your loved one is requesting, stop!
- If you discover you are trying to do something for your family member or friend that he or she would rather do independently or with minimal assistance, stop!
- If you realize you are pitying your loved one instead of respecting and realistically encouraging him or her, stop!

As you keep these guidelines in mind, you will begin to break one of the toughest habits that happens to almost anyone who's in your situation. You will learn how to stop treating your loved one as a "sick person," and instead begin helping and respecting him or her.

In Webster's dictionary, the word *respect* is defined with two important meanings:

> To consider worthy of high regard or esteem.
> To refrain from interfering with.

When you are sitting in front of your loved one, ask yourself how to put into action these two elements of respect. Focus on the things about your loved one that you consider worthy of high regard or esteem. Make sure you refrain from interfering with the abilities that were not taken away by the ailment. Out of a sense of respect rather than of pity, a deeper connection and warmth is likely to occur between the two of you.

Do your best to start noticing the nonverbal ways your loved one communicates, and to begin connecting more deeply in the silent moments.

Most of us exert so much energy trying to make conversation and say the right things that we miss some great opportunities to get closer to our loved ones in nonverbal and silent ways. For example, here are three success stories of people who stopped trying to find the right words and instead connected with their ailing loved ones in a more profound way.

Sylvia, fifty-three, used to feel anxious whenever she visited her ailing husband in the hospital. Then she realized:

> The most satisfying and memorable times have come when he and I said nothing at all to each other, but simply sat there holding each other's hand. In those moments I felt more love and connection with my husband than we've had in years. Even though he's seriously ill, I actually have felt a sense of joy and happiness

during those moments when we're silent and I take his hand or he holds tightly to mine.

Jonathan, forty-six, used to dread visiting his father, but recently something changed about their time together. He explains:

> I used to argue a lot with my dad—about money and politics or what he should be eating or whether I'll be getting married again. But in the past few weeks I tried something new. I stopped arguing with him and started to look at the spirit that's inside him. He's always had an amazing spirit—very alive, energetic, and colorful. Now even with his body in failing health, I can still see that colorful spirit burning inside him. Focusing on what's inside my dad, rather than his health or his personality, has made it so much easier to spend time with him.

Kirsten, thirty-nine, used to feel cut off and unable to connect with her youngest child, who has a serious brain disorder. Yet recently she has found:

> I stopped waiting for verbal clues as to what my child needs or how I can relate to her better. Now I focus on nonverbal messages, little things she does or the way her face or her body reveal what she's needing. Knowing how to tune into my daughter's nonverbal world has made us so much closer. It's as though we're finally speaking the same language, only we don't use words any longer.

If you are like most people, you've been raised and trained in a society that emphasizes verbal rather than nonverbal and silent communication. In order to get closer to your loved one, you may need to supplement your verbal skills by adding a few nonverbal and silent abilities that can make an enormous difference in how you connect with your family member or friend.

To begin your development of these important communication skills, you may want to experiment with some or all of the following nonverbal techniques.

Giving comfort with your eyes. Many of us feel a lot inside but show very little of our emotions, even to the family members and friends we care about most. If there was ever a time to start showing your love and support through your eye contact and facial expressions, now is that time!

You may want to look in the mirror to see how your eyes communicate what you're feeling inside. What do your eyes and your face look like when you are feeling supportive, encouraging, appreciative, and loving? What does your face look like when you're feeling anxious, self-conscious, impatient, or judgmental?

The reason for looking in the mirror is not to be vain or to become a phony and pretend to have emotions you're not feeling. Rather, the benefit of looking carefully at the power of your own nonverbal expressions is to help you bring out the warmth and caring you feel inside.

The next time you are with your loved one who's ailing, remember to get beyond words and express your support and love with your eyes as well. At the same time, stop focusing only on the words and opinions that are vocalized by your family member or friend. Notice the caring and the love that are in this person's eyes. Even if this person has trouble expressing affection verbally, start to see the warmth that is spoken by the eyes.

Giving comfort with your tears. Don't be afraid to cry or to let your loved one cry during your moments together. Unfortunately, many people suppress their warm tears and inhibit their loved ones with comments like, "Don't cry" or "Don't start that!"

Rather than being afraid of tears, look at them as a chance to break through the isolation and finally connect with your loved one. If tears begin to well up in your eyes, let them come. They will communicate to your family member or friend that you care deeply. Your tears will also give permission to your loved one that he or she can cry as well without feeling uneasy.

If the other person says, "Don't cry" or "Don't get me started," just respond gently by saying, "I'm crying because I care about you." Or if they try to inhibit and block their own tears, you can say gently, "Let the tears come. I'm here to be with you."

Many people fail to get close to their family member or friend in need because they're always trying to be "up" and pretend they have it all together. Sometimes you can say a lot more about how much you care and how strongly you support your loved one by your tears rather than your empty assertions that everything's fine.

Giving comfort with your hands. Occasionally the best way to communicate your support and your caring is to simply rest your hand gently on your loved one's wrist, hand, back, neck, or head. Yet it's very important not to be more physical than you or the other person are comfortable with, and you should be sensitive to your own good reasons for not being physical with certain relatives and friends. For example, with a parent or sibling who was physically or emotionally abusive to you in the past, you might want to hold back from touching, bathing, massaging, or other physical interaction.

However, with those loved ones you can trust, your physical contact can be extremely comforting. Holding this person's hand, stroking a forehead, giving a foot massage or a back rub, or helping this person overcome his or her physical difficulties is an important way of becoming closer.

Human touch can be the most healing and relaxing remedy for someone with mild discomforts. However, you should be careful not to be too physical with anyone whose bones are fragile or who has other medical reasons for not being touched. If you have questions about how to use your hands to relieve discomforts for your loved one, be sure to ask a qualified massage therapist, physical therapist, or nurse.

Giving comfort with your calmness. In the middle of difficult times or tough decisions, your ability to be calm and focused might be among the greatest gifts you can offer your loved one. If your family member or friend tends to be impatient or frustrated when he or she can't do something because of the ailment, your calmness and support might be just the right antidote to help restore this person's self-confidence.

But how do you regain your own calm when there are so many stresses? The secret once again lies in how well you take care of yourself, making sure you get sufficient sleep, good food, vitamins, exercise, spiritual guidance, support from your own network of friends, and, especially, time off to unwind at least once a week.

There is one other thing you can do to regain your sense of calm and be a better listener when you are with an agitated or distressed loved one. It has to do with noticing your breathing.

When you are with your family member or friend, take a moment every so often to notice if you are breathing rapidly, smoothly, or hardly at all. If you are holding your breath, if your chest or stomach feel tight, or if your shoulders feel locked forward, then you need to remember to breathe slowly and calmly in and out.

If you are breathing too rapidly and feeling as though your internal motor is in high gear because of all the things that are racing across your mind, then you need to take a moment to slow down your breathing and relax. Inhale and exhale very slowly and smoothly a few long, luxurious breaths —gently, in and out.

Remember the metaphor of the oxygen masks on an airplane. Unless you are breathing calmly and sufficiently, you will be of little help to the person next to you. The goal is to make sure your breathing isn't too rushed or too constrained. Only by inhaling and exhaling smoothly and evenly can you maintain the calmness and endurance necessary to help your loved one.

***Don't be afraid to talk with your loved one about what's
really going on for both of you.***

Many people complain that they have nothing to talk
about with a family member or friend who's ailing. In fact,
what that usually means is they're afraid to talk openly
about the thoughts and feelings that are running through
their minds.

For example, do you really know what your loved one
feels when he or she is in pain or discomfort? Instead of
avoiding this topic as a social taboo—"Thou shalt not speak
about heavy subjects!"—you might learn a lot about your
loved one and what he or she needs if you simply ask for a
description of what the symptoms feel like.

You can initiate some fascinating conversations and really
be of service to your family member or friend if you are
willing to relax, listen, and ask, "What does it actually feel
like when the illness flares up?"

It shouldn't be an off-limits subject to discuss with your
loved one how he or she copes with physical pain and
discomforts, especially if that is an important part of this
person's life. In fact, if you were in this person's shoes,
wouldn't you feel better if someone you cared about took
the time to ask exactly what you've been experiencing and
actually listened patiently as you tried to put it in words?

Francine's story illustrates the importance of broaching
certain taboo subjects, such as what the ailment actually
feels like for the person who's dealing with it moment to
moment.

Francine is a forty-two-year-old woman whose closest friend
Gene has AIDS. According to Francine:

> For a long time I thought of Gene's illness as a news
> headline, a terrifying epidemic, or a political controversy.
> Yet I couldn't get close enough to the reality of his AIDS
> to actually think about what he is feeling on a day-to-day
> basis.

Then one night we were talking on the phone and I
asked my friend. 'What does it feel like when your immune system goes out to lunch and you're not sure how
to get it going again?'

It was the first time we actually started talking about
the reality of Gene's daily life. He told me what it's like
physically to notice your body is not doing what you'd
like it to do to throw off the illness. He also opened up
and began to describe emotionally what it feels like to be
unsure of whether you're on an endless downward cycle
or whether you're going to get your strength back.

For some reason, I'd always shied away from actually
discussing what the illness is really about. I must have
been afraid that if I asked simple questions it would
reveal my own ignorance.

But my fear of admitting how much I don't know and
how much I'd like to understand only put up a wall
between us. I'm relieved that we finally started talking
about what's actually happening in Gene's daily struggle.
He's my friend and I love him. It felt strange to be so
distant from him when he's so very important to me.

The flip side of being more willing to talk about your
loved one's illness is being more willing to talk about your
own fears and uncertainties. If you can find the courage to
honestly admit to your family member or friend that this
situation isn't easy for you and that you need his or her
support and love as well, that can bring the two of you much
closer.

For example, Gretchen is a twenty-nine-year-old woman
whose first experience of dealing with a serious illness happened recently when her eighty-four-year-old grandmother
was hospitalized. According to Gretchen:

For the first couple weeks I'd go to the hospital and
feel all bottled up. I didn't know how to be myself there
and I could see my grandmother was too tired and dis-

tracted by all the tubes and monitors to be able to reach out and help me open up to her.

Normally we've had a great relationship. I love my grandma and she's often been my closest friend and confidante during hard times. But now that she was in the hospital, I didn't know how to relate to her.

Then one morning when everyone else had left the room and I was alone with my grandmother, I just told her the truth. I said, 'Grandma, I don't know how to be real in this cold and sterile place. I want to be close to you, but I'm not sure how to do that.'

As soon as I'd said that, we both got tears in our eyes. All it took was for me to tell her the truth and all the walls between us came down. For the next several weeks, I felt so much freer to go see my grandmother and talk openly about what my daily life was like and what her daily life was like. Instead of becoming strangers, we were closer than ever.

If you have been feeling "all bottled up" and unable to be yourself when you're with your loved one who's ailing, now is an opportunity to start feeling a little freer. If you want to initiate a conversation that is more honest and intimate than the usual small talk that keeps loved ones distant from each other, here are some possibilities for you to consider:

- Ask your loved one to tell you exactly how it feels during the moments when there's discomfort and the moments when the pain subsides.
- Ask your loved one what he or she misses as a result of the current situation, and see if the two of you might brainstorm together to find a creative way to fill that need in a different fashion.
- Ask your family member or friend what kinds of visitors, conversations, activities, or entertainments he or she would find enjoyable, and then work together to make those wishes a reality.

- Admit to your loved one when you feel inadequate or insecure in your role as a caregiver. Rather than trying to hide or cover up your fears, ask your loved one to help you become a better friend and ally. Find out the specific things your loved one needs from you, and the unnecessary things you've been busting your rear end to do.
- Admit to your family member or friend when you feel shut out or painfully distant from him or her. Then work together to find a way that you can connect better despite the obstacles brought on by the illness.
- Talk to your companion who's ailing about the daily struggles he or she is having with physical challenges, other people, mood swings, and important questions about hope and persistence. You and your loved one are partners on a journey—make sure there are no aspects of that journey that are considered off-limits or taboo.

Do employ a sense of humor to lighten up your conversations whenever possible.

Most people have the tendency to put on their gloomiest face and most cautious tone of voice when they are dealing with an illness or disability. Yet one of the things your loved one probably hasn't lost is his or her sense of humor.

Like a breath of fresh air, your witty comments or humorous perspective can transform a moment of anxiety into a moment of comradery and closeness. Recent studies by Norman Cousins and others have demonstrated that humor is good for the healing process. A good laugh and a smile lights up our faces, generating a physiological response that has numerous positive benefits.

While some people are naturally funny and love to tell jokes or come up with a humorous way of looking at even the most distressing subject, many people feel unsure of themselves in the area of humor. If that's true for you—if you have always felt that if you tried to be funny it would invariably bomb—there is still hope.

There are several ways to bring a sense of humor to your conversations with your ailing loved one. You might bring along a book of witty observations, stories, or jokes. Even if humor isn't *your* talent, you certainly can read aloud the humorous talents of others.

Perhaps you can rent a video of your loved one's favorite funny films. Instead of spending all your time together in worry or anxiety, you can spend some of it in laughter and enjoyment. Or send away for a one-month free rental of old Candid Camera shows on videocassette by writing: Laughter Therapy, Allen Funt Productions, 2359 Nichols Canyon Rd., Los Angeles, CA 90046.

If possible, have your ailing relative or friend spend time with any newborn baby, small infant, or cute child in the family. Quite often simply watching an adorable child can be the most humorous and enlivening activity. Or arrange a phone call or a visit from a relative or friend of your loved one's who is always good for a laugh.

If you find some old family photos, home movies, or other nostalgic items, those can be a source of humorous storytelling. If you know of some great family adventures you haven't heard for a while, ask your loved one, "Tell me the one about Uncle Pete" or "Do you remember the story about the time you traveled on your own?" Frequently even those who can't remember recent events can recall in great detail humorous incidents from long ago.

Ask your public librarian or your local audio store owner for suggestions of humorous records or cassettes that your loved one might enjoy. Pretty soon you might have your family member or friend with headphones or a Walkman on, listening intently to Lily Tomlin, Bill Cosby, George Carlin, Bob Newhart, Robin Williams, Richard Pryor, Billy Crystal, Roseanne Barr, or George Burns on tape.

While humor can be wonderful, be careful that you don't overdo it. If you or someone else try to *force* humor into a serious or inappropriate moment, it can be worse than no humor at all. Make sure you use good judgment on when *not* to employ jokes and which comedians or humorous subjects might offend your loved one. Your best guide is to pay attention to what your family member or friend desires and not to impose your tastes.

Don't deny the fact that you have unfinished business to resolve in order to get genuinely close to the person who's ill.

Many people think that an illness in the family means it's time to sweep all the disagreements and past hurts under the rug. They think it's time to pretend to feel all "lovey-dovey" with the ill person, even if there's some unfinished business from the past that makes the kisses and hugs slightly dishonest. In an effort to avoid trouble, many caregivers and relatives simply smile and say, "Yes dear," no matter how much their loved one irritates them.

While there's nothing wrong with being nice, there's something terribly wrong about holding all your frustrations inside until you feel like exploding. Just because your loved one is ailing doesn't mean you no longer have disagreements or issues that need to be resolved.

For example, what are some of the things that get on your nerves? What recent disagreements or personality clashes have been left unspoken? What unresolved tensions from the past are still keeping you somewhat apart?

I bring these things up not to create added distance, but to help you identify what specific frustrations might need to be addressed so you can be closer again.

Here's an illustration of the dilemma you might be facing. Brenda is a woman in her late forties whose best friend Irene has cancer. You will notice that Brenda has ambivalent feelings about whether to discuss or suppress her unresolved tensions with her good friend. She doesn't want to hurt Irene, but she also doesn't want to become distant. Brenda explains:

Before Irene became ill, we had an amazing friendship that goes back many years. I wouldn't say it was perfect; sometimes we argued about things, especially about Irene's disastrous taste in men.

But even when we were upset with each other, we knew we could say what was on our minds and still remain best friends.

Now that Irene's ill, I no longer feel the same freedom to be honest with her. I'm always afraid that if I say something critical or controversial, she'll get terribly hurt, or pull away from me forever.

Yet the more I keep things to myself or I let her do things that irritate me without my speaking up, the more I feel like I'm losing her as a friend.

Because of Irene's medications and her exhausting treatments, she gets moody at times and she says things to me that I know she doesn't mean. One night a few weeks ago Irene and I went to a restaurant with my current lover. For some reason, Irene started criticizing my lover and I just sat there and took it.

I thought my bad feelings would pass in a day or two, but I find I still resent some of the things she said and I feel frustrated that I sat there and said nothing.

Do I have to pretend I don't have feelings just because Irene isn't always in control of what she says these days? I know she's ill right now and that I need to be understanding, but do I have to keep silent and smile when she hurts me or someone I love?

If you are like most people, you've tried to forgive and forget the things your loved one has done that hurt you. But let's not kid ourselves. Have you really forgiven this individual or are you pretending that everything's fine between you because it's too scary to deal with unfinished business now?

I'm not saying you don't love this person and want to do whatever you can to help her or him. But it's dangerous and distancing to start pretending your loved one is a saint, or to deny the tensions in your relationship.

By trying to ignore or suppress your unfinished business with this person, you essentially put a wall around your heart. You may say you want to get closer to your loved one, but your unresolved hurts make that impossible. You may be pretending that everything's fine but there's still something unspoken which causes you to hold back.

If your intention is to find a way to get closer at a deeper level than superficial smiles, something has to be done about the unresolved issues between you. If you want to get beyond this emotional barrier and truly have meaningful moments with your family member or friend while there's still time, you need to come to terms with some of the emotional baggage you've been carrying around regarding this individual.

Based on what I've seen with hundreds of people dealing with this crucial issue, I've come to the conclusion that we each have three choices of how to resolve unfinished business. Two of these options are potentially disastrous, while the third can lead to a positive breakthrough in your relationship. Your three options are:

Keep all your hurts and anger locked inside.

This is the choice most people make and it usually doesn't work. In the attempt to pretend everything's fine between you, one of two things is likely to happen. Either your resentments and unfinished business will slip out in sarcastic or impatient remarks you later regret. Or by keeping so much inside, you soon become physically ill yourself.

For example, Andy has a reputation of being a "nice guy," and when his wife became seriously ill he attempted to suppress all the tensions he was feeling and do everything to help her cope with her illness. Yet like any relationship, their marriage has its good moments and its disagreements. The more Andy kept his feelings and frustrations a secret, the more he noticed he was letting sarcastic, impatient, and critical remarks slip out to his wife. Pretty soon this "nice guy" was suffering from recurring headaches and back problems, even as he kept saying to his wife, "Don't worry about me, I'm fine."

If you or someone you know has been trying to pretend that the illness of a loved one doesn't present you with occasional irritations and frustrations, now might be a good time to end the charade. Keeping all your tensions from past or current incidents locked inside is the surest way to create additional distance between you and your loved one and put your own health at risk.

To dump all your anger in this person's lap and get everything off your chest at once.

This is the choice selected by only a small percentage of people and it doesn't work either. If you've been saving up anger for days, months, or years, now is not the time to dump all of it on your loved one. The last thing you want to do is bombard your loved one with a tirade of insults and accusations at a time when this person is unable to defend himself or herself. Dumping all your anger might feel good for a brief moment, but you will surely feel remorseful soon afterward.

I remember vividly the story of a woman I met several years ago who took the opportunity of her father's terminal illness to let him know every negative feeling and rageful emotion she'd ever felt about their difficult relationship. The day after she unloaded her anger on her father, his condition worsened and he slipped into a coma for several days before he eventually died. Instead of feeling relieved or complete, this woman felt awful.

Since that time, I have heard several other stories of people who dumped their entire load of anger on someone who was ailing. In almost every case, it caused more harm than good.

Some individuals even go so far as to physically strike a disabled loved one, something which absolutely must be avoided no matter how stressful things might be. "Elderabuse," the physical or emotional mistreatment of frail elderly relatives by their family members, is becoming a widespread crisis in our society. One recent study estimated that in the United States alone, between six hundred thousand and one million frail elderly are mistreated each year by overstressed family members.

If you find yourself furious, screaming, or close to striking someone who's disabled or mentally or physically ill, it's essential that you immediately stop and remove yourself to a safe distance. Certainly if you've been keeping too much inside for too long, it's not easy to stop yourself in time. But you can do it and you must find a way to catch yourself before mistreating an ailing loved one with physical or verbal abuse. Whether your anger is justified or not, taking it out on this person is *not* the answer. You absolutely must pull back and stop yourself from doing anything that harms the person who needs your love and support.

But what do you do with the unfinished business and daily frustrations you have regarding your loved one? How do you get those feelings out of your system and connect with him or her while there's still time? Is there a healthy and appropriate way to release the emotional baggage without harming yourself or the other person?

That brings us to the third option, the one that works.

Make sure you first find a safe and harmless way to release your frustrations, and build a healthier relationship with this person.

The best way to reconnect and overcome your tensions with someone who's ailing is to use a two-step process that requires *both* steps in order to be successful. Keep them in mind when you want to get closer to someone you love a great deal but who is difficult to be with at times, either because of the ailment or because of a personality clash.

Step 1: Find a safe and harmless way to get most of the anger or frustration out of your system.

There are several creative ways to release your rage and anger *without* dumping on your loved one. You can try one

or more of the following until you feel lighter and less
burdened by the tensions you've been carrying inside.

Write an angry letter to this person but do not send it.
There are two reasons you must tear up the letter after
you've written several pages of your frustrations. The first is
that if you know you won't be sharing the letter with anyone, it's easier to be uninhibited and completely honest as
you release your angry feelings. The second reason is that
there are other, more constructive ways to be assertive and
stand up for yourself than dumping a huge load of hurtful
anger on your loved one.

*Talk to a supportive counselor, friend, clergy member,
social worker, support group, or therapist about your frustrations and anger.* You *do* have the right to be upset when
anyone treats you badly, even if that someone can't control
his or her actions. Make sure you find a supportive listener
so you won't have to keep all your feelings locked inside.

*Keep a journal of your daily struggles, frustrations, hopes,
and feelings during this challenging time.* Make sure your
journal is kept private and that anyone who lives with you
knows they are not to look in your journal notebook.

Take time out to forgive the ailing person. Do this not by
whitewashing the incidents and pretending they didn't occur, but by understanding why you were mistreated and
what can be done to prevent it from happening again. Forgiveness doesn't mean to pretend all is forgotten or ignored.
Rather, it means to let go of your grudge or your need for
revenge, seeking instead to understand what happened, why
it happened, and how you can take better care of yourself
the next time. Forgiveness is an opportunity to learn from
the past without getting stuck in it. It can be the most
healing thing not only for your relationship with this person
but also for your own peace of mind.

*Take a long walk, go swimming, do some exercise or yoga,
or meditate quietly to let your feelings be released.* As you do
one or more of these activities, picture your frustrations
being sent aloft out into the atmosphere as you breathe in

and out. When you inhale, take in the strength to see your situation more clearly. As you exhale, envision your anger or frustration being released out of your body and far into the distance in a harmless burst of energy.

By finding a healthy way to get your tensions out, you will no longer need to remain silent or fear that you are going to explode. You can use these simple techniques to sustain your physical and emotional health in spite of the daily challenges you face.

Step 2: Be assertive and stand up for yourself without blaming, attacking, or belittling your loved one.

Once you've gotten most of the anger out of your system using the techniques in Step 1, it's a lot easier to be assertive without becoming hostile or aggressive.

Don't forget you have the right to take good care of yourself, even if you're with someone who, because of an illness, can't help doing things that may be hurtful or frustrating. When conflicts arise, remember you can stand up for yourself without harming the other person.

If your family member or friend begins to criticize you or bombard you with unsolicited advice, you have the right to say, "Hold it! I'm getting overwhelmed. Let's slow down and take it one point at a time. I want to hear what you're saying but I need you to be specific and constructive."

By taking charge in this way, you can become a better listener and at the same time avoid bombardment with more advice and criticism than you can handle.

Sometimes when a person is very anxious or in physical discomfort, he or she says cruel things that aren't true, occasionally directed at those whom this person cares about dearly.

If your loved one is insulting to you or someone who's important to you, you have the right to say, "Stop! I can't listen to this. I love you and I want to be there for you, but I can't sit here and listen to these hurtful remarks."

In many cases, this simple act of assertiveness will cause

your loved one to stop the insults. If they continue, however, you have the right to leave the room and explain, "I'll be back as soon as you're done saying things that are hurtful."

It's important to let your troubled loved one know that you care, but that you are also a person whose feelings and needs count as well.

If your loved one hurts you physically or emotionally, even if it's unintentional, you need to acknowledge that hurt immediately and not lug it around for a long time afterward. You can stop building up resentments if you remember to say at the moment something painful or frustrating happens: "Hold it for a second! Something just happened and I need to let you know how I'm feeling." Then, without attacking your loved one, describe what hurt you and begin to explore together how to prevent it from happening again.

It's important to keep in mind that you and the other person need to work together as allies and not become adversaries as a result of the illness. When you stand up for yourself and say, "This isn't working. We need to try something else," you're not criticizing or attacking your loved one. Rather, these kinds of assertive/nonaggressive statements allow you to keep building a two-way relationship in which both sides count, and in which both sides work together to improve what's been painful or frustrating.

In each of these techniques, there is an important underlying principle—finding a safe and harmless way to release your frustrations rather than letting them build up and explode later on. The suggestions listed above each allow you to resolve your angry or hurt feelings without taking them out on your loved one. By using the release techniques in Step 1 and the assertion techniques in Step 2, you will no longer have to put up as much distance between you and your loved one. Rather than feeling like a helpless victim, you will become more able to connect with one another in spite of the challenges brought on by the illness.

To illustrate briefly how these techniques can help, here are three examples of people like you and me who used these suggestions to resolve tensions and get closer to a loved one who is ailing. I hope these examples give you some idea of how you might use the above techniques in your own situation.

Albert is a forty-one-year-old father of a thirteen-year-old girl named Jocelyn. He recalls:

> When my wife and I first found out that Jocelyn has a serious illness, we began treating her like a fragile porcelain doll. But we soon discovered that Jocelyn is a real-life teenager. Despite her illness, she's got the same rebelliousness, moodiness, and need for us to set limits that most kids have.
>
> It's not easy to say "No" or "Cut that out" or "Stop being such a brat" to someone like Jocelyn who may never see her twenty-first birthday. But once we learned how to stand up for ourselves and not let Jocelyn push us around, my wife and I actually got closer to her. I think Jocelyn feels better having a "normal" child-parent relationship with us than she did when we were treating her with kid gloves and letting her walk all over us.

Gwen is a fifty-nine-year-old woman whose husband Walter is hospitalized with a chronic illness. As Gwen describes:

> Walter used to be so full of life and have a great sense of humor. But lately he's depressed a lot and he can get very critical and almost nasty at times.
>
> When I used to smile and be the "good wife" in spite of his angry remarks about me or the kids, I essentially took my frustrations home with me. Pretty soon I needed two or three drinks to unwind at night and even then I usually couldn't sleep.
>
> What changed things around for me is that I began

standing up for myself with Walter. I'm still a good wife and I love my husband, but when he starts making cruel comments about me or the kids, I stop him and say, "Hold it a minute! If you want to talk to me, you've got to treat me with some respect." At first I didn't know how he would react. But when I stand up for myself in a loving way like that, Walter smiles and I can see in his eyes how much he does respect me. It doesn't work every time, but even when his moodiness persists, I feel a lot more relaxed and close to Walter knowing that I've stood up for myself.

It's a change in our relationship for me to be this assertive with Walter. But I think the last thing he'd want is for his angry moods to bowl me over. He can't help being discouraged and upset at times. It's my job to make sure those moods don't ruin the warmth and trust we've built up over the years. When I talk back to my husband, it's not out of disrespect but because I want us to be close.

Corinne is a thirty-two-year-old woman whose mother has a terminal illness. Corinne admits:

I love my mother, but she can be an extremely controlling and criticizing person. So in order to spend time with my mom and not get anxious or defensive, I've started doing a few things to take better care of myself.

I've begun to see a counselor once a week to have someone who can help me explore all my positive and negative feelings about my mom. I've started taking a long walk each morning to let my feelings and thoughts run free for a while. I've written a few angry letters to my mother that I've torn up and thrown away. Each time I get my frustrations out in an angry letter, I feel much more open and more relaxed when I'm with her.

For years I was afraid to let her in too much, but now that I'm standing up for myself it's a lot easier to get close and not feel she's going to overwhelm me with her strong personality. Now instead of sitting there with my armor on, I can actually take my mother's hand and say, "I love you Mom. I'm here for you."

Starting Today

Even if it's been several years since you and your loved one let down your defenses and truly connected with each other, now is a good time to try again. You care about this person and yet there's been something keeping you distant from one another. Make sure you find out what that obstacle might be and then do what you can to overcome it.

It's important to be realistic in what you can expect from your interactions with your loved one. You should be careful not to expect overnight miracles. For example, if your family member or friend is stubborn, don't wait for the stubbornness to disappear before you can get close. You may need to love this person along with his or her stubbornness. Or if your family member or friend is opinionated and inflexible when it comes to religion, politics, or lifestyles, don't expect this person to suddenly become open minded. The important goal is that you connect as two people who care about one another, even if you still have lots of different ways of viewing the world.

One of the great lessons that can be learned when caring for someone who's ailing is to discover the power of unconditional love. Quite often we want other people to love us without judging or criticizing us, yet we tend to be quite judgmental and critical of others, especially our family and friends.

The next time you are with your loved one, take a moment to look at him or her through the eyes of unconditional love. Can you love him or her exactly as is, without judging any trait or trying to change anything? Can you feel at one with this person's spirit regardless of all the tensions you've experienced with each other?

If you successfully reach a feeling of unconditional love, even if it's only for a moment, you will have achieved one of the great satisfactions of life—to know that your heart and another's heart have touched deeply. That profound sense of connection with this person is something neither illness nor death can diminish.

CHAPTER SIX

Different Reactions: How to Take Care of Other Family Members Who Might Be Disguising Their Pain

If you've ever seen the movie *Annie Hall*, you probably remember one of the funnier moments in which there were subtitles flashed on the screen to let us know the main characters' true feelings. On their first date together, the Woody Allen character and the Diane Keaton character kept saying relaxed and charming things out loud, but the subtitles revealed how anxious and awkward they felt.

That split between what people are pretending and what they are feeling inside is a lot like what goes on in most families when a loved one is ailing or disabled. Many people who are affected by the condition of a family member will say one thing but mean another. They pretend to have it all together when actually they are falling apart. They insist, "I'm fine," yet in fact they are becoming worn out or physically ill themselves.

How Are People Reacting in Your Family?

When someone you love is ill or disabled, you may find yourself worrying not only about the ailing person's health and well-being, but also about other family members who are adversely affected by the situation.

For example, how are the different family members who care about your loved one reacting to his or her condition? Is there someone who seems to be doing too many things at once and who is beginning to get irritable? Is there a family member or friend who seems depressed or upset but won't talk about it? Is there someone who refuses to accept the reality of your loved one's situation? Is anyone in your family using alcohol or drugs excessively as a result of the family crisis?

Quite often you can feel an underlying tension in your family as a result of the illness of a loved one. People are not themselves lately, but no one wants to admit it or talk about it. Several family members are acting strangely, yet they will deny that anything is out of the ordinary.

Stop for a moment and ask yourself:

• What has changed in your family as a result of the illness or disability of a family member?
• In what ways has your family gotten stronger or pulled together?
• In what ways have family members become more distant, silent, or easily upset in recent weeks or months?
• Which family members seem to be coping well and which seem to be having trouble adjusting to the realities of the situation?
• Which relatives and friends are pretending to be fine, when in fact they are hurting inside and needing some support?

"They Seem to Retreat into Their Own Separate Worlds"

Dori is a forty-five-year-old woman with three children. Her husband Lionel recently suffered a serious illness and is undergoing treatments. She describes:

> Ever since Lionel got out of the hospital, I've begun to notice a lot of unspoken tension in our family. Everyone is pretending to be coping just fine with Lionel's illness, yet I can feel a lot of agitation just under the surface.
>
> For instance, our kids are doing their best to adjust to the upheavals in our family, yet they each seem to retreat into their own separate worlds. Our eldest son has begun hanging around a group of kids who drink a lot, and that worries me. Our middle child tries to keep busy in school and several outside activities, as though she wants to keep her distance from the family. Our youngest daughter has been staring at the television set, as if it were a numbing drug to help her avoid what's going on around her.
>
> My in-laws will come over several times a week now, but not really have anything to say to me if Lionel is taking a nap. I've always done my best to be nice to Lionel's parents, yet now they're here so often and we don't really have all that much in common besides Lionel. Sometimes we sit there with nothing to say beyond news, weather, and sports.
>
> Even my own parents seem to be pretty upset about Lionel's illness, but they're also silent about it. They have this worried, sad expression in their eyes whenever I see them. I don't think they ever imagined this would happen so young to someone they love.

What Can Be Done?

If you would like to help those members of your family who are having trouble dealing with the ailment of a loved one, where do you begin?

How can you feel less anxious and more effective when you're around certain family members who are covering up their true feelings?

In the next several pages, you will be given a number of guidelines and successful examples for helping your family respond more effectively to the situation at hand, and for helping yourself cope better with your family's eccentricities during this difficult challenge.

Please don't think yours is the only family that has gone through twists and turns because of the illness or disability of a relative. By learning from the success stories of others, you will have a better chance to make a positive impact on your own family situation.

Identifying the Reaction Styles in Your Family

If you want to be more successful at helping those members of your family who are having difficulty with the changing condition of a family member, the first step is to recognize the underlying reasons these individuals are reacting as they are. What makes one family member open up as a result of the illness of a loved one while another person shuts down? What makes some family members reach out while others pull back and become isolated or withdrawn? Why do some relatives act in a bossy or controlling fashion when there's turmoil in your family? Why do some members of your family keep their needs silent when they are hurting inside?

I have found that in most families when there is a disability or a serious physical or mental illness, people tend to respond in one or more of the following reaction styles. Which of these five most common types resemble certain members of your family:

The "Super Trooper"

This is the person who tries to keep extremely busy in order that he or she won't have to experience the pain and anxiety of the situation. You'll recognize this person as the one who keeps saying things like:

Don't worry about me. I'm not tired.

I don't need sleep. I just drink a lot of coffee.

Let me do it! I can run those errands and still be back in an hour.

If I remember to keep busy, I won't have time to get depressed.

Don't ask me to slow down. That's not my way.

Is there someone in your family who is rushing around constantly and can't relax or unwind? Is there a family member who's so busy doing things to help others that she or he doesn't have time to be human?

In some ways the Super Trooper's keeping busy is a positive coping mechanism. This person can certainly get a lot of things done. It's also true that, for a while at least, rushing around like a chicken with its head cut off does allow someone to avoid feeling much pain or anxiety.

However, there are a few harmful aspects to the Super Trooper's way of coping. First, the person who keeps rushing around and is too busy to relax and unwind eventually becomes unpleasant to be with. Super Troopers often get cranky or irritable, especially if circumstances force them to slow down for a while. For example, if the family is waiting anxiously for test results, surgery results, or other important news that seems to be arriving by snail delivery, the high-strung Super Trooper often becomes so agitated that he or she makes everyone else more anxious.

Second, if you need a calm and empathetic listener, it's sometimes a mistake to turn to a Super Trooper. Since most Super Troopers always seem to be in a hurry, they may be unable to sit patiently and listen to your concerns. You may feel rushed whenever you attempt to talk about emotional subjects with this person, especially if the Super Trooper starts saying things like, "Hurry up," "Get to the point," "Stop feeling that way," or "Stop being so sensitive." You may need to find someone else to be your empathetic listener.

The other harmful aspect of the Super Trooper approach is that by keeping so frantically busy, this person has no time to relax and recharge his or her batteries. Super Troopers often become physically ill after keeping their feelings suppressed for too long. If certain members of your family are like this, they will keep rushing around and insisting they don't need to slow down right up to the moment when they come down with a bad cold, the flu, or something much worse.

The following case illustrates how to respond to a Super Trooper in your family.

Like many adults who have a parent in declining health, Gina and her older sister Kate have been taking care of their aging mother for several years. While Gina tends to pace herself and avoid burning out, her older sister Kate tends to act like a Super Trooper and keeps herself extremely busy juggling all her various responsibilities. Like the person who can't say no, Kate is always doing something to help others, especially her aging mother. But she often becomes weary and irritable in the process.

As Gina described to me, "For a long time I felt jealous and competitive with Kate. Why was Kate doing so much more than I do for Mom? Why was she such a martyr all the time, taking on too many responsibilities and then feeling burdened by it all? Was she a better daughter? Was she a more caring person?"

Recently, however, Gina has begun to see a different side of Kate's Super Trooper style. She explains: "My sister

Kate is not the all-giving saint she pretends to be. In fact, she's a very angry person inside and her resentments seem to come out every so often."

Looking back, Gina recalls, "Even when we were very young, Kate was always trying to please everyone. As the older sister, she was forced to be the responsible one, the goody-goody, the one who had to take care of everyone else. Now that Mom needs us a lot, I see Kate rushing in to do more than is needed sometimes, and then getting exhausted or sick in the process. I wouldn't want to be like her, yet sometimes I wonder if her inability to say no is the reason she seems to be Mom's favorite."

Like anyone who lives with or is related to an extremely busy Super Trooper, Gina has a decision to make: Should she try to change her sister's habit of working too hard and burning out? Or should she accept that her sister has been that way most of her life and isn't likely to change now, especially with the added pressures of taking care of their aging mother?

If you are also feeling jealous, competitive, or frustrated with a Super Trooper in your family who seems to do much more than anyone else and tends to get a lot of sympathy and attention as a result, what are your options?

Or if you're worried that one of your Super Trooper relatives is doing too much and becoming ill as a result, what can you do to intervene? What's the best way to respond effectively to a parent, sibling, or child who is unable to slow down?

As I recommended to Gina, when someone you care about is a Super Trooper, the healthiest course of action for everyone's benefit is:

Stop comparing your way of helping to the Super Trooper's way of helping. Each of us has a different style and no one way is all good or all bad. You need to focus on how to improve your own way of helping your ailing family member and stop comparing your contribution to anyone else's.

If your Super Trooper becomes irritable or frustrated from working too hard, don't blame yourself. Recognize that this person has a problem of not being able to slow down and unwind.

Offer suggestions to your Super Trooper on how to set aside time to relax. But don't require this person to change an underlying personality trait or give up a lifelong habit. Without expecting overnight miracles, simply remind your stressed-out relative that you care about him or her, and that there's no crime in taking a refresher break every so often.

Brainstorm with your Super Trooper on ways that she or he can get others to help out. Possibly there are other family members who can ease the burden. Probably there are community resources you can call to assist this person. Definitely there are ways to do less and accomplish more as you work together to help an ailing family member.

Have your own individual relationship with the ailing member of your family and don't consider it less worthy than the relationship your Super Trooper relative has with him or her. Not every relationship has to be based on "How much have you done for me lately." You may find that even though your Super Trooper relative gets a lot of appreciation for hard work, your relationships within the family may be stronger on the emotional or personal level.

When Gina applied these guidelines to her situation with her older sister, she noticed two gradual improvements. She explains:

> First of all, I began to stop comparing myself to my sister Kate and that helped a lot. We're different people and my way of helping our mom is just as valuable as Kate's way.
>
> The second issue that has begun to change is that I'm a lot more relaxed now when I give Kate suggestions about how to slow down, recharge, and stop pushing herself beyond her limits. I recognize that Kate probably won't give up her hard-driving personality overnight. So I offer

her suggestions on how to stay healthy and say no once in a while. But I don't stand on my head waiting for her to listen to my advice in every situation.

Sometimes Kate does follow what I suggest, and sometimes she goes right back to overscheduling herself into a frenzy. I love her a lot, and fortunately I'm learning to stay out of her way when she's doing her anxious rush routine.

The key to helping a Super Trooper is to recognize that this person usually has a long history of rushing around and burning out in stressful situations. You need to understand the background for this person's reaction style and learn to accept the aspects that aren't likely to change. Yet whenever your Super Trooper relative is open to suggestions, let this person know you care and that you support him or her taking a break every so often to replenish and renew.

The "Can't-Be-Bothered"

In many families, there is at least one significant relative who simply "Can't Be Bothered" by the situation of an ailing family member. This person tends to downplay the seriousness of the problem and insists that everyone else is overreacting. He or she finds a way to be absent or unavailable whenever the family needs some help. The Can't-Be-Bothered prefers not to get involved, even when the family desperately asks for support.

You can identify a Can't-Be-Bothered family member by the following sayings or attitudes:

Don't get so worked up. Everything's gonna be fine.

I'm too busy to deal with this now. Maybe later.

Why do you need *me*? You've got enough people there already.

I don't have an opinion. *You* take care of it.

Is there someone in your family who has pulled away like this as a result of the family crisis? Is there a member of your family who tends to put up a wall whenever the family needs him or her?

While it may seem as though this Can't-Be-Bothered person is insensitive or doesn't care, in fact this individual may be disguising some deep insecurities. More often than not, the Can't-Be-Bothered actually is too afraid to get involved, or too unsure of how he or she will perform in an emotionally charged setting. Just like someone who freezes up under pressure, the Can't-Be-Bothered relative might be pulling away because he or she is overwhelmed.

For example, I have talked with numerous families in which one or more people expressed frustration that a certain family member was avoiding responsibility or couldn't be bothered. They invariably felt that this nonparticipating family member was being cold or insensitive.

While in a few cases it does happen that a certain family member simply doesn't care, in the majority of families quite the opposite is true. When I would meet with the seemingly Can't-Be-Bothered family member, I usually found him or her to be wracked with guilt and a sense of uneasiness. Quite often I would hear comments like:

I don't know what to do. I keep putting off getting involved and the longer I put it off the harder it gets.

I'm afraid to get too close to the situation because I might say or do the wrong thing.

I'm so busy with my work right now that if I get involved with the family crisis I'm afraid it will consume all my energies.

I have to keep my distance, because if I go there I'm afraid I'll fall apart.

It's not that I don't care. I *do* care. But I don't know how to show it.

If someone in your family hasn't been doing his or her fair share, you may be reluctant to feel anything but contempt. You may have decided already that your Can't-Be-Bothered is simply an insensitive person. But I urge you to give this individual another chance.

Regarding your Can't-Be-Bothered family member, ask yourself the following:

• Is there something unspoken that's causing this person to put up so much distance?
• Is there a possibility that this individual would like to get more involved and show more love, but doesn't know how to get past certain emotional obstacles?
• Is there some alternative manner by which this person can help out?

It's essential to find out how this individual views family responsibilities. Quite often the Can't-Be-Bothered person makes the mistake of thinking that caring for an ailing family member is an all-or-nothing proposition—either you have to spend all your time making sacrifices for the ill person or you have to keep your distance and do nothing. As a result of this inaccurate perspective, the person feels overwhelmed at the prospect of getting involved and therefore remains aloof.

What can you do to remedy the situation? As someone who seeks to understand the Can't-Be-Bothered person in your family, you can help this individual overcome an all-or-nothing way of thinking. To encourage a reluctant or anxious family member to get more involved, try the following:

Find out, from this person's point of view, what he or she thinks is involved in taking care of your ailing loved one. By simply listening to this person's assessment of the situation, you will probably find out why he or she has pulled away.

Assure this individual that an all-consuming commitment of time or money is not required. Do what you can to help this person understand that this is not an all-or-nothing situation. This person can help out in small ways without becoming overwhelmed or stressed out.

Let this family member know he or she isn't the only one who's having trouble responding to the ailment of someone else in your family. This person probably thinks everyone else is 100 percent comfortable with their caregiving roles and only he or she is feeling uncertain. Be sure to explain your own hesitations, fears, and decision-making process. If your Can't-Be-Bothered knows that you have similar uncertainties and worries about getting swept away by the family crisis, he or she will feel less alienated and afraid to open up.

Focus on small, easily accomplished tasks as a way of getting this person involved again. Don't start by urging this person to do something which feels overwhelming, such as becoming the twenty-four-hour-a-day companion to the ailing individual. Start with something that's relatively easy and comfortable. If this person discovers that small tasks can help the ailing person and that doing one's share doesn't have to lead to burnout or overinvolvement, it may dispel some of the fears that led this person to pull away so dramatically.

Loretta's story illustrates a successful way of dealing with a Can't-Be-Bothered family member. Loretta and her husband Jason have a five-year-old daughter named Marie who is severely disabled. According to Loretta,

Ever since Marie was born, Jason hasn't been his usual caring self. Almost from the day we learned about Marie's condition, Jason began to pull away. He began working long hours most nights and taking frequent out-of-town business trips. Whenever I asked him to get more involved, Jason claimed to be too busy and he'd say, "Loretta, you take care of it."

I couldn't just dismiss Jason as an uncaring person. I know he cares, but at the same time he had this irritating "I can't be bothered" attitude that dumped all the responsibility in my lap.

Loretta made some progress in helping Jason stop avoiding Marie by taking the following steps:

She began by looking at her own hesitations about getting swept away by Marie's condition. Once Loretta began to talk with a support group about her own feelings of being overwhelmed and her fears of "doing the wrong thing" when taking care of Marie, she became more understanding of Jason's reasons for pulling back. Quite often the more you admit your own insecurities, the less judgmental and distant you will feel toward another family member who is insecure about how to help a dependent loved one.

She encouraged Jason to discuss his unspoken feelings about their daughter's condition. Ever since Marie was born, Loretta and Jason had been afraid to admit to each other how overwhelmed they felt at times. Now they began to open up to one another. And instead of feeling alone with their fears, they began to support each other in a much more deliberate way. Loretta discovered that Jason's greatest fear was that he would fail to do "the right thing" for his family. Now that they could discuss their fears openly, both of them realized that neither should have to do all the work alone, and that they definitely needed each other's support and patience.

Loretta helped Jason develop small, nonthreatening ways for him to become more involved in Marie's daily life. Once Jason became comfortable relating to Marie in thirty-minute and sixty-minute activities, he eventually felt less anxious about spending an entire afternoon or weekend with his daughter. When you are attempting to help a Can't-Be-Bothered to get more involved with an ailing family member, it's important to start slowly and build up confidence one step at a time.

Loretta and Jason began to arrange for more opportunities to have fun with Marie. Whereas they had previously viewed Marie as "someone with problems," and took care of her as though it were a duty or a burden, Loretta and Jason began to see things differently after a while. They developed cre-

ative ways of having more fun with Marie and enjoying her
lovableness and vibrant personality. Eventually, Jason wanted
to spend time with Marie not because it was his responsibility as a parent but because he began to appreciate the
specialness of his daughter.

While not every Can't-Be-Bothered makes as much progress as Jason did, quite often you will be surprised by the
results you achieve. If you can understand why your family
member is holding back and help this person find small,
nonthreatening ways to get more involved, you may discover that many seemingly uncaring relatives actually have a
lot they can offer.

"The Boss"

Some family members tend to bombard you with advice
and criticism at times like these. As a result of one person in
the family being ill or disabled, certain others in the family
feel this is a crisis that needs strict rules and tough leadership. They start giving orders or saying things like:

> You're not doing it right.
> You're doing it all wrong.
> You're being much too emotional.
> You're not being emotional enough.
> Let me tell you the right way.
> Someone needs to be in charge right now, and that
> someone is me.

When someone assumes they have the right to start giving
orders in a crisis, it reminds me of what happened in 1981
when Secretary of State Alexander Haig thought he was in
charge of the United States government for a few hours
after the attempt on President Reagan's life. Incorrectly
assuming he was next in line, Haig burst into the White
House press room and declared, "I'm in control here." It
was humorous and frightening at the same time to see this
man's ego get the best of him in such a public way.

In our families, there are often one or two individuals who feel a similar need to throw their weight around and give out orders during stressful moments such as the illness of a loved one. They have a specific idea of how they want others to react during the crisis and they tend to be judgmental and intolerant if anyone doesn't comply when they say, "Let me tell you the right way." Sometimes people who are mildly authoritative during tranquil times become extremely bossy during a family illness.

Ask yourself for a moment: Who in your family is the bossy one, the one who likes to give out unsolicited advice and criticism, or the one who panics in a crisis and starts giving orders? Who is the person who keeps telling everyone else they're not reacting right, when in fact most members of the family are doing quite well under the circumstances?

Here are a few helpful suggestions on how to deal with the human tendency of asserting one's preferred way of responding to an ailing or disabled family member:

Make sure you don't become equally intolerant. Be careful that your way of responding does not become the only "right" way as well.

Appreciate that there is no "right" way to react when a loved one is ailing. We all have our own styles of responding.

For example, some people are more expressive emotionally than others. Some are "get the job done" types and others pursue a slower, more cautious style of reacting. Some are focused on getting rid of the illness or disability while others are focused on how to cope even if your loved one's condition remains the same. Each approach has its strengths and limitations. Each variation of style is necessary to complement the other.

If a family member continues to bombard you with advice or criticism, recognize that this person is being dogmatic not because he or she is "right" but probably because this individual is anxious. People who bombard you with advice or criticism usually feel the need to control a situation that seems uncertain and out of control.

Rather than feeling belittled by the advice or criticism, take a moment to remind yourself that there are several different ways to be of service to a loved one who's ailing. You can listen to the advice, decide whether or not it's appropriate for you, and then make your own decision.

No one can force you to act in a certain way. When you remember that you always have the option to agree or disagree with someone's advice, you can stop feeling so put upon by the demands. Simply look at the advice and criticism as the person's way of discharging anxious feelings and not as a statement about your worth as a person.

Be prepared to stand up for yourself. If someone's unsolicited advice and criticism begins to get on your nerves or disrupts your effectiveness as a caregiver for your loved one in need, you have the right to speak up and take good care of yourself. Be aware, however, that what you resist often persists. The more you resist this person's advice, the more she or he will persist in saying it over and over again.

Instead of battling with your critical or advice-giving family member, make sure this person feels appreciated and acknowledged. You might say, "I understand what you're saying. I've listened to your advice and I'll consider it." Or you can say, "I appreciate what you're suggesting and I'll keep it in mind." Even if you choose not to follow the advice, let this person know you have understood it, valued it, and will consider it again in the future.

If your family member feels offended when you don't follow 100 percent of his or her advice, you can say, "I care about you and I appreciate your suggestions. But we each have our own way of responding to this situation. I'll respect your way and I hope you'll respect mine." Instead of a confrontation, I recommend an invitation—invite your dogmatic family member to stop arguing over whose way is right and instead join with you in helping your ailing family member by using your two separate styles. You can agree to be different from each other and stop wasting your energy arguing over who's way of responding is better.

Norma's case is a good illustration of how to deal more effectively with a family member who starts giving orders or insisting there's only one right way to respond to an illness in the family.

Norma is a thirty-six-year-old woman with three children and a career in the fashion industry. When Norma's father became seriously ill, she realized that her toughest problem wasn't her ailing father—she felt close to her dad and could help him a lot during this challenging time. Norma's toughest problem was her mother, who out of a sense of panic had become extremely controlling and dogmatic since her husband's illness was diagnosed.

Norma's mother began calling Norma three and four times a day with unsolicited advice and criticism. If Norma was planning to visit her father at seven that night, Norma's mother would call her in the morning and anxiously insist, "You need to get there by six. Don't wait until seven." If Norma said she was coming at six, her mother would call an hour later and say, "That's a busy time. Maybe you should come at half past five."

If Norma brought her dad a bouquet of flowers, her mother would criticize her selection. "That's such a waste of money," she'd complain. "You could have bought something much nicer for half as much."

When Norma would talk with her dad openly about his fears and hopes regarding his illness, Norma's mother pulled her aside and warned her, "You don't know what you're doing. There are certain things people just don't talk about."

After several weeks of these kinds of incidents, Norma began to resent her mother for being so anxious and controlling. She explained, "I can understand that this isn't easy for my mother, but why does she have to be so critical of me? No matter what I do, she finds fault."

If Norma's struggle with her mom sounds like something in your family, what can you do to break the vicious cycle of criticism and defensiveness? Does a family illness have to bring out the worst in people, or is there an alternative?

I reassured Norma that her situation with her mother was not uncommon. Many times when a loved one is ailing, quite sensible and rational people become extremely anxious and controlling. Since the illness of a family member feels like a loss of control, very often the other relatives may try to regain a sense of control by giving orders or criticizing every little thing you do.

What Norma did to work more effectively with her mother is something you can do whenever you are faced with an anxious family member who has become controlling or dogmatic in response to a family crisis.

Norma began by taking better care of herself whenever her mother bombarded her with unsolicited advice or criticism. She explains:

> If my mother calls me at eight in the morning to start giving me advice about how I should do this or that for my father, I make sure to acknowledge her suggestions, cut the phone call short, and then take a few minutes immediately after the call to unwind. Usually I write in my journal or I do some stretching exercises to get most of the anxiety out of my system. After ten or fifteen minutes of working out my feelings from the phone call, I'm ready to begin my day again without carrying a huge load of tension from my mom.

The next step for Norma was to set some limits with her mother. Instead of talking three or four times a day, Norma urged her mother to save up her questions and concerns for a once-a-day call. While it took several weeks for Norma's mother to stop calling so often, eventually Norma was able to convince her that once-a-day calls could be just as effective and would cause fewer arguments.

Finally, Norma began to help her mom find creative ways of relaxing and feeling less anxious. She arranged to have a cleaning person come once a week for her mother and also paid for her mom to get a weekly massage at a nearby health club. Norma spoke to two of her mother's close friends to urge them to call her mother more often and see how she's doing. Rather than feeling victimized by her mother and powerless to help her, Norma had begun to make an impact.

She admits,
I still get irritated occasionally when my mother finds something to criticize. She hasn't become a different person, I assure you. But the more I've helped her relax and set some limits with her, the easier it's been to deal with her panic over Dad's illness. My relationship with my mother is far from perfect, but it's so much less upsetting than it was before.

The "Time Bomb"

In many families, there is at least one person who claims to be coping just fine, but in fact he or she is keeping too much inside and is about to explode. Like a "Time Bomb," this person may be at risk. With so much pressure building up, she or he may be close to the breaking point.

As you think about the different members of your own family, is there someone who exhibits one or more of the following warning signs:

- Refusing to go to a doctor for a recurring physical discomfort
- Not being able to sleep night after night
- Using an increasing amount of alcohol, drugs, or medications to keep going
- Snapping angrily at small irritations and not being able to control his or her temper
- Showing a dramatic change in personality or abrupt mood fluctuations
- Being unable to face the realities of the situation

- Becoming isolated and withdrawn, even from those individuals to whom this person has confided in the past.

With so much attention focused on the ailing member of your family, this other individual may not be getting the attention and care he or she needs. Month after month, the Time Bomb symptoms get louder but nothing is done to relieve the pressure on this other family member.

Quite often a Time Bomb is likely to refuse your help. You urge this relative to stop drinking so much or to see a doctor about a recurring physical discomfort, but instead of compliance you get resistance and anger. Your Time Bomb might even deny that the problem exists. This person has become so focused on the ailing member of your family that he or she can't see anything realistically any longer.

How then do you help a member of your family who may be at risk of becoming seriously ill but who refuses to seek help? How do you respond to a relative who is about to explode but says, "Don't worry about me, I'm fine."

Here are some steps that have worked for others in a similar situation:

Talk with your Time Bomb relative about the need to discuss his or her feelings. Encourage him or her to make an appointment with a physician, a psychiatrist, a clergy member, or a counselor to address the tensions and symptoms before they get worse. Remind your family member that it's the intelligent and courageous choice to seek help and not a sign of weakness.

Sometimes a relative who won't accept help or advice from you or other family members may listen and respond when that same advice comes from an outside professional. If your Time Bomb refuses to listen to your suggestions, do your best to get this person to a qualified specialist. But don't be surprised if your relative is reluctant to make an appointment. Frequently it's easier to get a mule to change direction than to get a tense family member to seek help.

Accept what you cannot change. If your Time Bomb is unwilling to take care of a potentially serious physical problem or emotional situation, you need to take a step back for a moment and identify those things you can control and those things you simply have to accept. For example, here are some guidelines that others have used when trying to help a family member who is close to the breaking point:

Can Do	Can't Do
Let this person know you love him or her.	Don't expect to turn a non-expressive person into an emotionally expressive person overnight.
Express the fact that you're worried about her or his health.	Don't try to turn a person who's always been a worrier into someone who never worries about anything.
Educate yourself on what affordable options are available for relieving some of the burden on this individual.	Don't blame or attack.
Suggest a realistic next step to reduce some of the pressure.	Don't treat your Time Bomb as an adversary, but rather as an ally with whom you want to work together to help your other ailing family member, without either of you becoming ill in the process.
Find someone who can listen to your concerns about this person and help you develop ways to cope with this person's stubbornness.	Don't give up if this person is resistant or stubborn.
Listen empathetically to this person's legitimate fears and reasons for not wanting to seek help. The more you listen to and acknowledge this person's reluctance, the sooner that reluctance will lessen.	Don't put the entire burden of helping this individual on your own shoulders. Ask for help from other family members, community resources or a qualified counselor or social worker.

Initiate a "Family Intervention." If the situation keeps getting worse and your Time Bomb absolutely refuses to do anything about it, you have a last-resort option to consider. In cases where your family member is physically or verbally hurting others or if alcoholism, drug abuse, or untreated physical discomfort is seriously damaging this person's own health, it may be time to initiate a "Family Intervention."

Most people misunderstand the concept of a "Family Intervention." They mistakenly think it's a time to blame, attack, or verbally gang up on a troubled family member. That's an incorrect assumption and can be damaging to your loved one.

In a true family intervention, your job is to gather several relatives together to urge your troubled family member to seek help for a serious condition, such as alcoholism, a drug problem, self-destructive behaviors, potentially violent outbursts, or an untreated physical ailment. There are four steps to a successful intervention:

1. Invite your Time Bomb relative to a family gathering that is perceived to be nonthreatening. You do not need to tell this person ahead of time that there will be a family discussion at this event. The intention is not to be disrespectful, but to make sure your Time Bomb relative does show up.

2. At the family gathering, have each of the concerned relatives read a personal letter, prepared ahead of time, that focuses on the problem without attacking the individual's self-worth or basic personality. These letters should be loving, supportive, and hopeful, while asserting firmly that the relative must make an appointment within forty-eight hours to seek outside help.

3. Make sure the family intervention remains supportive and focused on a positive next step, rather than an opportunity to attack or belittle the Time Bomb. No matter what resistances or hostile remarks come from

the person who needs help, remember to keep focusing the conversation toward the positive next step.
4. Continue to express love and encouragement to your
family member throughout the long process of recovery. You can't do the work for this individual, but you
can remind him or her that your love and support are
unwavering.

(For more information about how to initiate a family
intervention that is not harmful or destructive, please contact your local hospital, chemical dependency treatment center, or chapter of Alcoholics Anonymous. Three excellent
books that describe in greater detail how to conduct a successful intervention are *How To Stop the One You Love
from Drinking*, by Mary Ellen Pinkham and Families in
Crisis, Inc., published by G.P. Putnam's, New York (1986);
Crisis Intervention, by Ed Storti and Janet Keller, published
by Crown, New York (1988); and *Family Intervention*, by
Joe Vaughn, published by Westminster, Louisville (1989).)
Zack's family situation is a good example of how to respond to a relative who is about to explode but who refuses
to seek help.
For the past two years, Zack and his three younger brothers and sisters have faced a double crisis. First, their mother
has been in and out of hospitals for a serious ailment. While
the doctors feel her hopes for recovery are still strong,
Zack's mother needs constant care.
The second dilemma is that Zack's father has a drinking
problem which has gotten much worse since his wife's illness. While at times Zack's father can be loving and nurturing to his ailing wife, at other times when he's had a few too
many drinks he becomes sarcastic and verbally abusive.
Zack and his siblings are afraid not only that their father's
verbal put-downs will hamper their mother's recovery but
also that his raging temper may cause him to hit or injure
her.
For several months the four siblings have tried unsuccess-

fully to get their dad to seek help for his drinking problem. Recently, when Zack brought up the subject, his dad flew into a rage and threatened, "If you bring that up one more time, you can leave and never come back. What a man does in the privacy of his own home is his business and no one else's."

Realizing that their father was not willing to do anything to resolve his drinking problem, Zack and his siblings met with a local social worker who specializes in family interventions and began to prepare for their own last-resort effort to help their dad.

In the middle of a family gathering for Zack's sister's birthday, the four siblings, along with two aunts and a close family friend, sat in a circle and began the conversation. First they each read a personal letter to Zack's father, which they had prepared ahead of time.

All of the letters were loving and supportive, but also firm and focused on Zack's father seeking help. Without attacking or blaming the father, each person at the family intervention explained why they needed him to summon up the courage to enter a rehabilitation program within forty-eight hours.

For example, the letter that Zack had written and which he read aloud at the family gathering, stated:

Dear Dad,
   This is hard for me to talk about because alcohol is such a difficult subject. I love you so very much and at the same time I'm worried about you and Mom.
   I'm worried that unless you stop drinking and find some healthier ways to let off steam, it's going to be extremely harmful to Mom. She needs us right now to be sober and coherent and patient and wise. She needs us to have the courage to handle our daily frustrations without alcohol. She needs us to prevent the kinds of angry blow-ups and sarcastic put-downs that have happened repeatedly in the past few months.

All of us love you, Dad, and that's why we want you to
enroll in this program. We'll stick by you no matter what.
You've given us a lot and you've taught us to be strong.
Now we need you to be strong and face this drinking
problem. We need you to do this for Mom and also for
yourself.

If we didn't love you so much, we'd sit quietly and
watch the problem get worse. But we do love you and we
hope you'll do what's best for the whole family and for
your own health.

While at first Zack's father tried to downplay the seriousness of it all, and insisted the family was overreacting to his
"having a few drinks every so often," eventually the family
intervention began to make an impact. After five letters had
been read, Zack's father became extremely quiet for a few
minutes and then asked to speak.

He admitted that he also was worried about his wife's
condition. He promised to do whatever was necessary to
help her recover. If that meant entering an alcohol treatment program, he'd do it.

It has been estimated by various sources that somewhere
between 60 and 90 percent of people will enter a treatment
program following a family intervention like the one described
above. While there still are many more hurdles to cross in
order to help a troubled family member recover from a
problem with drugs, alcohol, an untreated physical condition,
or an explosive temper, this first step is an important one.
If a member of your family is doing things that are harmful
to himself, herself, or others in the family, you may need to
initiate a group effort to urge this person to seek help.

The "Ones Who Feel Left Out"

There is one more special category of reaction styles. It
includes those family members who feel ignored, not taken
seriously, or left out of important conversations during a

family crisis. These significant individuals may also be suffering and need special attention: young children, non-blood relatives, and estranged family members.

Young Children

Quite often when a family member is ailing or disabled, the young children in the family feel left out or not taken seriously. Important decisions that affect these children's lives are made without consulting them. Frequently when a serious subject is being discussed, children are treated like unwelcome intruders to an adult event. The children walk into the room and everyone suddenly stops talking or puts on smiling faces that are supposed to convince the young person that everything's fine.

In many families, increasingly complicated lies get told, even though the young children often sense the underlying truth. When adults try to disguise their feelings in order to "protect" young children, the children know that something's wrong and they incorrectly assume they must be guilty somehow because of how uptight everyone gets when they are around.

If there are young children in your family, you have an important responsibility to treat them with respect during this difficult time. Here are some guidelines to follow when you are trying to decide how much to tell and how much to keep from young children about an illness in the family.

Put yourself in the shoes of this young person. How would you feel if the adults around you were lying or pretending that everything's fine when it clearly isn't? Wouldn't you rather have someone sit down and honestly tell you what's going on, what's truth and what's fiction? Wouldn't you rather be told what's causing all the commotion, what's being done to make things better, and what can be realistically hoped for? Wouldn't you rather have adults who could listen to your legitimate questions and concerns, rather than telling you, "Oh, don't you worry your little head about that. Everything's just fine."

Explain the situation in terms that make sense to this young person. If your child has ever experienced the illness of a grandparent, a close friend, a teacher, a pet animal, or a famous celebrity, you can compare and contrast the current ailment of a family member to that previous event. Or you can compare a relative being ill and seeking to recover with a recent illness and recovery in this young person's life.

Be open to even the strangest questions your child might ask. Don't be surprised if your child has serious questions and imagined scenarios that need to be addressed. Quite often you will find children go right to the bottom-line questions that everyone else is avoiding. Your child may ask, "Am I going to catch this illness?" "Is so-and-so going to die?" or "What will happen if so-and-so dies?" These are valid concerns and you need to explain honestly what is still uncertain and what is no longer a worry. You will need to spell out in understandable details what is being done to help this family member get better and what this child can rely on for love and care if things stay the same or get worse.

Allow the child to react in his or her own style. While some children will blurt out honest reactions immediately, others may need time and a few follow-up conversations before they fully understand and can react to important news. Be supportive and patient as you keep the communication channels open and active with your children. Recognize that no two children will react the same, and that each child has individual needs and concerns that have to be addressed.

Don't treat your children as younger or older than they actually are. Sometimes parents talk down to their children or become overprotective when another family member is ailing. The children sense that Mom or Dad is very uncomfortable about something, but they're not sure what. Be certain that you talk to your children with the same openness, honesty, respect, and authority with which you would discuss any other important issue. If you start treating your

children as younger or more fragile than they actually are,
you will be encouraging them to act irresponsibly or to rebel
against such condescending treatment.

On the other hand, don't force your children to become
"mini-adults" or to become the rescuer of the entire family.
Even though each member of the family will be making
adjustments because of the illness or disability of a family
member, that doesn't mean your children can no longer be
children. They still need a life of friendships, play, explora-
tion, and fun away from family responsibilities. Children
should not be required to spend twelve hours a day doing
chores or sitting silently in hospital rooms or other restrictive environments. It's OK to ask children to pitch in and
help, but not to discourage them from also having a life of
their own away from the family turmoil.

Marta's situation with her fifteen-year-old son Perry is a
good example of the delicate art of talking with a young
person about a serious illness in the family.

Marta is a single parent with two children and a stressful
job in computer sales. After Marta's seventeen-year-old
daughter Eileen was diagnosed with a serious illness, Marta
admits,

> I was too busy taking care of Eileen, working to pay
> the bills, and dealing with doctors and nurses to be aware
> of how the family chaos was affecting Perry. He seemed
> to be handling it all quite well. He never complained and
> he even offered to help with many of the household
> chores such as doing laundry and preparing meals for us.

What Marta didn't realize was that Perry had a series of
unanswered questions and unspoken feelings. As she later
discovered,

> He was spending a lot of time smoking marijuana after
> school and lying awake at night unable to sleep from
> either the drugs or the stresses of the day. I didn't know

about any of that until one of his teachers mentioned casually during a routine parents' evening at school that Perry had been falling asleep a lot in the classroom.

Gradually, over a period of months, Marta began to change the way she related to her younger son. She explains:

> For a long time I had been paying attention to Eileen and her problems, while at the same time ignoring Perry or taking him for granted. That had to stop.
>
> My next step was to start setting aside time to do things with Perry and find some opportunities to start talking to each other again. I realized that instead of exercising alone in the morning or after work, I could walk with Perry and get into some good discussions. We also started a ritual of going out to brunch on Saturdays, just the two of us.
>
> He didn't open up for the first few weeks, but then we began to have some real heart-to-heart talks. He's very perceptive and he had a lot of insight into what was going on in our family since Eileen's illness was diagnosed. Pretty soon we began talking honestly about what we each could do to reduce some of the pressures we were under.

In addition to her one-on-one conversations with Perry, Marta also encouraged him to begin talking to others who could understand the pressures and feelings he was experiencing. At Perry's school there was a peer counseling program of former drug users whom he met with on a weekly basis to talk about the steps involved in stopping a marijuana habit.

Perry also joined a sibling support group at a nearby clinic, where he met several people of all ages who were facing similar challenges as the brother or sister of someone with a serious illness or disability. Perry discovered that he wasn't alone with his feelings of being taken for granted as

the sibling who "doesn't have problems." He began to recognize some of the ways he had been trying too hard to
make everything "like it was before" in his family. He also
made several friends who understood the turmoil and guilt
feelings that many siblings experience when a brother or
sister is ailing.

For more information about finding a sibling support group
for yourself or another family member, see the section on
"Support Groups" in Chapter Three and also Appendix C.

Like many of us, Marta had no experience at first in
knowing how to deal with children who are faced with the
illness of a loved one. But through her own persistence and
by using outside resources, she helped her son Perry regain
his sense of well-being.

The "Non-Blood" Relatives

A second group of relatives who are often ignored or
taken for granted when a loved one is ailing are those who
are not "blood relatives"—in-laws, step-relatives, or non-
related friends or associates.

Quite often these "non-blood" relatives are treated like
outsiders, even when they are almost as powerfully affected
by the situation. For example, Noel is a good friend of mine
whose wife Arlene found out several months ago that her
father is terminally ill. All of the attention in the family has
been focused on Arlene, her mother, and Arlene's two
brothers. No one imagined that Noel also felt upset about
his father-in-law's illness.

But in fact Noel has a deep love for his father-in-law.
Since his own father died when Noel was quite young, his
father-in-law has been more than just a relative by marriage—
he's been a substitute father to Noel.

Like many in-laws and non-blood relatives and friends,
Noel has kept his needs and feelings silent. He thought he
didn't have the right to be upset or ask for support. He
assumed his grief was "so much less than those who were
more closely connected by blood."

As you look around at those who are deeply affected by the illness or disability of a family member, are there certain individuals who are just as much a part of the family as those with blood ties? Is there someone who is being left out of important conversations and decisions? Is there someone who needs support and inclusion, even if he or she hasn't been able to ask for it?

Without taking the entire responsibility on your own shoulders, make sure you and your other family members find a way to invite this individual into your inner circle. Find a way to let this individual know his or her feelings do matter and that you consider this person to be "family."

Quite possibly this person can also help pitch in to share the tasks of caring for the one who's ailing. It doesn't serve anyone to keep excluding this individual or ignoring the love and caring this person feels so strongly. If someone in your extended family has a strong bond with the family member who's ill or disabled, treat that person with the respect he or she deserves.

The "Exes" and Other Estranged Relatives

Now we come to the last and most delicate group of those who tend to be excluded when a loved one is ailing. What do you do about this person's ex-spouse, ex-lover, or relative whom he or she hasn't talked to in years?

On the one hand, the illness or disability of a family member can ironically become a key opportunity for people to resolve their unfinished business with one another. Very often a feud or running battle of many years duration can get worked out when one of the parties is seriously ill.

On the other hand, there's no law that says you need to bend over backwards trying to patch up every unresolved relationship in this person's life. Nor do you need to become best friends or roommates with your loved one's ex or exes.

To decide how to address the important subject of whether to reach out to those who are part of your loved one's history, here are some guidelines that have worked for many others in a similar dilemma:

Find out what the ill person wants and needs. Rather than assuming he or she wants to make amends with someone from the past, simply ask this person for guidance. You may find that you've overestimated this person's need to re-establish contact with someone from long ago, or you might discover that by helping your loved one arrange a face-to-face meeting with someone from the past a load of unresolved feelings can be healed. In either case, the first step is to ask, and not assume anything without asking.

Find out what the ex or other estranged relative wants or needs. If this person wants to have no contact with your ailing relative, you need to take that fact into account. Unless you are a dentist, it's not your job to pull teeth and there's no point in your pulling desperately on someone who simply refuses to reconcile a hurt from long ago.

On the other hand, if your loved one will benefit from a face-to-face meeting and you sense a glimmer of hope or an outright admission that this other person intends to be civil if they do meet, arranging such a meeting could have positive benefits for everyone involved.

Be honest about what you want or need. If you discover that you've taken on too much of a burden and you realize you don't want to keep trying to reach out to an ex-spouse or estranged relative you don't particularly like, then don't do it. You can either tell your ailing relative that you've tried your best and it's time to relax, or you can delegate the job of peacemaker to someone else who is far more willing to play that role.

One success story that happened recently may give you some ideas for your own family situation:

Curt has been married three times and has seven children from those marriages. When he recently was diagnosed with a serious illness, Curt's third wife Miriam had a tough decision to make: Should she reach out to his two ex-wives and his estranged son from his second marriage? Or should she take the safer route and not attempt to be the family peacemaker?

Miriam knew from talking to her husband that he deeply desired to work through some of his unfinished business with his ex-wives and his estranged son. Yet when Miriam tried to set up some face-to-face meetings, she got nothing but resistance. Both ex-wives were unpleasant to talk with on the phone and locating the estranged son was next to impossible.

When Curt continued to insist that he needed to talk with these individuals from his past in order to gain a sense of completion, Miriam felt caught in a bind. She admits, "I didn't want to go against the wishes of my ailing husband, but I wasn't willing to put myself through another round of begging his ex-wives or playing detective to track down his long-lost son."

Then Miriam had a good idea. Her eldest son Rick works as an account executive for an advertising firm. As Miriam explains,

> Rick is an expert at bringing people together and doing research. I realized there was no point in my continuing to beat my head against the wall with this dilemma, so I asked Rick to be in charge of it. And wouldn't you know it—the two ex-wives didn't give *him* a hard time at all. The second wife even helped Rick find the estranged son that Curt wanted to see so desperately.

Four weeks after she had delegated this unpleasant task to her son, Miriam watched with satisfaction as her husband Curt presided over three "peace summits" with three important individuals from his past. As Miriam discovered, "There's nothing more gratifying than to know I got the job done, and in this case I did it by delegating it to someone who could get it done more easily than if I tried to do it myself."

If one of the responsibilities in your family is to reach out to individuals you don't particularly like or who seem to be giving you a hard time, make sure you don't try to do it all by yourself. Is there someone in your family who can take over this unpleasant task? Is there anyone who has more experience or expertise in the diplomat or peacemaking role? Is there a supportive relative who wouldn't mind taking this or another burden off your shoulders?

Once again, it's important to remember when you are trying to help an ailing loved one or the other members of your family who might be disguising their pain that it's not your job to be a martyr or a victim. You can give a lot more love and nurturance to those you care about if you remember to take good care of your own needs as well.

CHAPTER SEVEN

Dealing with the Financial Challenges

At various times in our lives, we discover that certain myths we've been believing are no longer true.

For instance, at five years old I found out there's no such thing as Santa Claus. I was nine when I learned that babies don't get delivered by storks.

It was upsetting to realize I'd been believing something that simply wasn't true. But one of the most startling discoveries in my life came a few years ago when another myth of mine got shattered.

Like most adults, I had assumed that health insurance or Medicare would handle the financial burden if a family member became ill or disabled. Then I found out that the myth of being "covered" or "protected" is a lot like my earlier beliefs in Santa Claus and storks. It's simply not true! I was amazed to find out just how much isn't covered by insurance policies or government assistance. I was shocked to discover how complex and confusing it is to deal with the financial challenges of caring for an ailing loved one.

From my own experiences and from talking with numerous other people and experts in the field, I realized that nearly every family in which someone is seriously ill or disabled faces a series of aftershocks that follow the news of a loved one's diagnosis:

- Aftershock #1 is the medical uncertainty. Will your family member or friend get better, stay the same, or get worse?
- Aftershock #2 is the psychological uncertainty. How do you respond to the many emotional issues raised by a loved one being ill or disabled?
- Aftershock #3 is the financial uncertainty. How do you deal with the escalating costs of medical care, nursing care, and medications, and how do you handle the increasing number of forms and procedures?

The financial uncertainty can at times feel the most confusing. Like a runaway train, the costs of taking care of an ailing loved one keep racing out of control. The average bill for a single day in intensive care at many hospitals now runs into thousands of dollars. The current average yearly cost of staying in a nursing home is greater than thirty thousand dollars. The prices of various therapies and medications have escalated dramatically in recent years, while at the same time some insurance companies have become more restrictive in their coverage.

When a loved one is receiving professional care for an extended amount of time, you may be faced with financial challenges you never anticipated, such as:

- What happens if your private or group health insurance only covers a portion of the expenses?
- What happens if your loved one has Medicare but it doesn't cover the cost of "custodial care" (having someone do the back-breaking chores of lifting, transporting, bathing, cleaning, feeding, and changing the bedding for a seriously disabled or physically dependent relative)?

- What happens if your family member formerly provided an important income source and now can no longer work or can no longer find a job?
- What happens if you or someone else who cares for this person should become seriously or fatally ill? Who then would be legally responsible to care for your dependent family member or handle financial matters?
- What happens when someone says you may have to give up your home, your car, or your entire savings to pay for long-term care? How can this be prevented?
- What happens if you lose your job, or if you need to reduce your hours or stay home frequently to care for your loved one? What options are available to help you pay the bills?

In addition, many people find themselves in what is called the "sandwich generation"—those who have aging parents and growing children who each need financial assistance at the same time. How do you simultaneously find the resources to help both your parents and your children? What if providing for one generation means you have insufficient funds to assist the other?

"I'm Allergic to Financial Details."

If you are like most people, this is not your favorite subject. No matter how intelligent or educated you might be, it's still common to feel inept when it comes to medical finances and bureaucratic paperwork.

Elena's case illustrates how most of us feel about filling out forms and dealing with health costs.

Elena, forty-nine, is a commercial artist and divorced mother of four children, one of whom needs ongoing medical care. In addition, Elena's eighty-three-year-old mother often requires financial assistance and advice.

Like most individuals, Elena can't stand filling out insurance forms or dealing with the complicated details of medical reimbursements. She explains, "One of my close friends likes to explain financial issues to me until she's blue in the face. But I simply find it impossible to stay focused and interested in what she's explaining. I guess you could say I'm allergic to financial details."

While there's no such thing as an actual allergic response to money matters, many of us have a troublesome reaction when we have to sort through legal and financial instructions in order to figure out how to assist our loved ones. Here are some clues that you might have a similar "allergy" to financial details.

- Do you put off having to deal with insurance forms, legal documents, and financial decisions until the last possible moment?
- Do you sometimes notice your attention drifting when a friend, lawyer, accountant, or insurance representative starts explaining various coverage options or financial strategies?
- Do you ever resent that you are being forced to become an expert at filling out documents and dealing with bureaucratic red tape?
- Do you occasionally sign forms you don't fully understand or settle for something that probably isn't the best decision for your situation?
- Do you at times feel more stressed out by the financial and legal issues of caring for a loved one than by the actual ailment itself?
- Do you sometimes wish someone else would simply handle all of this for you?

How to Proceed

Even if you're the kind of person who finds medical paperwork to be almost as fun as root canal therapy, there are ways to make this important task a lot less unpleasant. You don't need to be a lover of graphs, charts, rules, and

delays to become more skillful and comfortable at the for-
midable decision-making that is so crucial to your loved
one's situation.

I will attempt here to give you a creative approach to
dealing more effectively with many of the pragmatic challenges that you currently face, or might face in the not-so-
distant future. While many of the specific details of health
insurance and government assistance are beyond the scope
of this book, there are nevertheless some key principles that
can help you do a much better job of addressing your loved
one's medical finances without having an "allergic reaction." (For more detailed and technical advice, there are
several books and pamphlets recommended in Appendix A).

As you explore the guidelines that follow, you may want
to curl up with a cup of hot tea, a relaxing back pillow, and
a note pad for jotting ideas. This section may not be as
captivating as a romance novel or a spy thriller, but it
certainly can improve the way you cope with the financial
uncertainties and crucial decisions that have entered your
life.

For each of the four steps described below, make sure
you include any relevant family members in these important
conversations. If your loved one is well enough, be certain
that she or he is consulted before any financial strategies are
chosen. If there are others who might be offended by not
being included in an important decision, go the extra mile to
keep these individuals informed. Try not to let anyone significant feel left out of decisions that affect them personally.

Failing to communicate about financial choices is often
the cause of long-standing family feuds, especially where
important issues such as the spending of family assets, the
search for affordable medical options, decisions about the
future, and the costs of long-term care are concerned. You
may want to check with other relatives to make sure everyone who should be consulted is being included in important
decisions.

Step 1: Identifying Your Information Gaps.

Don't feel embarrassed if you discover you don't have all the financial and legal information you need to help your ailing family member or friend. None of us learned in high school or college how to sort through the maze of insurance plans and government assistance programs that help people pay for medical care. Nor do very many of us learn these details as part of our daily lives or careers.

Recent surveys reveal that most intelligent adult Americans feel ill-informed about making competent decisions about paying for quality care. For example, a recent study by the American Association of Retired Persons (AARP) interviewed more than two thousand randomly selected adults over the age of forty-five to see how much they understood about Medicare coverage and reimbursement. The survey demonstrated that:

- *Seventy-five percent of the adults questioned said they knew "Not Much" or "Only Some" about how to pay for their family members' medical and long-term health-care costs.* Most of us either don't know or don't understand our own health insurance policies and what they cover and don't cover.
- *Sixty-two percent of the adults surveyed had never heard of the DRG System (Diagnosis-Related Groups), which is the method by which the government decides how much Medicare will reimburse you for particular medical procedures and treatment programs.* Quite often the actual costs are higher than what Medicare will cover. This has led to hospitals discharging patients quicker than is advisable and has surprised many family members who thought their coverage was sufficient to avoid costly out-of-pocket expenses.
- *The vast majority of adults surveyed held the belief that Medicare would pay the entire cost of extended nursing home stays, when in fact that isn't true.* Medicare pays for only certain medical and rehabilitation costs in par-

ticipating skilled nursing facilities, but does not pay for numerous other costs such as "custodial care" and services to meet personal needs. Too many families who need this information ahead of time are shocked and confused when they discover that they have to find another way to pay the "gap" between Medicare and actual nursing home costs.

In addition most middle-class families don't take the time to understand how government Medicaid works, often because they assume they will never need to apply for it. Medicaid (which is called MediCal in California) is a government insurance program to pay for the medical care of low-income citizens of all ages. Even though most people think of it as "welfare," in fact a huge number of middle-class families can qualify an ailing loved one for Medicaid to pay for long-term care and nursing home costs. But you need to understand the Medicaid regulations in your particular state well in advance of applying for assistance. In most states, you need to "spend down" or transfer assets to another family member two years before applying for Medicaid. The longer you wait to become fully informed about Medicaid rules, the longer it takes to qualify for the program.

"I Wish People Would Start Asking the Right Questions Sooner."

Our shortage of information about medical coverage is understandable, but it's also dangerous. Unless you begin to find ways to overcome your uncertainties and misinformation about how to pay for quality care, you or your loved one might suffer as a result.

I recently spoke with an expert in health-care coverage named Cornelia. She has worked the last twelve years as an "intake nurse," the person who fills out the paperwork on patients when they are enrolled in an excellent long-term care facility not far from where I live. Every day Cornelia meets families who walk in the door expecting that their health insurance policy plus Medicare will cover most, if not all, of the expenses.

Cornelia's difficult task is to explain to each family as they arrive that they need to reexamine their coverage. In most cases, she finds the families either don't understand their coverage, have purchased the wrong insurance plan, or are insufficiently protected against many of the costs of long-term care.

Cornelia admits,

> It breaks my heart to have to tell families all day long that they may lose their homes, their cars, or their savings in order to pay for their loved one receiving quality care. Usually I try to work with the family to offer them some alternatives. But in many cases, they've waited too long to make the necessary arrangements, or they haven't kept files of the right information they will need to apply for certain kinds of assistance. I wish people would start asking the right questions sooner and getting their financial details straightened out *before* they're at the entrance of the facility and it's often too late.

To make sure you don't wind up being told you've purchased the wrong policy or that you're unable to pay for the quality care your loved one deserves, begin this week to identify your own information gaps. Even if you'd rather be doing other things, take approximately an hour per day for the next seven workdays to do the following:

Find out exactly what your insurance covers. Sit down with your insurance representative and be sure you understand exactly what your family member's private or group health plan covers and doesn't cover. Find out what options you have for improving the coverage without adding any unnecessary costs.

Talk with a caseworker at your local hospital, senior center, Catholic Social Services, Jewish Family Service, or another denominational program in your area—ask your minister, priest, or rabbi for a suggestion. Find out what specific financial concerns you must resolve to make sure there are no surprises or gaps in your loved one's coverage. Or talk with an accountant or financial planner who understands medical finances and can explore the best strategies with you.

Be sure to ask about how to apply for SSI (Supplemental Security Income), Medicare, Medicaid, and Veteran's Administration (V.A.) Benefits. You may be pleased to find out your loved one is entitled to assistance you never knew about previously. If you have any questions or problems regarding Social Security, Medicare, or Supplemental Security Income (SSI), you can call the 24-hour toll-free number 1-800-234-5772.

Send for some of the free or low-cost information sources listed in Appendix A that explain specific financial strategies for family members in your situation. Most of these publications are written in understandable language to help you make more informed decisions.

Ask yourself the following questions:

"What financial or legal areas do I need to understand better than I do now so that I don't make a bad decision for my loved one?"

"What person or agency can I call or visit in the next seven days who will explain this to me in the clearest language?"

Unfortunately, most people put off this information-gathering step and wind up facing an embarrassing situation of having to settle for insufficient care or risking a severe financial setback for yourself or your family member. I have heard countless horror stories of people who were victims of financial catastrophes simply because they lacked important information about the right strategies for avoiding disaster. If only they had overcome their "allergy" to financial details for just a few days and sought competent advice, their financial hardships might have been prevented.

"This Is Not What We Expected."

Nina and Bruce are good examples of people who lacked important information but were reluctant to seek advice. When Nina's mother began having dizzy spells and eventually had to be hospitalized, Nina and her husband Bruce started using up their savings and their children's college funds in order to pay for quality care.

Month after month the bills escalated and the tensions in their relationship increased. Nina explains, "Bruce cares a lot about my aging mother, but he also resented that most of our plans for the future were going out the window because we were spending all our hard-earned savings."

Like many people who want to help a family member in need, Nina and Bruce were becoming "downwardly mobile." Bruce describes their drop in financial security as follows:

> Once upon a time we were "comfortable" financially and thought that would continue. But ever since we began paying for medical costs, private nurses, and increased insurance bills to help Nina's mother, we've moved down in economic status from "comfortable" to "barely getting by." Some months we can pay our bills and some months we wind up going deeper into debt. This is not what we expected to happen when Nina's mother first became ill. Some months we're paying a lot more for my mother-in-law's care than we pay for our mortgage, our car loans, our kids, and our usual assortment of bills and expenses."

For a long time, Bruce and Nina refused to take the suggestion of one of their friends who advised them to talk to a caseworker.

Bruce expressed his feelings at the time:

> We weren't going to spill our guts to some social worker we'd never met. Social workers are for poor people on welfare. Nina and I aren't poor and we're not on welfare, thank goodness.

But as their financial situation and the money conflicts in their marriage got worse, Bruce and Nina's refusal to locate and talk with a caseworker became even more costly. Nina started having mild heart palpitations and underwent tests at a nearby hospital. Fortunately, the cardiology test results were favorable and Nina's heart was still in relatively good condition.

At the hospital, Nina met a medical social worker who was on staff and advised Nina on ways to pay for her cardiology tests. As Nina describes,

> This intelligent and helpful woman didn't fit any of my pictures of what a social worker is supposed to be. Talking to her, I realized you don't have to be poor or on welfare to need the information of someone who's trained to help people get through the bureaucracies of medical expenses. While we were discussing how I was going to pay for my cardiology tests, I happened to ask her about the problems we were having with the costs of my mother's long-term care. That led to a series of conversations and an eventual meeting where Bruce and I got to explore our options with this caseworker.

To their surprise, Nina and Bruce found out that the majority of health-care bills they'd been paying could have been taken care of by other means. Specifically, Nina's father had qualified for Veteran's Administration benefits and also for a retirement policy from one of his previous employers, both of which covered the medical care of spouses. Nina's mother was also qualified to apply for and receive a monthly check from SSI.

The caseworker also explained that they could receive several tax breaks they had failed to use because of the money they were spending on Nina's mother's medical care. She also recommended a less costly but equally respected nursing service.

While these conversations and financial strategies didn't

solve all of Nina and Bruce's problems, they did begin to ease the burden. Like most people, Nina and Bruce had never realized they were entitled to several different kinds of benefits. With continued advice and guidance from a caseworker and a financial planner, they eventually developed a monthly budget and long-term financial plan that allowed them to help Nina's mother, save for their kids' educations, and still pay their monthly expenses.

If you are like Bruce and Nina in that you have always believed that social workers are only for the poor or that financial planners are only for the rich, now is a good time to take another look at the professional advice that might be available to you. All of us need the expertise and contacts that certain caseworkers and financial advisers can provide. By talking with knowledgeable individuals who specialize in health-care finances, you may be able to relieve much of the burden you and your loved ones have been suffering.

Step 2: Discovering a Missing Source of Funds.

This is an extremely important step, especially when you are dealing with an Alzheimer's patient or someone who can no longer remember or communicate about financial details. Your family member may have an insurance policy, a savings account, a file of documents, or a series of investments you don't know about. You and the other family members may need to locate these resources with very little help. While it may be awkward or uncomfortable to be acting a little bit like a private detective, that may be necessary if you are to find all that is available to help your family member or friend afford quality care.

Here are some ways you might uncover some additional resources for helping your loved one:

Talk to this person's most recent employer and all previous employers. Ask for the Personnel Manager who specializes in Employee Benefits. Find out if there is additional help from group health plans, disability benefits, pensions, retirement programs, or other potential sources of funds.

Dig through your loved one's paperwork. Look for old receipts, bank statements, canceled checks, a safe deposit box key, passbooks, or other clues of additional savings accounts, investments, insurance policies, real estate holdings, or other liquid assets.

Check on any theft insurance application forms or home insurance policies to see what valuables, collections, jewelry, coins, and artwork were listed. Then discuss with other family members if these valuables should or should not be used to pay for long-term care.

Find out if your loved one has a written will. It probably lists available assets, investments, and valuables. Most wills are kept in a file cabinet, a home safe, a safe deposit box at the bank, or with an attorney.

If your family member has been married before, find out from a caseworker, lawyer, accountant, or from local court documents whether your loved one is entitled to Social Security benefits, pensions, retirement accounts, or other sources of funds from that previous spouse. There may also be alimony payments due as part of the court settlement. Occasionally in divorce settlements there is a provision of future support in the event that a spouse becomes ill or disabled.

If you or your relative have served in the armed forces, contact a Veteran's Administration representative about coverage plans, benefits, and facilities for veterans and their families. As in the previous case of Nina and Bruce, quite often people forget to utilize this important resource that can save thousands of dollars.

Be sure to photocopy and keep a record of all receipts, bills, bank statements, forms, and medical records. You can save yourself a lot of time and aggravation by having an accessible file of information, instead of having to search for documentation every time you are dealing with doctors, insurance companies, bureaucrats, and the Internal Revenue Service.

Brainstorm. Talk with a caseworker, a financial adviser, or other family members about other places where you might look to find additional financial resources and assistance that can help pay for quality care.

When asking about financial details like these, you may need a letter from a physician or an attorney before the bank, insurance company, or other source of funds will release details. In some cases, you may need to get a legal authorization to have access to certain information or to use the available funds to pay for your loved one's medical care. Be sure to get advice from a knowledgeable expert if you come up against some roadblocks.

"I Want to Do What I Can to Make His Final Years Comfortable."

Here's an illustration of the importance of becoming a bit of a detective in order to help your loved one:

Doris was fifty-seven when she married her second husband Graham, who also had been divorced previously. For sixteen years after their marriage, Doris and Graham led an exciting and fulfilling life. Graham loved to travel, paint, bake homemade breads, and sample fine wines.

But in his mid seventies, Graham began to lose his memory and eventually was diagnosed with Alzheimer's Disease. According to Doris,

> After years of being so energetic and lively, he was no longer himself. He'd go into the kitchen and turn on the oven to bake some bread, but then he'd forget why he'd done that and he'd sit there staring into space with the oven on and the ingredients spread all over the counterspace. Pretty soon he couldn't even remember if he'd gone to the bathroom or not, or he'd have an accident and be too disoriented to care. Each morning, I would have to lift his arms and dress him like a baby.

Yet like many caregivers, Doris took care of her husband out of a sense of pride. She explains, "I love my husband and sometimes I feel a sense of pure satisfaction knowing

I'm coming through for him. I want to do what I can to make his final years comfortable."

Doris's toughest challenge was finding a way to pay for all the costs of long-term care. She wanted to bring in a home-care nurse to help take better care of her incapacitated husband and help him get dressed and changed each day. Doris admits, "Lifting a two-hundred-pound man several times a day was beginning to wear me down and my doctor was worried about my back going out on me again."

However, Doris found that the cost of a home-care nurse was more than their insurance or Medicare would pay. She thought about applying for Medicaid, but was told her husband did not qualify according to the restrictions in their particular state. Doris considered putting Graham in a nursing home, but that also appeared to be too costly. She recalls, "This was the first time in my life when I felt all my choices were out of reach. No matter which option I picked, there was this sense that it would cause me to live the rest of my life in poverty."

Then Doris attended a support group of Alzheimer's Caregivers (see Appendixes B and C for details on locating or starting a support group for your loved one's ailment). At one of the meetings, she heard of another spouse in a similar situation, but the wife in this case had begun to act like a private detective and tracked down several sources of missing funds that could help pay for home-care assistance or a quality nursing home.

With the help of her daughter, Doris began to do some research. She hit a few dead ends and roadblocks, but eventually came up with several additional sources of funds.

Doris discovered in a stashed-away file folder a pension plan from one of Graham's former employers, a job he'd held for twelve years in his thirties and forties. It had a provision whereby employees of the firm could receive substantial medical coverage after retirement from certain preferred providers. She also discovered that Graham held passbooks for two savings accounts at another bank, which he had established before their marriage. In a safe deposit box, she discovered an old Army medal—a clue to look for Veterans Administration benefits.

Rather than losing her home or having to resort to desperate measures to care for her husband, Doris now had some viable options. While not every person who searches for missing funds comes up with as much as Doris found, in many cases you will be surprised at how much we don't know about the financial details of loved ones. Even if you think you know everything about your spouse, your parents, your children, or your siblings, you may find there are financial documents or overlooked employee benefits that can make a difference.

Searching for missing funds is an important step to take even when you're pretty sure you won't find any additional sources of support. In some cases, it can prevent the frustration and embarrassment that happens to many families when they apply for assistance and the missing funds are uncovered by the government agency instead of by you. For example, if you are applying for Medicaid you will need to prove that your loved one truly qualifies. This may take several months or even years to accomplish. Wouldn't it be frustrating to go through all the paperwork and procedures, only to have the Medicaid office call up and tell you about a savings account or hidden asset that disqualifies your loved one and forces you to start over again? I've seen this happen to people who were reluctant to play the role of private detective. Even if it seems uncomfortable at first to be researching your loved one's financial resources, it can help him or her afford quality care.

Step 3: Have a Brainstorming Session with Close Relatives.

In your family, is everyone pitching in financially? Or is the responsibility of caring for an ailing loved one falling too heavily on one or two individuals?

In most families, one individual or couple usually tries to handle the entire financial situation by themselves. While this may seem noble at first, in fact it is often a shortsighted or foolish strategy. Many spouses, parents, and children of ailing family members needlessly jeopardize their own health and financial security by trying to do too much and not being willing to ask for help from others who are quite capable of making a significant contribution.

Sometimes we're too proud to ask anyone for help. In other cases, we need others to pitch in but we don't know how to ask for assistance.

If you stop and think about it, there may be several additional sources of family funds that can be identified and used. That's why it's essential for you to have a brainstorming session with close relatives as soon as possible to identify financial resources and strategies you may have overlooked.

Your brainstorming session can take place in one of three ways:

- By getting as many family members as possible together for a problem-solving meeting.
- By making a series of telephone calls to those who live too far away to attend the meeting, for those who claim to be too busy to attend the session, and for those who won't show up because of personal reasons or ongoing feuds.
- By combining both of the above. Have a family gathering to discuss practical issues and also make sure to contact the members not present by telephone during the meeting.

I call this step a brainstorming session because that's precisely what it is—a chance to generate good ideas and creative solutions. Besides, the word *brainstorming* is a lot less threatening than the term family meeting, which causes some relatives to assume it will be confrontational and accusatory.

At the brainstorming session, you should have one family member take notes and send out the results of the meeting to all family members, present or absent. A second family member can be the discussion leader, or you can bring in a caseworker, clergy person, or counselor to serve as facilitator.

The discussion should eventually cover each of the following topics:

- What ideas does each family member have about possible sources of funds for quality care?
- What information does anyone have about where there might be hidden sources of funds or assets that could help pay for long-term care?
- What connections does the family have for locating the right doctors, nurses, specialists, lawyers, financial advisers, social service agencies, medical supplies, and resources at affordable rates?
- Which members of the immediate family could help out financially more than they are currently offering?
- Which distant relatives can be called upon to provide assistance, even if it's been years since they were active in family gatherings?
- Who can offer assistance or suggest resources to ease the burden on the one or two family members who have been doing most of the caregiving, research, errand running, and physical chores?

I must warn you ahead of time that many of the underlying tensions in your family might emerge during the planning, execution, and follow-up of a family gathering such as this. Old sibling rivalries may flare up. Long-standing feuds and bad feelings may be expressed overtly or covertly. Miscommunications and power struggles should not surprise you.

Yet with all the family history and drama, remind one another that what's important is whether this task gets accomplished: Can this family pull together sufficiently to give the ailing loved one the best care possible? Can the family battles be ignored long enough to make sure everyone pitches in to the best of their resources and abilities?

Don't expect your relatives to suddenly start communicating as well as the Huxtables on the television show, *Cosby*. Rather than miracles, you need your relatives to join together in a common cause. Even if it's been years since your family has gotten along at family gatherings, it's still likely that some new information and participation will be achieved by gathering the relatives together in person or by telephone.

I'm not promising that it will be easy to arrange a brainstorming session, but I do guarantee you that it will be worthwhile in terms of additional help for your loved one. No matter how resistant you may feel about including other family members in your loved one's medical situation, this is a good time to move beyond family rivalries and focus on solutions that can help right away.

"We're Family and I Want to Help."

Marna's story is a good illustration of the importance of having a brainstorming session with close relatives. Marna's younger sister Alice is a single parent whose twelve-year-old son Christopher is seriously disabled.

According to Marna,

> I've known for several years that my sister Alice is struggling financially and could use some help to pay for my nephew Christopher's medical and physical therapy costs. Yet in our family, money matters are very private and there's a sense of pride involved. No one wants to admit to anyone else in the family that we may need assistance.
>
> Several times I've offered to help my younger sister Alice out of a financial jam, but she always says, "No, I'm fine," even when she's heavily in debt and having to make difficult decisions. On a few occasions, Alice had to say no to getting the right doctors or therapists for Christopher because she didn't have the money and she

had too much "pride" to let us help out. That breaks my heart to see my own sister struggling so hard and coming up short again and again.

Recently Marna took Alice out to lunch and asked her permission to set up a brainstorming session that could address the rising costs of taking care of Christopher. At first Alice was opposed to the idea, saying that her financial struggles were not anyone else's problem.

But then Marna explained to her, "Alice, I'm your sister and I care about you. We're family and I want to help. It hurts me that you won't let any of us chip in."

Reluctantly, Alice agreed to let her older sister Marna call a brainstorming session in two weeks. At the family gathering, which began with an enjoyable potluck meal and exquisite desserts, everyone took turns describing what they could do to ease the burden on Alice and Christopher.

Here are some of the results of Marna and Alice's family brainstorming session. These commitments may provide you with some ideas about what can be achieved if a similar gathering were to occur in your own family.

- Marna's older brother Pete admitted that he didn't have much to offer financially, but that he'd be willing to run errands one day a week so that Alice could take some time off for herself.
- Marna's parents wanted to help pay for Alice's rent and utilities, so that Alice could use more of her monthly paycheck for Christopher's therapy and rehabilitation costs.
- Alice's ex-husband, who didn't show up for the family brainstorming session, said over the telephone that he'd do his best to start sending his alimony checks on time. He also promised to take Christopher on a pleasurable outing at least once a month. Alice's response was, "I'll believe it when I see it."

- Marna and Alice's rich Uncle Walter, also reached by telephone, agreed to give a yearly gift to Alice with no strings attached. They had called him to ask for a very small amount and were surprised by the size of his generosity.
- Marna's husband Bill offered to use his connections in the health-care field to stay abreast of new information about research and treatment programs that might be useful for Christopher.
- Marna offered to start doing some information gathering of her own to see if there were any additional sources of money or better insurance policies for Christopher's condition.

Instead of remaining cut off from each other because of "pride" or "privacy," this family pulled together and discovered what each family member was capable of contributing. They still had their personality quirks and occasional dislikes, yet they got beyond their differences long enough to pitch in for Christopher's care.

As you think about the members of your own extended family, consider whether there is anyone who could help your financial or caregiving situation, but whom you have been reluctant to ask. While you might have a personal rule against asking anyone for help, this could be a good time to make an exception. Don't let an initial hesitance or a long-standing family disagreement prevent your loved one from receiving the best possible care. If additional resources are available somewhere in your extended family, don't be afraid to admit, "We could use your help."

Please note: In some emergency cases, such as when a family member requires a lifesaving medical procedure that is beyond your financial resources, you may need to ask for help to an even wider "extended family." In certain situations, it may be appropriate to consider asking for a special one-time donation through your local church, synagogue, or community religious newspaper. You might ask for support from specific co-workers or old friends. Or you might consider a request for emergency donations on a local radio or television program.

While this kind of appeal should be used only in very special emergencies, I have seen dozens of justifiable situations in which it has saved the life of a cherished relative. Quite often there are generous people around us—either in our families or in our communities—who want to help if only we would let them know. You may want to talk with a caseworker at a social service agency or a priest, minister, or rabbi if you feel your loved one needs emergency funds and you're not sure where to turn for help.

Step 4: Protecting Your Loved One and Your Family in Case the Situation Gets Worse

Most people don't like to think about what might happen if a loved one's condition worsens or if he or she can no longer manage financial affairs.

"Think positive" is what most people say. "Everything will be all right."

I agree that having a positive attitude is important. Yet if you sincerely want to help a loved one who's ill, part of your responsibility is to prepare well in advance for this person to be taken care of in the event that physical or mental abilities diminish. Planning ahead for someone else to be legally authorized to make financial and personal decisions doesn't mean you're pessimistic—it means you're sensible and you're taking good care of your family member.

For example, if your elderly parent or spouse is beginning to lose memory or find it difficult to focus on important decisions, you need to begin preparing to have someone else be legally authorized to take charge. Or if a family member is mentally ill and is unable to make rational choices for a long period of time, steps must be taken for the intelligent handling of financial affairs.

In addition, it's important to be certain your relative will be cared for if something should happen to you or another primary caregiver. Even if you plan on living forever and always having a coherent mind, for your loved one's benefit it's a good idea to think ahead. Who should be legally authorized to help make financial decisions and take care of your ailing loved one if you or another relative are unable to continue doing it? What can be done right away to make sure there won't be legal problems if you or another primary caregiver should become incapacitated?

To handle situations like these, there are several types of financial and legal arrangements that must be planned well in advance. For additional information about any or all of the following options, consult one of the books listed in Appendix A or talk with a lawyer, caseworker, or social services agency representative about:

Durable Power of Attorney. This will permit others to act on the ill person's behalf in the event of major incapacity— for example, in signing documents, making financial decisions, and having access to authorized accounts. It can be created well in advance of need (some states call this a "Springer Power of Attorney," which goes into effect only when the person becomes incapacitated). The power of attorney role can be broad or limited, depending on what you and your family members feel is best. It is fairly inexpensive to establish, but must be done correctly if it is to be enforceable.

A Living Trust. This is a more detailed method for managing and distributing assets contained within a specified trust account. The legal document of a living trust describes exactly how the person wants to be cared for when he or she can no longer manage financial decisions. This is more complex and expensive to establish and often requires substantial legal fees, but may be necessary for managing a sizeable estate.

Guardianships or Conservatorships. These terms are used to describe someone who is legally empowered, usually through a court proceeding, to handle the financial affairs of someone who is mentally or physically unable to do so, or who might be incompetent at some future time. Many states have all-or-nothing guardianship laws, and if your loved one still has some ability to make financial and personal decisions this setup would needlessly restrict her or his independence. In some states, more enlightened guardianship laws have been established. You may want to talk with a knowledgeable attorney or caseworker to see if guardianship or conservatorship is the appropriate step for your family.

While you are thinking about legal and financial issues, there are two other important things to discuss with your loved ones.

A Living Will

When asked, most people say that they don't want the "extraordinary measures" of medical technology to keep them alive but unaware for months or years. In the United States, you have the constitutional right to specify that you don't want to be kept alive by "heroic measures" in cases of irreversible brain damage or painful terminal illness.

Yet unless you and your family members specify in writing through a "living will" that the doctors are not to persist in keeping a patient alive past a certain point, it is difficult to prevent this from happening. Most people who refuse to draft a properly executed living will or who wait until a loved one is unable to sign such a document unfortunately may be faced with the prospect of a loved one kept alive against his or her wishes with tubes, transfusions, and monitors.

Each state has various restrictions and procedures about living wills and you should seek knowledgeable advice on this emotionally charged issue. In most states, if past a certain point you wish artificial nutrition and hydration withheld or withdrawn, it must be specified in the living will document. You must also notify the doctors well in advance about a living will and its terms. In most situations, if you fail to remind the doctors and nurses of the terms of the document, they will assume that extraordinary measures should be carried out.

This is a complicated legal and moral issue that is currently in transition in many states. If you or your loved one are interested in making sure ahead of time that the ailing person's wishes will determine whether or not heroic measures are taken, you should consult an attorney or case worker to have a living will drafted and signed by two witnesses. For more information, contact the Society for the Right to Die, 250 West 57th Street, New York, NY 10107. While it's a difficult decision to make and an uncomfortable topic for most people to discuss, it should be talked about early enough so that the choice is made while a loved one is fully coherent.

Contingency Instructions

This is the one safeguard that doesn't require an attorney or a properly executed legal document. I recommend that you take a few moments in the next few days to sit down and make a list of important information that you can give to another friend or relative who would take care of these details for your ailing loved one if something should happen to you.

On your list, attempt to spell out all the things you do for the ill person that you probably take for granted. What phone numbers should someone have if they're going to be taking care of your loved one? What should this person know about your loved one's medications and medical problems? What about bank accounts, wills, insurance policies, monthly bills, and other business matters—where are these located and how would someone else gain access to everything? What about daily money management—how do you and the person who's ailing handle the day-to-day specifics of making financial decisions and having cash on hand?

These contingency instructions can make the difference as to whether or not your loved one will receive excellent care if you are unavailable. Even though most people fail to take this important step to protect their loved one's well-being, make sure you take a few minutes to get it down on paper and then give copies of this list to one or two reliable family members.

"We Just Didn't Want to Talk About It."

Cheryl's predicament demonstrates the importance of protecting your loved one through planning ahead of time for a smooth transition of legal and financial authority.

Cheryl, forty-six, has an older sister named Bonnie, forty-nine, who has been diagnosed with schizophrenia and has been in and out of hospitals and treatment programs for almost thirty years. For most of her life, Bonnie has been cared for by her mother.

According to Cheryl, who has a husband and three children of her own:

> I often wondered whether I would be ready to take care of Bonnie if anything ever happened to my mother and the responsibility passed to me. Yet for years we just didn't want to talk about it. I'd heard legal terms like "power of attorney," "conservatorship," and "guardianship," but to talk about those things with my mother meant I would have to broach two painful subjects.
>
> First of all, talking about Bonnie's future has never been a pleasant topic of conversation. Her options have often alternated between "bad" and "worse." Second, I couldn't just sit down and say to my mother, "Hi Ma, let's talk about what will happen to Bonnie if you pass away." I mean, how do you get someone to consider the possibility of their own demise in order to plan responsibly for the future?

I would like to be able to write that Cheryl found the courage to discuss with her mother how to take care of Bonnie in the future. But it didn't happen that way. Cheryl avoided the conversation for several years. Then she brought it up hesitantly and dropped it when her mother complained, "Oh, let's not think about that right now."

Seven months ago, Cheryl's mother suffered a debilitating stroke with serious brain damage that left her unable to authorize Cheryl to take over the complicated financial and legal details of caring for Bonnie. For seven months, Cheryl has gone to numerous lawyers, doctors, nurses, social workers, and court proceedings in a frustrating effort to gain access to her mother's bank accounts, insurance policies, and a trust fund set up to pay for Bonnie's ongoing care.

According to Cheryl:

If only I had been more persistent bringing this up to my mother when she was still coherent enough to deal with it. Of course it would have been uncomfortable to talk about contingency plans and go through legal documents that would authorize me to take over caring for Bonnie at some future time.

But I wish I had just scheduled a meeting with an attorney or a social worker and said, "Mom, let's do it! This is hard for both of us, but we need to take care of this for Bonnie's sake."

Instead I waited for a magical "right moment" that never came. Now I'm in constant battles to get this mess corrected. It's costing so much more in legal fees this way, not to mention the frustration of having to battle a system that won't budge unless we have written proof that my mother wants me to take care of her and Bonnie.

Why Wait?

Quite often there is a huge time gap between when we realize we need to resolve a financial or legal issue and when we actually get off the fence to do something about it. Months and years go by, and we keep repeating the immortal words of Scarlett O'Hara, "I'll think about it tomorrow."

Even if you feel uncomfortable about issues like contingency plans, financial strategies, and legal authorizations, it pays not to wait much longer. As Cheryl wishes she had done, you must find the courage to say to your loved ones, "Let's take care of this right now and then put it out of our minds. The longer we wait, the more we risk the possibility of problems later on."

If someone in your family refuses to face these realities, have empathy and find out what their fears might be. Then locate a supportive doctor, lawyer, accountant, caseworker, or relative whom this person respects and who can say, "Now's the time to clear up these financial and legal issues. We can do it correctly and then not have to worry about it any longer."

Rather than risking a financial disaster or setting yourself up for endless legal battles, take time now to learn more about your financial options and other responsibilities. There are patient and understanding individuals available to you who can explain the choices and answer your questions—but only if you take the initiative to seek their assistance.

CHAPTER EIGHT

Conquering the Nasty "G-Word" (Guilt!)

I once saw a fascinating demonstration of the hidden power of guilt. A doctor who specializes in neuromuscular research stood in front of a forty-year-old woman who was allergic to chocolate and ragweed. When the doctor asked this woman to lift a relatively heavy object, she could do so fairly easily. But when the doctor gave her a piece of chocolate to eat or had her sniff a handful of ragweed, she was barely able to raise the object. Her strength had been diminished substantially by exposure to certain allergy-producing substances.

Next, the doctor did the demonstration once again in a slightly different way. After several minutes away from chocolate or ragweed, the woman was asked to lift the heavy object and she did so easily. Then the doctor asked the woman, "Think about something for which you feel guilty or self-critical." The woman thought about her physically disabled younger brother, whom she hadn't called or visited for several days.

When the doctor asked her to lift the heavy object one more time, she couldn't do it. She strained with all her might, but the object proved too heavy for her to lift. Just as her energy had been dissipated earlier by the allergic substances, so it was again weakened by her guilt feelings.

Quite clearly, our physical and emotional strengths are lessened when we are beset by self-criticism and guilt, which can cause us to feel sluggish, depressed, or indecisive. They can disrupt our ability to handle stressful challenges and undermine our patience for helping an ailing relative. While some people might say that guilt is no big deal, in fact it can be a primary obstacle during times when you are needed most.

What Can Be Done?

I can't take away all your guilt feelings with a magic wand. Nor can I guarantee that self-critical thoughts won't reappear from time to time. But there *are* several positive techniques for resolving the majority of your guilt feelings so they don't continue to wear you down or make you feel impatient with an ailing loved one.

You can learn some helpful methods for understanding and mastering the feelings of self-blame we all experience when a family member is ill or disabled. Remember, these techniques are not intended to make you less sensitive or compassionate to the person who's ailing. These guilt-reduction steps should not be viewed as an excuse for shirking your responsibilities to care for a loved one in need. Rather, by defusing some of your strongest guilt feelings it should help you to become better able to be of service to this individual.

In addition, you will experience positive benefits for your own health and well-being. By reducing the guilt that clouds your thinking, you will make clearer decisions and have more energy to give those individuals who are depending on you. Instead of wallowing in self-reproach, you will be given some creative ways to overcome it.

Is Anyone Immune?

Some people insist that guilt is an ethnic trait. They point out that Jews have a greater tendency to feel guilty, that Catholics have a corner on the guilt market, or that Asian-Americans feel more responsible for family members than other groups do.

I tend to disagree with generalizations like these. Based on my observations of people from various religions and ethnicities, I would argue that guilt is one of the most equal-opportunity employers, especially when it comes to family matters of illness and health Different people express their guilt feelings in different ways—some keep them hidden inside while others are quite obvious about their feelings of remorse. However, you don't have to be Jewish, Catholic, Asian, or anything but human in order to worry that you're not doing enough for someone who needs so very much. Except for certain sociopaths, criminals, and narcissists who've lost their ability to feel concern for anyone but themselves, the rest of us have a tendency to feel guilty from time to time.

The Two Different Kinds of Guilt

Everyone has some occasional pangs of guilt, but it becomes a serious problem if these nagging feelings begin to disrupt your concentration or sap your energy every day. Yet how much is "too much?" How do you decide whether your guilt feelings are reasonable or excessive?

The dictionary describes two different kinds of guilt—one that is useful and manageable, and another that is harmful and unnecessary. Knowing the difference between these two kinds of guilt is essential in learning how to deal with this complex emotion.

According to *Webster's Dictionary*, the first definition of guilt describes a useful function—guilt is a necessary and proper response to the violation of a law or the conscious commission of an offense against another person. This guilt is like a teacher of good behavior, that says to us, "Be kinder, be more respectful, don't break the law, don't be insensitive." If it weren't for this useful kind of guilt, there would be even more callousness and cruelty in this world. This kind of guilt is valuable, for it reminds us to consider the consequences of our actions.

Surely there have been times in each of our lives when we did something insensitive, and guilt was the emotion which helped us learn not to do it again. I can recall several incidents in my own life when I needlessly opened my big mouth and said things that hurt someone I cared about. The guilt I felt afterward became my inner teacher, helping me to ask, "What can I do differently not to hurt someone again?"

But *Webster* also describes a second kind of guilt that is potentially harmful and self-destructive. According to the dictionary, guilt can also mean "feelings of culpability for imagined offenses or from a sense of inadequacy." These are not things you did wrong, but rather the worries and painful insecurities that unfortunately cause us to beat ourselves up with self-punishment we don't deserve.

Some examples of these imagined offenses and inadequacies are:

- You feel guilty about something you did or failed to do, but in fact your loved one felt fine about it and the second-guessing is entirely your own.
- You feel guilty because your ailing relative seems agitated or tends to criticize you, even though the agitation is not your fault and the criticism is inaccurate.
- You stop yourself in the middle of a good day or a weekend outing with thoughts of "Do I have the right to feel OK when this other person is in such dire straits?"
- You are afraid to do anything independently of your loved one because it might seem selfish.

- You blame yourself for your loved one's condition, or you worry that God or fate is punishing you.
- You can't forgive yourself for a small oversight or an innocent mistake, or you spend hours or days ruminating about a fairly minor incident.

Excess guilt can be detrimental to your health and to your effectiveness as a caregiver. It's not fair to be inundated with self-criticism in spite of your good efforts to care for a family member or friend. When every step you take is clouded by chronic second-guessing that makes your daily life a painful struggle, then reasonable guilt has become harmful guilt. If you begin to feel drained emotionally or physically because of lingering feelings of "Am I doing this right?," then it's time to do something positive to lighten up.

Identifying the Harmful Guilt

You would be amazed at how many caring and helpful individuals unnecessarily beat themselves up with excess guilt. For example, Anthony is a business consultant in his fifties currently taking care of his ailing wife, who has a serious heart condition, and his aging father, who has Parkinson's disease.

According to Anthony:

I try to do the best I can for both of them, but I invariably feel guilty. I feel badly that I've had to put my dad in a nursing home. Every time I visit him there, I see his tired and lonely eyes. And I wonder if I'm being a good son.

With my wife I feel guilty whenever I have to work late or travel on business. Each minute I'm not with her, I worry about how she's doing.

The hardest thing with both my dad and my wife is when *they* feel guilty for being so dependent on me. Last week my wife looked at me with tears in her eyes and said, "I'm such a burden on you, I know I am. I feel terrible when I see how hard you're working and still managing to be there for my needs, too."

When she says that or when my dad complains that he's becoming a burden on his children, I feel terrible. It's so hard to see someone unhappy and not get hooked in yourself.

As a result of his guilt feelings, Anthony was beginning to experience a number of side effects. He found it hard to concentrate at work. He had become more short-tempered with clients, his secretary, and others who got on his nerves. He also began experiencing stress-related symptoms—back problems, skin flare-ups, and headaches—that possibly were linked to his increased level of guilt feelings. Anthony comments, "I've never been the kind of person who spends a lot of time mulling over things or feeling guilty. Yet lately with my wife and my father in so much distress, I've become a bit of an emotional wreck."

When I asked Anthony to make a list of some of the guilt feelings that were on his mind, he was surprised by just how much self-blame he was carrying inside himself. On his list of "Things About Which I Feel Upset with Myself," he wrote:

I'm upset that I can't be with my wife more of the time.

I feel guilty that the best nursing home I could afford for my dad is less attractive than what I'd like it to be.

I'm not pleased with the fact that I once spent ten years not talking very much to my dad and staying away from family holidays during my "rebel days."

I can't forgive myself that my wife and I had a terrible argument the night before her first heart attack.

I feel selfish for fantasizing every so often about getting away from all of this.

I feel guilty that my wife is unable to do many of the activities she used to enjoy.

I feel ashamed of the fact that I once said to my father a long time ago, "I wish you were dead."

I'm a little embarrassed that the private nurses seem to like my dad and get along with him better than I do.

I'm ashamed to admit that on a few occasions I've secretly wished my dad would pass away already and end his misery.

I criticize myself every time my dad needs something to ease his pain and all I can do is stand there like an idiot.

I feel badly whenever I think about making love with my wife and we can't because of her heart condition.

I feel guilty for all the times I've been impatient or critical of my wife.

I often wonder what it is I've done wrong in the past to deserve all this.

I feel like I don't have the right to be concerned about my headaches and backaches or how hard things are right now, because bottom-line I've still got my health for the most part and they don't.

The Tendency to Overreact

Like Anthony, many of us have a long list of regrets and self-criticisms that relate to our ailing loved ones. Maybe you're still feeling guilty for something you said or did many years ago. Maybe you continue to second-guess an unresolved situation that happened a while back.

Unfortunately, these bad feelings can cause additional problems now and in the future. You may find yourself pulling away from your loved one out of guilt or embarrassment. Or you might be overbearing and overprotective, thus smothering him or her with your guilt-induced efforts to please.

You might be like Anthony and suffer from stressful physical symptoms or an inability to concentrate on your daily activities. Or like Shakespeare's Lady Macbeth, you may feel a compulsive urge to engage in obsessive behaviors to relieve your conscience. In Lady Macbeth's case, her feelings of guilt led to excessive handwashing. For most people these days, chronic guilt feelings, deserved or undeserved, are acted out in binge eating or dieting, escapist love affairs, excess smoking, drinking, or workaholic tendencies. It's common for people to overreact and overcompensate for their guilt feelings. If you notice yourself feeling out of control since your loved one's ailment, now is a good time to start unraveling the reasons.

Taking Action Against Chronic Guilt

The best way of coming to terms with these debilitating feelings is not to ignore them or become obsessed with them. Rather, by understanding where your guilt feelings come from and how to turn them into less harmful emotions, you can make significant progress in regaining your peace of mind and renewing your competence as a caregiver.

If, like Anthony, you are a compassionate individual who does a lot for an ailing relative yet are plagued by guilt, what are your options? Here are some specific steps that worked for Anthony and many others. They can help you conquer the "Nasty G-Word"—maybe not all the time, but enough to dramatically improve your daily functioning.

Step 1: Sort Out the Constructive Criticisms from the Unnecessary Guilt Trips

There's an old expression that says, "The less you run away from something, the shorter distance it takes to return." That's precisely the situation with guilt. The less you run away from your guilt feelings, the easier it is to face them and sort out the ones that are constructive from the ones that are inaccurate and harmful.

An important step for anyone who is feeling guilty for real and imagined offenses is to sit down and separate these emotions into two distinct categories. Using the insightful philosophy of Reinhold Neibuhr I mentioned earlier, your task is to "accept with serenity the things that cannot be changed," find the "courage to change the things that should be changed," and seek "the wisdom to distinguish the one from the other."

I recommend that you take at least a half hour of quiet time with no interruptions and write out your own list of regrets, guilt feelings, and things you feel upset with yourself about. Just as Anthony discovered some valuable clues about the extent of his own guilt feelings, so will your list help you understand what's been making you feel so sluggish or indecisive.

As soon as you've made a list of guilt feelings, separate that list into two categories:

Category A	Category B
The useful guilt feelings that suggest an area which needs improvement. Rather than beating yourself up with additional self-criticism, simply make a note of what you can do in the future to improve this situation for your ailing loved one and yourself.	The unnecessary guilt feelings that are inaccurate, impossible to change, or have to do with past incidents that are no longer relevant. These are the self-criticisms that are useless and harmful. Yet they are often a substantial percentage of the guilt load we carry around each day.

Next to each guilt feeling, write down some constructive activity that can help you overcome it. Instead of remaining powerless against your inner critic, these action steps can help you take charge to feel strong again.

For example, Anthony separated his earlier list of guilt feelings into these *A* and *B* categories. Looking at his list and the action steps he wrote next to it, you may see some possibilities of how to turn your own self-criticisms into more productive reactions:

On his 'A' list of Things that Could Be Improved, Anthony Included:

Then to resolve the guilt, he began to explore as an Action Step:

His wanting to spend more time with his wife.

Ways to be more assertive with his clients and coworkers so they might understand his need to spend more time with his wife and less time working away from home.

His secretive guilt feelings about wanting to make love with his wife in spite of her heart condition.

Talking with a physician about the risk factors and talking with his wife about other ways of being intimate (such as hugging, kissing, touching, massage, and romantic evenings) that were less risky.

His frustration at not knowing what to do to relieve his father's pain symptoms.

Reading books on pain management and talking with a specialist about new techniques that might help his father.

On his 'B' list of Things that Were Inaccurate, Impossible to Change, or Irrelevancies from the Past, Anthony included:

Then to resolve the guilt, he began to explore as an Action Step:

His guilt feelings about being a rebel or saying harsh things to his father many years ago.

Accepting the fact that every family and personal relationship has its angry moments.

Those "rebel days" are no longer as important as his current efforts to help his father. We all need to appreciate that angry moments from long ago need *not* condemn us to a life of feeling guilty.

His secret wishes that his father would pass away and end his misery.

Talking with a support group or a counselor about why this is such a common thought that enters the minds of many good people. Wishing that someone would pass away and end the current crisis is nothing more than an idle thought that often comes during moments of discouragement and frustration, even to the best of us. As long as you don't act on it, it's harmless and innocent. It doesn't mean you're a bad person. Nor do you need to fear that this idle thought will adversely affect your loved one.

His regret that he and his wife had a serious argument the night before her first heart attack.

Since that incident is in the past and can no longer be changed, the important issue now is how to be a loving support to his ailing wife. Without going overboard to make up for that guilt feeling, or pulling away out of shame or embarrassment, Anthony's task is to do his best for his wife and accept that they both are human.

Step 2: Take a Moment to Forgive Yorself for Not Being Perfect.

Many of us seem to find it easier to forgive others than to forgive ourselves. Yet it's impossible to stop feeling guilty and letting your self-criticisms undermine your health unless you find a way to forgive yourself for not being perfect. If you sincerely want to reduce your level of guilt and anxiety, you need to take a moment to resolve some of the things for which you have been judging yourself.

For example, one of the issues on Anthony's list of guilt feelings deserves special attention. Like many family members, he felt twinges of guilt that his father had been put in a nursing home, even though two caseworkers and the doctor had all agreed that a long-term nursing facility was the most loving and appropriate decision in his father's circumstances.

While it's common for people to feel uncertain about needing to send a family member to a residential-care facility, in the majority of cases it is the correct decision and the guilt is unfounded. If you feel bad about a decision like this, it's important to find a way to forgive yourself for something that isn't your fault. You didn't cause your loved one to become so ill that he or she needed constant care. Nor did you make this decision impulsively or without considering how hard it is to send a family member away from home. Now that you've made the best arrangements possible to provide the care your family member needs, take a deep breath and say, "I forgive myself. I did the best I could under the circumstances. Feeling guilty about it doesn't help my loved one or myself."

This crucial step of pulling yourself out of the painful flames of self-criticism may seem at first like a waste of time to you. You might be saying, "I don't need to forgive myself. This is childish." But you would be amazed to know just how many good people are walking around with emotional and physical symptoms because of their unwillingness to forgive themselves for things that weren't their fault or that happened long ago.

For instance, Marlene is a former New Yorker in her forties who got married eight years ago and moved with her husband to California, where they both had been offered new jobs. Three years after Marlene's move to the West Coast, Marlene's divorced mother in New York became seriously ill. For the past five years, Marlene has felt guilty for a number of reasons. She explains:

> I know rationally that my moving far away from home didn't cause my mother's illness. Yet I feel terrible that I'm not with her more often.
> I'm fortunate she's cared for by my aunts and my older brother. And I try to call and visit her as often as I can. But there's still this lingering feeling of guilt that I'm a bad daughter or a selfish person because I can't be there 100 percent for my ailing mom.

As we discussed her feelings about her mother, it became clear that Marlene had been told repeatedly from the time she was very small that a "good daughter" is one who stays close to home and takes care of her family, including her aging mother. Marlene could recall dozens of overt and subtle messages from her mother that said, "I'm counting on you. Just as I've raised you and taken care of you for many years, eventually it will be your job to take care of me."

Yet with Marlene's marriage and career decisions, and her improved job opportunity in California, the parent-child roles hadn't turned out as her mother had hoped. As a result, Marlene, like many other daughters who have desired a life of their own, felt guilty that somehow her independence was hurting her aging mother.

The challenge for Marlene and for anyone else who simply cannot always be physically available for an ailing loved one is to *focus on what you can realistically provide for this person and forgive yourself for not living up to the expectations this person placed on you.*

As I explained to Marlene, by her mother's definition of a "good daughter," she simply could not win. Unless she could magically become the same kind of stay-at-home, take-care-of-everyone-else-but-don't-think-of-yourself kind of person her mother was raised to be by *her* mother, she would fall short.

But by a less restrictive definition, she could certainly be a "good daughter." Why not focus on how much she could do to be there for her mother in spite of the geographic distance? Marlene needed to recognize that her phone calls, letters, visits, and long-distance caregiving arrangements have made a significant difference in helping her mother cope with her illness.

It was unrealistic of Marlene to expect there to be no feelings of regret over her mother's illness—we all have things we wish we could have done differently. While it would have been easier if Marlene had lived closer to home, or if her mother had moved with her to California, she has still been a steady and loving presence in her mother's life. Despite the distance, she has done the very best that she could under difficult circumstances.

In addition to focusing on what she's done right rather than becoming obsessed with what her mother feels she's done wrong, I also urged Marlene to do a specific self-forgiveness exercise. This exercise has been useful for many people who were feeling unnecessarily guilty about a situation in which they had done their best despite many obstacles. You can use this powerful technique whenever you notice yourself feeling caught up in guilt or regrets for things you didn't intentionally do wrong, as well as for things you cannot change.

Here is a helpful self-forgiveness exercise:

Find a photograph of yourself with your ailing family member. Or visualize in your mind's eye an image of the two of you together.

Looking at your own face in the photo with your loved one (or in the imagined scene in your mind's eye), say to yourself, "I can see how hard this has been. I can see how much you've been trying to adjust to this stressful situation. I forgive you for the things you did that weren't perfect. I applaud you for all the things you did that were helpful and loving. You don't deserve to be punished. I forgive you."

You may feel some hesitation about saying these words of forgiveness or accepting them as true. Maybe you're afraid that forgiving yourself is selfish or self-indulgent. Maybe you have a habit of being so self-critical that you don't know how to give yourself a break.

But ask yourself, "What's so terrible about forgiving myself for being human, as long as my intention is to restore my energy to serve my loved one? What's so shameful about admitting I'm not perfect and appreciating that I've tried very hard to do what was best for my family member?"

If you are reluctant to forgive yourself and reduce your level of self-criticism, make sure that you don't stop trying. Go back and repeat the photo visualization exercise once again. It's worthwhile to cut through some of your guilt, because forgiveness allows you more energy *for giving* to your loved one.

When Marlene sat down with a photograph of her mother and herself, she found it difficult at first to be forgiven for living so far away and not always being available to help her ailing mom. Marlene admits, "I had this big lump in my throat that said, 'You don't deserve to be forgiven. If you let yourself off the hook, you'll become an even more selfish daughter.' "

Marlene's fear of becoming "selfish" unless she continued to whip herself with undeserved guilt is a common feeling. Many of us are our own worst critics, and somehow we fear that if we treat ourselves less harshly it will turn us into self-absorbed narcissists.

Ironically, I've seen repeatedly that quite the opposite is true. If you are already a caring, giving person, then being more gentle with yourself won't make you narcissistic. It will simply make you an already compassionate person who is no longer overburdened by unnecessary guilt.

Using up your time and energy on guilt and self-criticism is what tends to make people self-absorbed. Obsessive fear that you're going to make a terrible mistake or somehow fail your loved one can get in the way of being a supportive caregiver. Your task is to come through for the person who's ailing or disabled. Yet it's very hard to be gentle and nurturing to someone else when you are refusing to be gentle and nurturing to yourself. That's why I recommend to family members that they need to stop being so guilt-ridden—it's a weight you don't need to carry in order to help your loved one.

When Marlene attempted this self-forgiveness exercise a second time, she found it useful. She explains:

> I began to realize that punishing myself with criticism was not helping either my mother or myself. By sitting down and looking at a photo of the two of us, I had to admit that I've been doing a heck of a lot to help her. It hasn't been easy, but I've really tried to be there for her.
>
> When I finally said those three words, 'I forgive you,' I got tears in my eyes. It felt strange and kind of wonderful to finally be appreciated that I am a good daughter, even if my mother could never say that to me directly.
>
> The funny thing is that I can be a lot less critical of myself and still get a lot more accomplished for my mom. Now when I call her or visit her or make long-distance arrangements to take care of her, I feel a lot less stressed out. Forgiving myself didn't make me selfish—in fact, it's giving me more energy to do more things to help out. I love her a lot, and I know she loves me even though I'll never be exactly the kind of daughter she was hoping for. But isn't that the way life is sometimes?

If guilt has been a problem for you recently, now might be a good time to sit down and do this powerful self-forgiveness exercise. Simply looking at a photograph of yourself and this person you care about won't make *all* the guilt feelings disappear immediately. But it's a start. I urge you to use this opportunity to lighten your load a bit and start focusing not on your shortcomings but on the more positive things you can do that will actually help your loved one.

Step 3: Learn to Laugh at Your Own Human Foibles.

Sometimes when we feel clumsy or inadequate in our efforts to care for an ailing family member, the healthiest way to respond is to laugh at our own imperfections. We human beings have an amazing capacity to be awkward, to say the wrong thing, or to mess up at the most inopportune moments. But if you can't laugh at your own guilt feelings, all you can do is cry.

For example, most of us expend a lot of time and energy dwelling on what's gone wrong and what we should have done differently. We bombard ourselves with comments like, "If only I had done this" or "If only I had done that." Maybe instead of feeling guilt about these "if only's" it would be more productive to laugh at them.

A wise and witty relative of mine named Ena Felder once taught me a useful way to laugh at these "if only" notions. She has a beloved expression that I remember whenever I notice I'm spending too much time with regrets about what might have happened if only I'd acted differently.

According to the homespun philosophy of Ena Felder, when someone starts mulling about "If only this" or "If only that," she remarks, "If . . . if . . . if . . . who needs if's! *If* my grandmother had had balls, she would have been my grandfather."

Laughing at your own human imperfections is a chance to break out of the sluggishness of guilt feelings and renew your energy for doing good. So let's take a moment to add some levity to this heavy subject of guilt.

Imagine just for fun that the *Guinness Book of World*

Records has asked you to be a finalist for a new category—
"The caregiving family member who has the most guilt
feelings in a single month."

Now imagine as well that the final competition for the
world's record is being held at Madison Square Garden in
New York with a live cheering audience and the cameras
rolling for television's *Wide World of Sports*. There you are
on stage, competing against two of the world's finest guilt-
ridden family members.

This is a tough competition. These two opponents feel
guilty about *everything*, even some incidents that couldn't
possibly be their fault.

But you haven't come all the way to Madison Square
Garden just to lose. You're describing to the audience and
the millions at home just how guilty you've felt about your
ailing family member. The mornings you woke up feeling
guilty about your good health while your loved one was
hurting or unhappy. The weekends you've felt caught in a
bind, torn between enjoying yourself and staying home,
pacing the floors, and worrying a lot. The nights you tossed
and turned in bed, mulling over a small thing you felt guilty
about.

After describing the amazing number of ways you've managed to feel guilty in a single month, the crowd cheers wildly
and the judges measure their response on a computerized
"Guilt-o-meter." Suddenly the contest officials declare you
the winner. You are the champion. The Gilded Grand Guru
of Guilt. Congratulations! No one does guilt better than you
do.

Within the next seventy-two hours, you would be interviewed on *Today, Good Morning America, Donahue, Oprah,
Geraldo*, and *Sixty Minutes*. A small article and a large color
photograph of you will appear in *U.S.A. Today*.

For the next several weeks, publishers wine and dine you
with offers for a six-figure book contract on *Smart Women,
Foolish Guilt* plus a sequel called *How to Feel Guilty and
Have Thin Thighs in Less than Thirty Days*.

Obviously, this is an exaggeration for comic purposes. Yet it's also a chance to laugh at how incredibly talented we each can be at making ourselves feel guilty. It's truly remarkable how we can spend twenty hours feeling bad about something that happened in less than ten seconds. Or we can expend thousands of words trying to justify, explain, or apologize for something we said clumsily in a sentence or two.

The next time you notice yourself feeling guilty enough to break the *Guinness Book* world's record, stop yourself and see the humor of it all. You're not really such a bad person, but you are terribly good at finding ways to feel guilty!

Alison's story illustrates the liberating power of laughter to triumph over unwarranted self-criticism. A thirty-six-year-old woman whose daughter has a congenital spinal disorder, Alison has a unique talent for guilt.

Alison explains:

I used to be a walking guilt factory. I felt unsure about everything. I worried that my daughter's ailment was somehow my fault, even though the doctors assured me I wasn't the cause of it. If my daughter was unhappy, I assumed it must be something I've done wrong. And if she was happy for a while, I felt guilty because I feared she'd never be quite as happy or fulfilled as other kids her age. If my husband got discouraged while helping out with our daughter, I felt responsible that I'm not doing it all for him. If my parents were sad or worried about their grandchild, I felt I was somehow to blame."

When I met Alison at a workshop and told her about the fantasy image of the world's record for guilt, she began to laugh and commented, "Oh God, that's me. I could probably win that competition and spend a whole day telling Oprah or Phil or even Barbara Walters all about it."

Seeing her guilt reactions in a comic light helped Alison begin to make some progress in reducing her tendency to blame herself for everything that went wrong for her daughter. As Alison recalls,

> The day after I imagined myself as the world's champion of guilt, I took a moment to look in the mirror and smile as I said, "My goodness, woman, are you going to spend the rest of your life feeling like a criminal just because your daughter is differently abled? Are you going to turn every struggle she has into guilt that it's your fault? Are you going to forget to love her because you're too busy feeling guilty?"

For the next several weeks, Alison and I talked about why she had taken on so much guilt as a result of her daughter's illness. While it's common for parents to feel responsible whenever a child is hurting, in fact they usually are not at fault.

We also discussed ways for Alison to catch herself and stop the guilt reactions as they arose. This can be the most constructive thing one can do with guilt feelings—notice them, take a deep breath, and remind yourself that you don't have to beat yourself up with unnecessary self-reproach for things you didn't cause or things you cannot change.

Whenever Alison began to engage in self-blame or harsh criticism, she knew it was time to stop, take a moment to relax, and tell herself, "You are *not* the cause of what is happening to your daughter. You can help her more if you stop feeling so guilty and start using your energy more productively."

I urge anyone who frequently feels self-critical to begin using a sense of humor and a sense of perspective to snap out of guilt whenever it begins to dominate your thoughts. We all need to laugh at ourselves every so often, especially when we are acting like the world's champion of guilt.

Step 4: Stop Viewing the Ailment as a Form of Punishment.

The most crucial step in reducing your guilt feelings is to get to the core emotion that nearly all of us experience when a loved one is ill or disabled. At the very root of most guilt feelings is an unspoken belief that can wear you down terribly. It is a subtle but powerful notion that you might not realize you have. Yet I've discovered repeatedly that almost every family member and friend of an ill person possesses this core guilt reaction to some extent.

The primary cause of guilt feelings when someone you care about suffers is a misguided belief that somehow you are being punished. That God or fate is getting back at you. That you must have done something terrible in the past to deserve this kind of misfortune. That your loved one is in pain because of something you did or something you failed to do.

Even if this belief makes no sense to your rational mind, it still might be operating on a deeper level. The subconscious mind is not always rational or logical. You might be feeling subconsciously that your loved one's ailment is somehow your fault, even though you know it's not logically true.

What are some of the signs that you might be experiencing this core guilt reaction? How can you tell if your subconscious guilt is making you feel sluggish or indecisive?

Here are some clues that you may need to resolve this underlying belief in order to regain your full capacity for serving your loved one:

You've been having thoughts of "Why me?," "Why did this have to happen to us?," or "What did I do to deserve this?" These questions are common and we all have them from time to time. But if you notice that at certain moments you feel depressed or defeated because you fear the ailment of a family member is somehow a punishment you have earned, then this belief may be causing you unnecessary harm.

One healthy way of dealing with these "Why me?" guilt

feelings is to turn the question around. Instead of asking "Why me?," you might ask *"Why not me?"* With millions of people becoming ill or disabled each year, why shouldn't it happen to someone you care about? With thousands of children born each year who are differently abled than the majority, what makes any of us think it can't happen to a member of our own family? It's not a punishment, it's a fact of life!

The question "Why me?" implies there's something you must have done wrong to deserve this fate. But in fact the human organism is very fragile and all sorts of things can happen to people we love. To assume it must be a punishment against you personally is clearly unfounded.

The key issue is not, "Why did this have to happen to us and not someone else?" but rather, "Now that we have this situation to confront, how are we responding to the challenge?" Instead of feeling guilty for a situation you didn't cause, it's more productive to feel motivated to handle the situation as best you can under the circumstances!

You worry that God or fate is getting back at you for something you did wrong in the past. This is a common fear, both for religious people and for those who don't consider themselves very religious. Based on my research with people from a variety of faiths, as well as atheists and agnostics, I've found repeatedly that during an illness in the family a loved one commonly thinks, "Am I being punished?," "Did I do something that made God angry?" or "Is God getting back at me?"

It seems that somewhere in our subconscious minds we click into that first childhood notion we learned about God. For most people, those first images of God were of an angry celestial parent, someone who would reward you when you are good and take away things you care about if you are bad.

Unfortunately, this materialistic, reward-and-punishment view of God sticks in our minds. Even for the majority of adults who pray to a compassionate and loving, rather than a punishing or vengeful, God, the fear of God's anger seems to return when a loved one is suffering.

How then do you get beyond the childlike notion of an angry, punitive God and return to a healthier image of a loving and supportive God? How do you stop feeling guilty that your family member's illness is God's way of reprimanding you?

There are at least three healthy options that can assist you in overcoming these unnecessary feelings that you are the cause of someone else's suffering.

Talk with someone you respect who has a more compassionate view of God. I don't know who might have taught you that God is punishing or cruel. But I do know a large number of priests, nuns, lay advisers, ministers, rabbis, theologians, and spiritual counselors who would disagree with that negative and outdated view of God.

I urge you to find someone to talk with who has outgrown their own childhood images of God-the-angry-parent and worked toward a healthier adult notion of a loving, supportive God or higher spirit.

Read books that give you a renewed sense of spiritual support. If you ask some friends or clergy members, "Is there a book you've read that can help me feel more connected with a loving God rather than a punitive God?" you will find there are several good choices available.

Great religious thinkers from a variety of faiths have struggled with these important questions and written some inspiring books that can help us when a family member or friend is ailing. I have found that during painful times such as these, certain spiritual writers have spoken to the deepest part of me with support rather than guilt. I've listed some of these books in Appendix A, and I recommend you ask for specific suggestions from someone who shares your particular religious or spiritual background.

Consider the possibility that rather than punishing you, God is actually providing you with loving support and strength. Instead of getting stuck in that earlier superstition of an angry deity that dishes out punishment to naughty "children," take some time to rethink your own personal notion of God.

For many people, seeing God not as a cruel deity but rather as a compassionate source of energy can make the difference between wallowing in guilt or feeling productive again. I recently read a moving description of one person's experience of seeing God in a new light. Perhaps this inspiring account will spark some ideas of your own. The following was written by an eleven-year-old cancer patient named Jason Gaes:*

When my friend Kim died from her cancer, I asked my Mom—if God was going to make Kim die when she was only six, why did he make her born at all? But my Mom said even though she was only six Kim changed people's lives. What that means is like her brother or sister would be the scientist that discovers the cure for cancer and they decided to do that because of Kim.

When you think about how much the illness or disability of a loved one has changed your life and the lives of many others, it makes you wonder, "Is there a deeper purpose here? Is there something good that can come from all of this?"

No one knows for sure if God plays a part in the hardships that happen to human beings. Maybe we are born with certain propensities and God must watch to see how it all turns out. Or maybe God wants to intervene, but the nature of life is that God cannot control everything. He or She must wait for us human beings to respond to these difficult challenges—to work toward cures, to be loving in spite of the stresses we face, to find strength to take care of one another.

It is my personal belief that God wants us to spend less

---

* *Life* Magazine, December 1988, page 78.

time asking, "Am I at fault for my loved one being ill?" and more time answering the question, "Now that a loved one is hurting, what can be done to help? What can I do to assist this person right now and to prevent suffering for others in the future?"

Responding to this important task requires a great deal of energy and perseverance, neither of which can be provided by guilt. Instead of wasting precious time and resources feeling guilty, I urge you to resolve some of your guilt and focus on being productive.

Chapter Nine:

Walking the Fine Line Between Hope and Realism

As a child, I used to be fascinated by the tightrope walkers at the circus. These high-wire acrobats somehow managed to keep their balance at an amazing height as they walked gracefully one step at a time along a narrow cord. If they leaned just a little too far to the right or left, they could easily fall.

Walking a tightrope between hope and realism is essentially what you and I do on a daily basis when a loved one has a mental, physical, or developmental disorder.

We fluctuate between hoping our family member will get better and feeling discouraged that the condition is getting worse. If we lean too far on the side of hoping, we can easily fall into what I call "The Danger of False Hope." If we lean too strongly on the side of being too realistic, we can make the mistake of "Giving Up Hope Too Soon."

For example, consider the following ambivalent feelings told to me recently by a good friend whose brother is mentally ill:

Last night my wife and I spent several hours visiting with my brother Curtis who is living in a board-and-care facility. It's so confusing when I think about Curtis. One minute he's just like any other twenty-eight-year-old—he's extremely intelligent, friendly, and articulate. The next minute he's hostile and abusive, yet I realize he's an innocent victim of a biochemical condition that his doctors still don't fully understand.

Whenever I'm with Curtis, I start asking myself, "Is it reasonable to hope he will eventually be free of these symptoms? Or is it more helpful to be realistic—to consider that he might have to live with this condition for a long time and we need to make the best of it?"

I can't help fluctuating between thinking his troubles are temporary and wondering if they might be permanent.

Even though these comments have to do with the fine line between hope and realism with regard to a mentally ill relative, they are similar if a loved one is physically ill or disabled. It's so hard to know whether to be hopeful, or whether to be pragmatic and stop expecting a dramatic improvement. At what point does being hopeful cause you to expect too much of a loved one, to the detriment of this person's progress? At what point does being realistic cause you to settle for less than what might be possible?

The Tendency to Give Up Hope Too Soon

Last year I participated in a conference of caregiving family members who had gathered together from all over the United States and Canada to talk about common concerns. One of the most valuable discussions took place on the topic of "Regaining Your Sense of Hope."

Whether your loved one is getting better, worse, or staying the same, hope is essential. We human beings need to be hopeful in order to stay motivated to do what's necessary to help a loved one. For each of us, hope can mean different things. Here are a few of the illustrations of hope that I heard at that conference from caring family members:

I'm not hoping for a miraculous recovery. I've accepted that my loved one will have this condition for as long as she lives. But I'm hopeful that her life can be better, that she and I can learn more about how to cope with this ailment and reduce its discomforts.

I'm hoping my family member can hang in there until they find a cure for his condition. And no matter how bad the situation gets, I'm still going to hold onto that glimmer of hope.

I see hope as a daily process of looking for something to feel good about. Every single day I try to find something to be grateful for—maybe that my father is still here with us, that I'm learning more about how to be a better caregiver, or that I can still say "I love you" even if he seems not to be listening.

I definitely haven't given up hope. No matter what happens, I still hold onto a strong sense that something positive will come from all of this. You can call it a crutch, but I get a lot of mileage out of my ability to remain hopeful.

There are times when I feel so discouraged and frustrated that I'm anything but hopeful. But somehow I regain a sense of hope when I'm out in the backyard doing my gardening. There is always some new life in my older plants, some new bud struggling to survive. Even on bad days, gardening boosts my spirits, calms me, and restores my hope that life goes on.

While each of these statements suggest the usefulness of being hopeful, what about those situations when the ailment seems permanent or there is no additional cure available? Is it ever appropriate to say to a patient or a family member, "Forget it. There's no more hope"?

Various experts disagree on this question, but the vast majority agree that even the most honest and factual discussion should still leave open the possibility of hope. Even with a person who has a condition for which there doesn't seem to be any realistic hope of recovery, there is still some benefit to be gained by leaving open the possibility of a change for the better.

For example, I know of a woman with a severe spinal disorder who was told incorrectly that she would never walk again. This was bad advice because in many spinal injury cases there is still some electrical activity in the muscles of the legs. While the odds of a recovery are small, there nevertheless are a few persistent and determined men and women who have worked for years with the help of physical therapists to regain their mobility. Giving up hope too soon would have been a mistake for them!

I also know of people who were diagnosed as being mentally or developmentally disabled and were told, "You'll never be able to hold a job" or "You'll never be able to live on your own." In these situations one should *never* say "never," because in fact some of these individuals do make sufficient progress to develop job skills or independent living skills. To tell someone that there's no hope is to take away a part of their dignity.

Finally, there are numerous cases each year of people who have been told they had no chance to recover from a serious physical ailment and yet they do recover. Sometimes it takes a second opinion, a third opinion, or a nontraditional approach. But there are countless individuals walking around today who at one time were told, "Forget it. You don't have a chance."

Twenty years ago Elisabeth Kübler-Ross revolutionized the health-care professions by instructing doctors, nurses, counselors, and relatives to start treating patients not as medical statistics but as human beings. That includes being more honest, less secretive, and more informative about medical options and risk factors. But Kübler-Ross also stressed the importance of being empathetic and respectful when giving difficult news to a patient. She made it clear that no one has the right to say, "Forget it. There's no hope. You don't have a chance." Nor is it respectful to say something unrealistic, such as, "Everything's just peachy. Don't worry about a thing."

Presenting the facts with too much finality can take away a person's energy and motivation. On the other hand, covering up with a false sense of hope can lead to feelings of betrayal. What Kübler-Ross and others have suggested is to be loving and involved, and to let the person know that you care and that even when the news is bad there are still reasons to be hopeful. A doctor, nurse, or relative can spell out the statistical likelihood of various alternatives and be honest about the probabilities, but there should always be a ray of hope that no one has the right to take away.

Yet even twenty years after Kübler-Ross's initial work, I still hear occasional stories of doctors who tell patients and relatives authoritatively, "I'm sorry, it's conclusive. There's no hope." Maybe in a few special cases, this kind of directness might be appropriate—when the patient knows the situation is permanent, for instance, and doesn't want to be deceived, or when the patient's denial of the seriousness of the condition is causing even more suffering.

But what about the cases when these "No Hope" physicians are simply wrong and it's not time to give up hope just yet? What about those instances when the results might be conclusive that no existing treatment can help, but there may be the hope of future remedies? What about those circumstances when it would be more helpful to the patient to say, "There's nothing more we can do *here*, but there may be other options," rather than closing out all hope by implying, "There's nothing more that *anyone* can do."

The best way to deal with this difficult question is to be as honest as you can. Disclose both the reasons to be realistic and the reasons to be hopeful. Patients have the right to know what's happening to them, and they also have the right to know that there are still reasons to keep going.

Even if there are times when you fear you've reached the end of possibilities for your family member, don't make the mistake of giving up hope too soon. I'm not recommending that you rush out and spend your money on every quack, charlatan, or miracle cure that you hear about. Nor should you put pressure on a loved one to accomplish something she or he can't do because of the ailment. Being hopeful doesn't mean falling into denial or having unrealistically high expectations that cause you to be impatient or judgmental toward your family member or friend.

But I do urge you to take an extra look at your options. Is there a reasonable treatment possibility you haven't considered yet? Is there an additional source of reliable information and quality care that could possibly be helpful without being harmful? Is there a way of reducing the discomfort and increasing the quality of life for your loved one? Is there a ray of hope that still exists for either an improvement or a lessening of the pain?

Getting a Second Opinion

In 1988, a fascinating book by Lawrence Horowitz, M.D., former director of the United States Senate Subcommittee on Health, was published. Called *Taking Charge of Your Medical Fate,* its essential message is that the doctor you choose and the way you work with him or her can make a significant difference in rates of improvement.

What most people don't realize is that we have the right to request the doctor of our choice. We have the right to ask doctors to explain technical decisions to us. We are entitled to ask about options, risks, and physicians' experience. We can inquire about drug side effects, treatment effectiveness, and second opinions.

Many physicians today welcome this kind of involvement from caring and intelligent family members. However, some doctors will be offended or act defensively. Even though it is a doctor's responsibility to consult openly with patients and family members about important decisions, this is not the most comfortable part of the job for many physicians.

But that's not your concern. You have the right to be given reliable information and viable choices, even from a doctor who claims to be too busy to answer your questions. If your doctor gives you a hard time, you may need to find a nurse, a social worker, an administrator or another doctor who can help you penetrate your physician's wall of secrecy. If your doctor refuses to explore realistic alternatives that you have been told by a reliable source can help your loved one, you may need to change doctors.

For example, Candace is a woman in her thirties who was worried about her four-year-old son, Max.

After having several seizures and blackouts over a six-month period, Max had been diagnosed with childhood epilepsy. One doctor, an eminent specialist who had a dozen interns taking note of his every word, insisted, "Your child is just going to have to live with these seizures. There's nothing that can be done about them in this particular case."

When Candace said she wanted a second opinion, the eminent specialist was appalled. He angrily remarked, "I assume you came to me because you wanted the most reliable assessment available. Well, you've received it. Now you can either wait for a cure to be developed in the next few years or you can waste your time and money chasing after someone who will tell you what you want to hear. But if you love your child, you'll stop being so selfish."

Candace felt as though she had just been reprimanded by a stern father figure. But after talking with a counselor and a support group about her continued feelings that there was still hope for Max, she asked around for a recommendation of someone who might have a different approach to childhood epilepsy.

For the next several weeks, Candace and a member of her support group went on a research quest. They called numerous experts, spoke with a variety of practitioners, and learned a great deal about what was being done to treat seizures in children. For a few days, Candace was considering the approach of one prominent doctor who had recommended a high-risk surgery that had been successful in many cases. But after talking it over with several other doctors, she decided it wasn't time yet for such a drastic solution.

Finally, Candace found a highly recommended acupuncturist who had worked successfully with several children diagnosed with epilepsy. Even though she was a little uncomfortable with the idea of acupuncture, Candace phoned several of the parents of these children to find out what their results had been. Each set of parents confirmed that the treatment was harmless and relatively painless. Most of the patients of this acupuncturist were still seizure-free after several years.

After several more phone calls to learn more about this practitioner and the techniques that would be used, Candace made the decision to give it a try. Following several months of treatments, Max's seizures lessened and eventually stopped altogether. Candace admits, "I'm not totally convinced that the seizures won't return, but I'm hopeful. Max seems to be back to his normal self and time will tell if the treatments worked."

Like many concerned family members, Candace had been put in a difficult position. On the one hand, she was being told by an eminent physician that it was selfish and counterproductive to keep looking for alternatives. On the other hand, she knew in her gut that she wasn't ready to simply give up hope or sit idly by and watch her four-year-old child have seizures. Fortunately, she was able to find a viable solution. Yet there is no guarantee that if we look for alternatives we will find one that can work for our loved one. In many ways Candace was lucky. Quite often the options are fewer and the results are not always as positive.

Some Guidelines for Making a Tough Decision

If you want to get a second opinion about an important medical situation—either to make sure your physician is proceeding correctly or to change doctors—where do you find one? There are a number of things to keep in mind.

Call or join one of the organizations listed in Appendix B. These information clearinghouses and support organizations are often the best way to locate up-to-date information on research, treatment, new options, and access to qualified specialists who can provide you with a second opinion.

Call the Second Surgical Opinion Hotline in Washington DC on their toll-free number, 1-800-638-6833. They will refer you to agencies in your area. These agencies will in turn refer you to three different qualified doctors.

Talk with patients who have undergone various approaches, and ask for their assessments of specific doctors, procedures, and medications. Make sure you have all the reliable information you need before making a decision.

Three cautions are in order whenever you start looking for second opinions or different treatment options:

Be wary of quack remedies and expensive programs that promise miraculous cures but refuse to document their results. If it sounds too good to be true, it probably is. You may need to take on the role of an investigative journalist to find out if patients are actually achieving the results claimed by the practitioners. Just because someone insists with apparent certainty, "It works, believe me it works," you still have the right to be skeptical until you have researched it thoroughly.

Watch out for the tendency of some research-oriented hospitals to use patients as human "guinea pigs" for testing unproven and potentially harmful new medications. If a doctor wants to try high-risk drugs or procedures on your loved one, make sure you get a second opinion from an independent expert who can evaluate side effects, risk factors, and potential benefits.

Don't give up on a highly competent doctor or treatment program too soon. Quite often families jump from one remedy to another without allowing the time and patience it takes to see definitive results. Rather than wasting time and money, or becoming exhausted from trying too many options, stick with the ones that seem most likely to benefit your loved one.

The Mistakes We Make Because of False Hope

Along with hopefulness comes the danger of having too much blind hope, clouding our ability to make good decisions. For example, as soon as I described Candace's success story, I felt a bit concerned and asked myself, "Is Candace's good fortune going to raise false hopes in situations where being realistic might be more appropriate? Will her story about an exciting improvement make readers rush out and start looking for practitioners who promise the moon and deliver nothing but disappointment? Am I giving anyone false hope or setting someone up for discouragement?"

The issue of false hope is extremely important and yet it's not often discussed. False hope can be dangerous when it causes you to become impatient or judgmental of your loved one, as if to say, "Why are you taking so long to get better? Why can't you try harder? Why can't you be like so and so?"

False hope tends to make you feel inadequate as you wonder, "Why are other people having these wonderful recoveries and we're not?" It can make you give up the slow one-step-at-a-time process of helping your loved one and instead search for hurried cures that are foolish or unlikely.

False hope is hard to avoid when every so often television and newspapers run bold stories about exciting new remedies or remarkable cures, or when a friend calls to tell about a powerful new therapy. Your curiosity gets aroused. Your hopes get raised. You think the bad luck streak might be reversing. But in most cases it is just a false promise that is not applicable to your family member's condition. Most "miracle cures" are not going to help the specific situation your loved one is facing. And the repeated adrenaline drain of hope followed by disappointment is maddening.

Josh Greenfeld describes dealing with lofty promises and false hopes in his book, *A Client Called Noah,* which is the story of Greenfeld's autistic son. The author writes, "The number of miracle workers who are quick to generalize from a false specific is frightening. And the effect is cruel beyond words on other parents."

It's a good policy whenever you hear about a new remedy or program to take a few precautions before you jump to the conclusion that your prayers have been answered.

Call several informed experts and find out if this new treatment or program is available yet, or if it won't be out for many years. Frequently, the reports that make news are the early findings of lengthy research and development projects that won't be available in useful form for quite some time, if ever. It may not be time to count on this new remedy yet.

Call for several opinions. Do some checking as to whether a new remedy can work on the specific symptoms your loved one is having, or whether it applies only to people in a different situation.

Find out all you can. Ask about side effects, risk factors, and potential benefits, so you can make an informed decision about whether it's a worthwhile possibility.

Only when you're convinced it's a good idea and you are aware of the risk factors is it time to let your hopes rise. Otherwise you will be on a constant roller coaster, overreacting to every false hope that comes along.

Monica's story is a good illustration of the importance of

checking out the details first before getting your hopes raised prematurely. Monica is a thirty-six-year-old woman whose younger brother Clark is living with AIDS. According to Monica:

For the first several months after Clark got diagnosed, I kept hearing about miracle cures and new discoveries almost once a week. Each time, I'd let my hopes soar and I'd be convinced, "This is it. They've found a cure. Clark isn't going to die."

But after numerous times getting all worked up over a false hope that turned out to be wishful thinking, I felt like a yo yo. My moods would go up and down, up and down. And I felt badly that I'd get Clark all ecstatic each time and then disappointed when the "miracle cure" turned out to be another empty promise. Or a drug that won't be available for several years.

Since those early days, I've learned how to deal with news reports and rumors about possible treatments. I'm still very hopeful and extremely involved in looking for viable approaches. Yet I'm a lot more realistic now when I read or hear about some new "Breakthrough Cure for AIDS." Rather than getting excited and then disappointed, I make sure to call several experts and talk to some people who can explain the details of this new remedy or medication. If possible, I call the actual people who are taking or administering the new treatment and ask them exactly what their side effects and results have been.

Usually I find out that Clark's current medications are the best course of action and we don't need to jump on the bandwagon of each new and unsubstantiated treatment. Every once in a while, however, my phone calls and questions do turn up a new alternative that can help Clark's situation. So I make sure that I bring up only the best possibilities to Clark and his doctor. Several of those discoveries have been extremely helpful, and those are the times when I let myself get excited and hopeful.

Can Hope Do It Alone?

I want to alert you to a growing phenomenon that has been causing some dangerous false hopes for many individuals. In recent years, there have been numerous gurus, seminars, books, and articles that suggest to many gullible people that hope alone can cure anything.

You probably have been exposed to some of this thinking. The two premises of this rapidly growing phenomenon of people who rely on hope alone to cure ailments are:

- That the only factor which causes most ailments in the first place is the presence of "negative thoughts," "toxic beliefs," or a lack of love.

- That since fearful thoughts or a lack of love are what cause most illnesses, the only way to cure an illness is through positive thinking, affirmations, and love.

While I am a strong believer in the power of the mind and the importance of being optimistic, I am also very concerned about the mistakes many people make when they engage in oversimplistic thinking such as this. Yes, it's quite possible that our beliefs and ability to love and be loved may play a role in our overall health. But unfortunately there are people who have jeopardized their own recoveries from serious ailments by attempting to rely on hope and affirmations alone.

For example, I met a woman named Bridgitte who was undergoing treatments for cancer and beginning to make some progress until she stopped her treatments because she mistakenly drew the wrong conclusion from a popular book a friend gave her. The book, *Love, Medicine and Miracles* by Bernie Siegel, M.D., has a lot of excellent points as it discusses the importance of love and hope as healing influences. Siegel describes several cases of "exceptional patients" who defied the odds and were cured in part because of their positive mental attitudes.

Unfortunately, Bridgitte and numerous other individuals have incorrectly concluded that the message of Dr. Siegel's book was, "Stop your treatments and rely on love and positive affirmations alone to cure yourself."

Ironically, Dr. Siegel himself has stated on several occasions that this is not what his book is recommending. He commented on *The Phil Donahue Show* that the reason he continues to work as a medical surgeon is because he still recognizes that traditional procedures often are necessary, for positive beliefs and affirmations are only a part of the healing process. On *The Oprah Winfrey Show,* he also spoke out against the belief that "negative thoughts" are the sole cause of disease when he said, "There are lousy friends who make you feel guilty [by blaming the patient for the disease]. There are terrible therapists who make you feel you caused the disease."

Please don't fall into the simplistic trap that "negative thinking" is the sole reason for a loved one's illness. Although our attitudes and beliefs can affect our health and our healing processes, blaming the patient or pinning the entire cause of an ailment on a negative mental attitude is inaccurate and insensitive.

If someone starts insisting that "all you need is love" and recommends stopping a worthwhile treatment, make sure you don't get swept up in this kind of false hope. Optimism, affirmations, and love are extremely important for rallying the body's healing forces, but putting your reliance on hope alone could be a tragic mistake. I consider myself a strong believer in religion and spirituality, yet I recognize that faith works best when combined with responsible action.

If a dogmatic person starts insisting that you ought to put your trust in some guru, philosophy, or other magical thinking, here's what you can do: Use the jargon of the New Age and tell this person, "Thank you for sharing!" Then use the jargon of urban survival and say, "Now get out of my face."

Being Realistic with Ailments that are Hard to See

Finally, there is one more type of false hope that you may need to watch out for. With certain illnesses, since your loved one appears to be fine most of the time, you may start questioning the reality of the ailment.

For example, one of the cruel tricks that certain disorders play on us is when we can't *see* the ailment even though we've been told it's there. With Alzheimer's, Parkinson's, epilepsy, schizophrenia, or manic depression you can't *see* the brain chemistry that is out of sync. So when your loved one appears to be fine for a few hours, a few days, or a few months, it's tempting to conclude, "The illness is gone. Let's forget about the medications or the long-term care planning we've been doing. The problem is over."

In a similar fashion many tumors, viruses, and heart conditions present no reliable clues to the naked eye that your loved one needs special care. Your family member or friend may look fine, showing no outward signs that a malignancy or other serious condition is festering underneath. So it's tempting to fall into denial and say, "Maybe the doctors are wrong and we don't need to follow these precautions and prescriptions." It's enticing to engage in wishful thinking and say, "Maybe we can wait a while longer and hope it goes away."

If your loved one had a broken arm or a broken leg, you'd know for certain it was real and you wouldn't be prone to wondering, "Is the illness gone? Are we overreacting? Is this person pretending to be ill or doing this on purpose? Can he or she control the symptoms?"

With most ailments, there is no broken arm or leg staring you in the face. Your loved one looks fine for the most part, and yet the illness is just as real. Your family member or friend *isn't* making up the symptoms or doing all this just to be difficult.

Falling into denial is a very common reaction, especially when the ailment is hidden or elusive. For instance, here are some revealing comments from family members who were struggling to decide whether to focus on what they saw with their own eyes, or what they couldn't see but which was nonetheless true:
Esther has an aging mother who's been diagnosed with Alzheimer's disease. Yet Esther admits,

> When Mom looks good or has a few good days in a row, it's easy to slip back into denial. We hear ourselves saying, "Oh, it's not really Alzheimer's" or "Oh, it's only temporary."
> These false hopes make us reluctant to take Mom in for tests or to seriously consider long-term care. Sometimes we rush from doctor to doctor hoping for a different diagnosis and exhausting Mom and ourselves in the process. Sometimes we just get lazy and say, "Let's not deal with the financial or medical issues until we're sure she really needs it." But in fact my mother does have Alzheimer's and we're just kidding ourselves when we pretend it's not so.

Bart is married to an intelligent and energetic woman named Kimberly who had a mild heart attack almost six months ago. Bart admits:

> For a long time I would listen to Kimberly complain about tiredness, chest pains, or heartburn, but I thought her symptoms were no big deal. I assumed she was being psychosomatic or looking for sympathy. But after her heart attack I realized these symptoms were for real, even though she seemed healthy and fine 95 percent of the time.

Quite often what appears to be "no big deal" needs to be checked carefully by a competent medical professional. In most cases, your loved one is *not* having these symptoms to be difficult or to gain sympathy. In many hard-to-detect illnesses, the person looks fine most of the time and can't control the actions or symptons that are clues to a more serious problem.

Yet until you face the reality that this person might need special care, you will continue to feel impatient or skeptical. Nearly every family member of someone with Alzheimer's, mental illness, or physical aches and pains has had moments of saying, "I wonder if this person is doing this on purpose." So don't feel guilty about it, but do make sure your loved one gets the proper testing and treatment from a qualified doctor. Sometimes the most loving thing you can do for a family member with a hard-to-see ailment is to stop expecting the symptoms to disappear and start accepting that it's time to take them seriously.

Finding the Balance

Now that you're aware of the variety of ways that people either fall into false hope or give up hope too soon, how do you achieve a healthy balance between hoping for the best and dealing realistically with a serious ailment?

What I recommend to patients and family members is not to think of hope or realism as two either-or, mutually exclusive choices. It's not a question of *either* "Should I hold onto some hopeful images" *or* "Should I let go of hope and prepare for the worst?" There's a middle ground in which you can find balance by paying attention to *both* hope and realism.

Here are some guidelines you can use to regain your balance one day at a time:

*Start each day with a sense of openness
to learning something new.*

Set as one of your goals each day that you will learn something new about your loved one, his or her condition, or something about yourself. These are highly realistic as well as hopeful goals.

For example, every single day there is the possibility of learning something new about your loved one—why he or she is a certain way; what makes this person feel supported and loved; what makes things easier or harder for your loved one; and what brings meaning and satisfaction to this person's life.

Each day there is the opportunity to learn more about your loved one's condition—what is realistically being done to help others in a similar situation; what are some hopeful developments that might be worth exploring; and what are some realities that you need to understand better and learn more about?

Every day is another chance to discover more about yourself—what are your strengths and limitations as a caregiver; what are you really like as a family member or friend; what are you learning about your own ability to express love, patience, and caring; and what are you discovering about your priorities in life?

If one of your daily goals is to learn and grow from these insights, you will feel a sense of hopeful momentum each day regardless of whether your loved one's ailment gets better, worse, or stays the same. Even if you think you know all there is to know about these issues, there is still a lot more to discover.

For example, I recall an extremely brilliant scholar in his sixties who once told me:

I thought I was intelligent and well-learned until I faced the illness of my older brother. I found out just how little I really knew about who he is and who I am. I've had many great teachers, but none more revealing than facing life and asking the hard questions with my ailing brother.

When you view your loved one's illness as a source of new learning and new meaning, it puts a different light on your daily activities. Your day-to-day tasks become a chance to grow and develop as a human being, rather than feel burdened or victimized.

For example, Gretchen's case demonstrates the fact that the illness of a loved one is often a powerful source of learning, growth, and new insights.

Gretchen is a forty-eight-year-old woman who recalls:

My life was pretty stable and predictable until six years ago when my husband became seriously ill. That crisis started a whole new set of challenges for me. It wasn't just the challenge of helping him cope with his ailment and the fact that he was no longer going to the office each day. His illness also became the stimulus that got me thinking, "What do I want to be doing with my life? What am I capable of achieving in the work world? Who are the friends and relatives that I can count on to help us through this difficult time?"

"Looking back at these six years of turmoil and change, I see myself having grown up a great deal. I went back to finish my education, I got an important job that has helped us stay afloat financially, and I learned how to stand up for myself and my family in ways I never had to before my husband's illness. I'm not pleased that my husband had to suffer so much in order to push me onto this productive path, but I am pleased at how I responded to the challenge."

Don't lose hope because of bad news or setbacks that might be temporary.

Quite often people give up hope or stop trying because they keep running into brick walls. Now I'm not saying that it's fun to run into brick walls, but I urge you to make sure you restore your sense of hope and strength no matter what obstacles block your path.

With many illnesses that are lengthy or hard to treat, there is a long and twisting path you may need to walk to find the right doctors, medications, and treatments. But whether you find the right help for your family member on the first try or the twentieth the point is that you keep looking and that you eventually find it. Each piece of bad news is just a brief chapter in a long novel that is still being written. Each setback is just a temporary situation that challenges you to keep looking for answers to help your loved one deal with her or his ailment.

I recently counseled a woman named Katrina who was feeling burned out and frustrated after several years of trying to find the right doctors and treatments for her son's respiratory disorder. Each highly recommended doctor she was unable to help her son. Yet Katrina didn't give up. To help her deal with repeated disappointments and restore her energy for another round of searching, I urged her to do a simple exercise that any of us can do when we're feeling discouraged.

First, take a relaxing and soothing bath in which you let your feelings of disappointment and sadness come up in a safe environment. After a good cry in the bathtub, you will not only be physically clean but also emotionally cleansed. You will feel a lot less weighed down by sadness or discouragement.

Then it's time for the second step. Stand in front of the mirror and remind yourself that you are one excellent human being for the caring and persistence you've shown in helping your ailing loved one. None of us is perfect, yet we can each take a moment from time to time to recognize that we're doing a good job in a difficult situation. I urge you to do this not for selfish reasons, but to restore your commitment to continue doing all you can for your ailing loved one.

When Katrina did this exercise, she first went to a nearby gourmet bath store and spent a few dollars on her favorite flavors of scented bath oils. Then she spent thirty minutes alone in her tub letting her feelings of sadness and frustration slowly come out as she soaked. Finally, she stood in front of the mirror and said the following:

Katrina, you are one persistent woman and I'm glad you're as committed to helping your son as you are. It's not time to give up yet. You can rest and regain your strength. But one of these days you're going to see some more encouraging results. Take good care of yourself because you're needed right now.

Instead of feeling exhausted and defeated, Katrina felt somewhat renewed. Her problems weren't solved by taking time out to unwind, but her determination and health were re-energized.

Maybe a bubble bath and a conversation in front of the mirror isn't your style. But what is your style? What are you willing to do to let out the sadness we all experience when our efforts to help someone don't always work? What are you willing to do to remind yourself that your patience and persistence are justified? Whether your style is to take a day off, take a long walk, have a counseling session, visit with a good friend, or schedule a relaxing massage at a health club, make sure you find the time to renew your energies. Not only for your sake, but for the sake of those who are relying on you.

Don't overreact to each piece of good news and start expecting more than is realistic from your ailing loved one.

Too often when something goes right you might notice relatives and friends start to overreact and raise their expectations dangerously high. A mentally ill loved one makes some progress in holding down a volunteer job for two days and suddenly a family member assumes he or she is ready to hold down a high-paying, high-pressure job. A physically ill loved one makes some progress in barely using a limb that was immobilized, and suddenly a family member assumes she's fine again, back to normal.

The key to staying balanced is to let yourself enjoy each small triumph and feel some hope *without* overreacting and expecting more than is realistic from your loved one. Putting unrealistic pressure on people who are ailing or disabled usually causes them to feel inadequate and defeated. Even if your intention is to prod this person on with your high hopes, the result is usually the opposite. Many ailing individuals feel like giving up when they find they are always accomplishing less than certain important relatives and friends expect of them.

For example, Marissa and Donald have a nineteen-year-old daughter named Patrice who has a rare birth defect that usually requires her to use a wheelchair or special walking braces to get around. For years Marissa and Donald have spent a great deal of time and money finding the right specialists and therapists to help Patrice get better and regain full mobility.

Like most family members who hope for the best for a loved one, Marissa and Donald don't want to be too realistic. They don't want to accept the possibility that Patrice might need a wheelchair or special walking braces for the rest of her life. They have their sights focused on a cure for the mysterious ailment and don't want to settle for less.

Sometimes, however, their determination to hope for the best has its downside. For instance, according to Patrice:

My parents have a lot of guilt and anger about the fact that their daughter is disabled. My mom keeps hoping I'll magically get better and refuses to listen to what's really going on with me. Part of her desperation is because she blames herself for the fact that she was exposed to some toxic paint fumes where she worked when she was pregnant with me. But I know she's not at fault. She never intended for that to happen and no one realized in those days that the paint fumes were dangerous. Yet her guilt makes it hard for her to accept that I am the way I am.

My father has a lot of frustration because his "little girl" has to suffer. He loves me a whole lot, but sometimes his anger at my disability causes him to be short-tempered and impatient. Sometimes he frustrates me because he has such stubborn ideas of the "right way" and the "wrong way" to deal with an ailment. Unfortunately, his way and my way are not always in agreement and I often feel like giving up because I can't possibly live up to his expectations for me.

My parents want so badly for me to get better and walk on my own. They're good people and I know they love me, but I wish just once they would accept me as I am.

As you can see from Patrice's description, it's unfortunate when family members put too much pressure on each other because of their strong hopes for an improvement. These kinds of "oppressive expectations" take place not only between parents and children, but also between spouses, siblings, lovers, friends, and other relatives. It's quite common to see well-intentioned people feeling disappointed and impatient because their expectations aren't being met. In many cases, this causes extra problems for everyone.

To make sure you aren't expecting something unrealistic from your loved one that is adding to the pressure he or she is facing, ask yourself these questions:

- Are you willing to love and accept your family member exactly as is and be supportive even if the situation doesn't get better? Or is your love conditional on this person doing things the way you want them done?
- Are you willing to take a new look at your ideas of what this person is doing "right" or "wrong"? Are you willing to appreciate that your loved one has the right to face this ailment in his or her own way, regardless of

whether it agrees with how you would handle the situation?

- Are you willing to accept the realities of your loved one's condition and stop wishing everything could be the way it was before the ailment took hold? Are you willing to stop resisting the way things are and start making the best of this challenging situation?
- Can you hope for an improvement without becoming impatient or criticizing your loved one every time this person takes a step backward? Can you be hopeful and accepting at the same time?

These are not simple questions and you may want to talk with a good friend, a counselor, or a support group at least once a week about how to walk the fine line between hope and realism. Don't be surprised if there are days when you notice yourself tilting in a lopsided way toward acceptance or impatience, toward optimism or despair. We each have days when we wish it all were different and days when we forget that there's still hope.

What You're Doing is Worthwhile

If there is one thing I hope you have gained from this book, it is a deeper understanding of how to keep your sense of balance while helping a loved one who's ailing. Life has its difficulties and we get to choose how to respond to them. Some people run away or slip into denial. Some feel like burdened victims and become worn out. Others rise to the occasion and remember to stay healthy in the process.

A few years ago my wife Linda and I lost a much-wanted pregnancy and were feeling pretty discouraged for a while. Then one of the people Linda works with wrote us a card that included an anonymous proverb which caught the essence of what happens when any of us faces a difficult time such as the ailment of a loved one. The proverb said:

There is in every true heart
a spark of heavenly fire,

which lies dormant
in the broad daylight of prosperity;

but which kindles up
and beams and blazes
in the dark hour of adversity.

The illness or disability of someone you care about is an opportunity to kindle a spark of heavenly fire. It's a chance to find out what's really important in your life and how to respond with your most heartfelt involvement. I don't think our purpose here on earth is to eat, sleep, pay taxes, and die. I think our deeper purpose is to love one another and to respond to the genuine human needs we all have for companionship.

After our loss, my wife Linda and I made a commitment not to give up hope. And I urge you and your family not to lose faith when there are setbacks in your own situation.

To be of service to someone who's hurting is no easy task. I hope this book has given you some ideas on how to come through for your loved ones and yourself during these stressful times. In the next few weeks and months, you may want to reread certain sections that apply to specific challenges you are facing. No matter how many times we experience the illness or disability of someone close to us, there is always more to learn.

As I think back on the times in my life when a special person was ailing or in need of care, I remember feeling scared. But I also recall having a deep sense of love and a strong sense of purpose. What you are doing to assist another human being is extremely worthwhile. Now if you can just remember to take good care of yourself, too, you'll do an even better job. Good luck!

Notes on Sources

Chapter One: page 5
The statistics on the number of caregivers were obtained from U.S. Government Statistics, The American Society on Aging, The American Association of Retired Persons, The National Information Center for Handicapped Children and Youth, and several other associations and research studies that compile data on various illnesses and disabilities.

Chapter Three: page 30
The stages of coping with a serious illness were first described in *On Death and Dying* by Elisabeth Kübler-Ross (New York: Macmillan, 1969).

Chapter Four: page 51–52
The "Caregiver Burnout Syndrome" is a term developed by Elaine Brody and other gerontologists to describe the psychological and health risks for people who take care of an ailing loved one without taking adequate care of themselves.

Chapter Four: page 66–74
The statistics on sleep disorders are available from Consumer's Union, publishers of *Consumer Reports*.

Chapter Five: page 100
Norman Cousins uses an approach to healing that includes a sense of humor and an active participation by the patient. His books describing these techniques include *The Healing Heart: Antidotes To Panic and Helplessness* (New York: Norton, 1983) and *Anatomy of an Illness as Perceived by the Patient* (New York: Bantam, 1981).

Chapter Five: page 105–106
The statistics on elderabuse were reported in *ParentCare*, a newsletter published by the School of Gerontology of the University of Kansas, and by researchers from the American Society on Aging.

Chapter Six: page 118
The expression "Super Trooper" was first described in the book *Body, Self and Soul: Sustaining Integration* by Jack Rosenberg, Marjorie Rand, and Diane Asay (Atlanta: Humanics Limited, 1985).

Chapter Nine: page 213
The book discussed on the trade-offs between hope and realism is *Love, Medicine and Miracles* by Bernie Siegel (New York: Harper and Row, 1986).

APPENDIX A

Additional Reading That Can Help

Many of the books that assisted me and that have helped thousands of others are listed below. You can find them in any of the following ways:

- Call your local public and university libraries to see if they carry a specific book. If they don't have it, ask if they know other libraries nearby that might carry it. Or ask if they could order the book for other library patrons like yourself.
- Call your local bookstores to see if they have a particular book in stock. Don't be surprised or upset if they don't have the book on the shelves. But do ask them to order it from a wholesaler, which only takes a few days if the wholesaler has the book, or directly from the publisher, which can take a few weeks.
- Call the organizations listed in Appendix B to see if they have access to these and other helpful books on specific caregiving topics.

- If none of the above approaches work, you may want to call the publisher directly to see if it's possible to order a copy. In some cases, you may need to write to the author in care of the publisher's address to see if the author has additional copies or updated information that can be ordered.

Excellent Books on Chronic Illnesses in General

We Are Not Alone: Learning to Live with Chronic Illness, by Sefra Kobrin Pitzele (New York: Workman, 1986)

Written by a chronically ill person, this book is practical and very helpful to patients, relatives, and friends. It provides dozens of creative strategies for adapting to everyday obstacles.

Mainstay: For the Well Spouse of the Chronically Ill, by Maggie Strong (Boston: Little, Brown, 1988)

A first-person story of the emotional and nuts-and-bolts aspects of responding well to a loved one's ailment. This book can be read by parents, children, siblings, lovers, and friends as well as spouses.

Caregiving: Helping an Aging Loved One, by Jo Horne (Prospect, IL: AARP Publications/Scott-Foresman, 1985)

An outstanding book by the administrator of an adult day-care center, this book has lots of practical information and helpful advice.

Helpful Books for Family Members of Disabled People

One Miracle At a Time: How To Get Help For Your Disabled Child—From the Experience of Other Parents, by Irving Dickman and Sol Gordon (New York: Simon and Schuster, 1985)

Using research from hundreds of families nationwide, this book is filled with personal stories and helpful suggestions for parents who want to make good decisions.

Hope for the Families: New Directions for Parents of Persons with Retardation or Other Disabilities, by Robert Perske (Nashville: Abingdon Press, 1981)

A down-to-earth and heartfelt description of the feelings and decisions parents go through. This author knows the experiences first hand and writes with a sense of empathy and humor while making practical suggestions.

A Difference in the Family: Living with a Disabled Child, by Helen Featherstone (New York: Penguin, 1981)

A classic in the field, this book deals with both the personal issues of helping your family respond well and the practical issues of coming through for a disabled loved one.

Disabled? Yes. Defeated? No, by Kathleen Cruzie (Englewood Cliffs, N.J.: Prentice-Hall/Spectrum, 1982)

This realistic but hopeful book has hundreds of resources and good ideas for making life fuller for the disabled and their families.

No Apologies: A Guide To Living with Disabilities, Written by the Real Authorities—People with Disabilities, Their Family and Friends, by Florence Weiner (New York: St. Martin's, 1986)

An inspiring and innovative book on the numerous ways that people with disabilities overcome obstacles in today's society.

The Source Book for the Disabled, by Glorya Hale (New York: Saunders/Holt, 1982)

Hundreds of good ideas on how to deal more effectively with day-to-day realities and find resources that can help.

Excellent Books on Specific Ailments

AIDS:

You Can Do Something About AIDS, by Sasha Alyson (Boston: The Stop AIDS Project, 1988). Distributed free at most bookstores.

AIDS: A Catholic Call for Compassion, by Eileen Flynn (Kansas City, MO: Sheed and Ward, 1987)

And the Band Played On: Politics, People and The AIDS Epidemic, by Randy Shilts (New York: St. Martin's, 1987)

Someone Was Here: Profiles in the AIDS Epidemic, by George Whitmore (New York: New American Library, 1988)

When Someone You Know Has AIDS: A Practical Guide, by Leonard J. Martelli (New York: Crown, 1988)

ALZHEIMER'S:

The 36-Hour Day: A Family Guide to Caring for Persons with Alzheimer's Disease, Related Dementing Illnesses, and Memory Loss in Later Life, by Nancy Mace and Peter Rabins (New York: Warner, 1984)

Understanding Alzheimer's Disease: What It Is, How to Cope with It, Future Directions, by Miriam K. Aronson (New York: Scribner's, 1988)

The Loss of Self: A Family Resource for the Care of Alzheimer's Disease and Related Disorders, by Donna Cohen and Carl Eisdorfer (New York: Norton, 1986)

A.L.S.
(LOU GEHRIG'S
DISEASE):

In Sunshine and Shadow, by Judy Oliver (Sherman Oaks, CA: Amyotrophic Lateral Sclerosis Association, 1986)

Six Parts Love: One Family's Battle with Lou Gehrig's Disease (New York: Scribner's, 1985)

AUTISM:

A Child Called Noah (1972), A Place for Noah (1978), and A Client Called Noah (1987), by Josh Greenfeld (New York: Holt)

The Riddle of Autism: A Psychological Analysis, by George Victor (Lexington, MA: Lexington Books, 1983)

The Hidden Child: The Linwood Method for Reaching the Autistic Child, by Jeanne Simons (Kensington, MD: Woodbine House, 1987)

CANCER:

Taking Time: Support for People with Cancer and the People Who Care About Them, by Joan Hartman (Washington DC: National Cancer Institute, 1982)

From Victim to Victor: The Wellness Community Guide to Fighting for Recovery for Cancer Patients and Their Families, by Harold Benjamin (Los Angeles: Tarcher, 1987)

The Road Back to Health: Coping with the Emotional Side of Cancer, by Neil Fiore (New York: Bantam, 1984)

CEREBRAL
PALSY: *Handling the Young Cerebral Palsy
                         Child at Home,* by Nancie R. Finnie
                         (New York: Dutton, 1975)

                         Does She Know She's There? by Nicola
                         Schaefer (Garden City, NY: Double-
                         day, 1978)

DOWN'S
SYNDROME: *Your Down's Syndrome Child: Every-
                         thing Today's Parents Need to Know
                         About Raising Their Special Child,* by
                         Eunice McClurg (Garden City, NY:
                         Doubleday, 1986)

EPILEPSY: *Seizures, Epilepsy and Your Child: A
                         Handbook for Parents, Teachers and
                         Epileptics of All Ages,* by Jorge Lagos
                         (New York: Harper and Row, 1974)

                         *Children with Epilepsy: A Parent's
                         Guide,* by Helen Reisner (Kensington,
                         MD: Woodbine House, 1988)

HEART
DISEASE: *Heartmates: A Survival Guide for the
                         Cardiac Spouse,* by Rhoda Levin (New
                         York: Prentice-Hall, 1987)

LUPUS: *Understanding Lupus,* by Henrietta
                         Aladjem (New York, Scribner's, 1985)

MENTAL
ILLNESS: *Surviving Schizophrenia: A Family
                         Manual,* by E. Fuller Torrey (New
                         York: Harper and Row, 1983)

Families Helping Families Living with Schizophrenia, by Families of the Mentally Ill Collective (New York: Avon, 1987)

The Caring Family: Living with Chronic Mental Illness, by Kayla Bernheim (New York: Random House, 1982)

MULTIPLE
SCLEROSIS: *Understanding Multiple Sclerosis: A Guidebook for Families,* by Robert Shuman and Janice Schwartz (New York: Scribner's, 1988)

PARKINSON'S: For an eighty-page booklet to help patients and family adjust to the disease, contact The American Parkinson Disease Association, Box 8111, 660 South Euclid Street, St. Louis, MO 63110.

RETARDATION: *The Special Child: A Parents' Guide to Mental Disabilities* (Boston: Little, Brown, 1978)

We Have Been There: A Guidebook for Families of People with Mental Retardation (Nashville: Abingdon Press, 1983)

STROKE: *Stroke: A Guide for Patients and Their Families,* by John Sarno and Martha Taylor Sarno (New York: McGraw-Hill, 1979)

For books on other ailments, call the hotlines listed in Appendix B.

Specific Suggestions on Home Care and Nursing Skills

Home Care for the Elderly: A Complete Guide, by Jay Portnow and Martha Houtmann (New York: McGraw-Hill, 1987)

Caring for Your Own: Nursing the Ill at Home, by Darla J. Neidrick (New York: John Wiley, 1988)

Caring: Home Treatment for the Emotionally Disturbed, by Frederic Neuman (New York: Dial Press, 1980)

Home Health Care: A Complete Guide for Patients and Their Families (New York: Norton, 1986)

For free information to help select safe, efficient, and effective in-home services, contact The National Home Caring Council, 67 Irving Place, New York, NY 10003, (212) 674-4990.

Guidelines for Selecting and Working with a Nursing Home

Step by Step: How to Actively Ensure the Best Possible Care for Your Aging Relative, by Ted Rossi (New York: Warner, 1987)

The Nursing Home Dilemma: How to Make One of Life's Toughest Decisions, by Doug Manning (San Francisco: Harper and Row, 1985)

Living in a Nursing Home: A Complete Guide for Residents, Their Families and Friends, by Sarah Burger (New York: Seabury, 1976)

A Home Away from Home: Consumer Information on Board and Care Homes, by Margaret Haske, available free from AARP Fulfillment, Box 2400, Long Beach, CA 90801. Ask for #12446.

Your Home, Your Choice: A Workbook for Families, available free from AARP Fulfillment, Box 2400, Long Beach, CA 90801. Ask for #12143.

For free brochures on choosing a nursing home, living independently and community services for older people living at home, send a self-addressed, stamped envelope and forty-five cents postage to The American Association of Homes for the Aging, 1129 20th Street NW, Suite 400, Washington, DC 20036.

Adult Day Care

For a Directory of Adult Day Care in America, with 847 centers listed, write to National Council on the Aging, 600 Maryland Avenue SW, West Wing 100, Washington, DC 20024. Ask for Order #2022.

Advice for Long-Distance Caregivers

A free booklet called "Miles Away and Still Caring: A Guide for Long-Distance Caregivers" (1986) is available from the AARP Fulfillment, Box 2400, Long Beach, CA 90801. Ask for Order #D-12748.

Suggestions on Helping an Ailing Parent

You and Your Aging Parent: The Modern Family's Guide to Emotional, Physical and Financial Problems, by Barbara Silverstone and Helen Kandel Hyman (New York: Pantheon, 1982)

A classic in the field, it has many good ideas on dealing with the emotional issues as well as the practical concerns.

Parentcare: A Commonsense Guide for Adult Children, by Lissy Jarvik and Gary Small (New York: Crown, 1988)

An outstanding new addition to the challenge of helping an aging parent and avoiding burnout in the process.

Making Peace with Your Parents: The Key to Enriching Your Life and All Your Relationships, by Harold Bloomfield and Leonard Felder (New York: Ballantine, 1985)

Filled with suggestions and case studies on how to resolve your tensions with mom or dad, especially when one or both of them are ailing.

How to Talk to Your Children About a Serious Illness in the Family

Should the Children Know? Encounters with Death in the Lives of Children, by Marguerita Rudolph (New York: Schocken, 1978)

An excellent book about how to help children face a serious illness of a loved one.

How Do We Tell the Children? A Parents' Guide to Helping Children Understand and Cope When Someone Dies, by Dan Schaefer (New York: Newmarket Press, 1986)

Looks at how families respond to illness and death, and how to help younger children deal with their questions and feelings.

Unspoken Grief: Coping with Childhood Sibling Loss, by Helen Rosen (Lexington, MA: Lexington books, 1986)

Very helpful for understanding what the well child goes through and how to assist the silent but troubled members of our families.

Useful Books on Financial and Legal Issues

The Age Care Sourcebook, by Jean Crichton (New York: Simon and Schuster/Fireside, 1987)

A wide variety of helpful information and practical advice on issues ranging from home nursing, nursing home decisions, and financial and legal issues. Easy to read and comprehensive.

How to Provide for Their Future: Suggestions for Parents Concerned with Providing Lifetime Protection for a Child with Mental Retardation, available from The Association for Retarded Citizens at PO Box 6109, Arlington, Texas 76011.

This recently updated practical guide can be used by parents of anyone who is unable to make financial and legal decisions for themselves. It's also helpful for siblings and friends of the mentally and emotionally disabled.

The Consumer's Guide to Long-Term Care, a free booklet available from the External Affairs Department, American Council of Life Insurance, 1001 Pennsylvania Avenue NW, Washington DC 20004, (202) 624-2000.

This booklet has updated information on some of the choices families have to protect themselves against financial devastation in the event of a long-term ailment.

Social Security, Medicare, and Pensions, by Joseph L. Matthews and Dorothy Matthews Berman (Berkley, CA: Nolo Press). To order, call 1-800-992-NOLO.

An easy-to-read layperson's guide to dealing with legal and financial issues.

Alternatives—A Family Guide to Legal and Financial Planning for the Disabled, avilable from the Russell M. First Publications, 1983, PO Box 1832, Evanston, IL 60204.

One of the best planning guides for anticipating the future needs of disabled family members.

How to Recover Your Medical Expenses: A Comprehensive Guide to Understanding and Unscrambling Medicare, by Kal Waller (New York: Collier Books, 1981)

This book walks the reader through the steps and hurdles that are involved when filling out medicare forms and negotiating with doctors and the government for reimbursements.

Your Medicare Handbook, available from your local Social Security Office or the Social Security Administration, Department of Health and Human Services, Washington, DC.

With Medicare laws and requirements changing in the past few years, it's essential that you know ahead of time what costs are covered and how to apply for benefits.

Spiritual and Religious Approaches to Illness and Dying Issues

When Bad Things Happen to Good People, by Harold Kushner (New York: Avon Books, 1981)
A wonderful description of how to get beyond feelings of anger and betrayal toward God or religion, and how to regain a positive sense of meaning and purpose.

A Gift of Hope: How We Survive Our Tragedies, by Robert Veninga (New York: Ballantine, 1985)
An inspiring book on the spiritual and practical aspects of coping with the illness or death of a loved one.

Man's Search for Meaning, by Viktor Frankl (New York: Pocket, 1985)
A classic on how to find meaning and strength even during the most horrific circumstances, written by a psychotherapist who lost his family in the Holocaust of World War II.

The Courage of Conviction: Prominent Contemporaries Discuss Their Beliefs and How They Put Them into Action, by Philip Berman (New York: Ballantine, 1986)
An easy-to-read and highly inspiring look at how some well-known celebrities, authors, scholars, and leaders come to terms with their spiritual questions and how they find strength in their various faiths.

On Death and Dying (1969), Living with Death and Dying (1981), On Children and Death (1983), by Elisabeth Kübler-Ross, New York: (Macmillan)
The serious illness of a loved one can be a fearful time or a time for new explorations of the meaning of life and the understanding of death. These books by Elisabeth Kübler-

Ross can help you discover how to relate to illness or dying as part of life itself and an opportunity for closeness and compassion.

Who Dies? An Investigation of Conscious Living and Conscious Dying (1982), Meetings at the Edge: Dialogues with the Grieving and the Dying, the Healing and the Healed (1984), Healing into Life and Death (1987), by Stephen Levine, Garden City, NY: (Anchor Press/Doubleday)

These are three fascinating books that have helped many people stop feeling terrified of illness or dying. They describe how to understand the healing and dying processes from a spiritual perspective and how to assist a loved one move through these transitions with much less emotional pain.

Books on Staying Healthy While Taking Care of Someone Else

Here are three excellent books on keeping a personal journal during the caregiving process:

One to One: Self-Understanding Through Journal Writing, by Christina Baldwin (New York: M. Evans, 1977)

The New Diary: How to Use a Journal for Self-Guidance and Expanded Creativity, by Tristine Rainer (Los Angeles: Tarcher, 1978)

Life-Study: Experiencing Creative Lives by the Journal Method, by Ira Progoff (New York: Dialogue House, 1983)

Here are some practical books on how to improve your chances for sleep and resolve a chronic sleep problem:

Inside Insomnia: How to Sleep Better Tonight, by Bernard Dryer and Ellen Kaplan (New York: Villard, 1986)

Somniquest: The 5 Types of Sleeplessness and How to Overcome Them, by Alice Kuhn Schwartz and Norma Aaron (New York: Harmony, 1979)

Good Night: The Easy and Natural Way to Sleep the Whole Night Through, by Norman Ford (Rockport, MA: Para Research, 1983)

The Sleep Book: Understanding and Preventing Sleep Problems in People Over 50, by Ernest Hartmann (Glenview, IL: AARP/Scott-Foresman, 1987)

Here are some popular works on how to boost your immune system and stay healthy even during stressful times:

The New York Times Guide to Personal Health, by Jane Brody (New York: Avon, 1987)

An excellent resource guide on how to prevent or treat many common ailments. These suggestions can help you remain healthy while caring for a loved one.

Immune for Life, by Arnold Fox and Barry Fox (Rocklin, CA: Prima Publishing, 1989)

A good overall look at how to adjust your diet, nutrition, stress levels, exercise, and psychology to boost your immune system.

Dr. Berger's Immune Power Diet, by Stuart Berger (New York: Signet, 1985)

An introduction to how diet, nutrition, and stress management can affect your susceptibility to some ailments. Has some helpful tips on how to boost your immune system and stay healthy as you work to help a loved one who needs you.

Some Excellent Books on Overcoming Chronic Guilt Feelings

What Did I Do Wrong?: Mothers, Children, Guilt, by Lynn Caine (New York: Arbor House, 1985)

A terrific book by a widowed mother who knows what it feels like to think everything is your fault, and who shows some ways to stop blaming yourself for things you didn't do or cannot change.

Good-Bye to Guilt: Releasing Fear Through Forgiveness, by Gerald Jampolsky (New York: Bantam, 1985)

An innovative approach to forgiving oneself and others in order to become more fully alive. This book can help you renew your sense of love and closeness, even with someone who has been difficult in the past.

Guilt: Letting Go, by Lucy Freeman and Herbert Strean (New York: John Wiley, 1986)

A comprehensive and insightful look at why we tend to feel guilty at times like these and how to work through many unnecessary guilt feelings.

How to Negotiate with Doctors, Insurance Companies, and Bureaucracies

Taking Charge of Your Medical Fate, by Lawrence Horowitz (New York: Random House, 1988)

A fascinating look at what happens if you don't become assertive with your loved one's doctors and clinics, and how to understand your rights as a caregiver.

Managing Your Doctor: How to Get the Best Possible Health Care, by Arthur Freese (New York: Stein and Day, 1975)

Instead of feeling like a helpless victim, this approach shows you how to manage your doctor and help these individuals do the best job possible for your loved one.

How to Talk to Your Doctor: The Questions to Ask, by Janet R. Maurer (New York: Simon and Schuster, 1986)

A must-read for anyone who cares about a loved one and wants to make sure they receive the best treatment available.

A Complete Guide to Understanding and Participating in Your Own Care, by Judith Nierenberg (New York: Bobbs-Merrill, 1978)

Shows the patient and family members how to become

more knowledgeable and creative in arranging for proper health care. Instead of waiting for someone else to find the time to address your concerns, this book helps you manage the healing process more successfully.

APPENDIX B

Phone Numbers of Specialized Resources and Referral Services

Whenever you have a question or a concern about your loved one's illness or disability, there are people you can call to get the most reliable, up-to-date information. In the next several pages there are dozens of helpful services listed alphabetically by the name of the ailments or groups they service.

In addition to asking your specific questions, don't forget to ask for other information that might help you become an even more effective caregiver. When you call the numbers listed below that relate to your family member or friend's ailment or disability, be sure to inquire about:

- Free pamphlets, booklets, and helpful information about the diagnosed condition and how family members can assist an ailing loved one.
- A referral to specialists, local chapters, or resource centers in your area that provide support for patients and family members.
- Information about joining or starting a support group in your area for concerned relatives and friends.

- Suggestions for addressing any of the day-to-day caregiving issues you have been facing, or referrals to other organizations that can help.
- How to obtain newsletters, periodicals, or book lists that can help you be more informed and more effective in assisting your loved one.
- How to join this organization or support it with volunteer time or fundraising assistance.
- Phone numbers and addresses of patients and families you can contact to exchange caregiving ideas or answer specialized questions.

Please be patient and persistent with these organizations. Most of them are nonprofit groups and many are understaffed. However, they often have meant the difference between a family member being isolated and ineffective, or successfully becoming well informed and useful.

ACQUIRED IMMUNE DEFICIENCY SYNDROME (AIDS)

National AIDS Hotline	800-342-AIDS
Computerized AIDS Information Network	213-854-3006
National Association of People with AIDS	202-429-2856
AIDS National Directory and Crisis Line	800-221-7044
American Foundation for AIDS Research	212-333-3118
Families Who Care	213-498-6366
Minority AIDS Project	213-936-4949

AGING (GENERAL RESOURCES)

National Association of Area Agencies on Aging	800-424-9126
American Association of Retired Persons	800-424-2277
National Council on the Aging	800-424-9046
National Support Center for Families of the Aging	215-544-5933
Children of Aging Parents	215-945-6900
The Family Survival Project (California)	800-445-8106

ALCOHOLISM
Alcoholics Anonymous   212-686-1100
Al-Anon Family Group Headquarters   212-302-7240
National Association for Children of Alcoholics 714-499-3889
National Council on Alcoholism   212-206-6770
National Referral Service of Doctor's Hospital 800-252-6465

ALZHEIMER'S
Alzheimer's Disease and Related Disorders
Association   800-621-0379
                                                 or if calling
                                                 from Illinois
                                                 800-572-6037

AMPUTATION
Amputee Service Association   312-274-2044
National Amputation Foundation   718-767-8400
Families with Amputee Children   213-828-4009

AMYOTROPHIC LATERAL SCLEROSIS (ALS) (Lou
Gehrig's Disease)
ALS Association   212-679-4016

ARTHRITIS
The Arthritis Foundation   404-872-7100
The American Juvenile Arthritis Foundation 404-872-7100

ARTHOROGRYPOSIS
Arthorogryposis Information   209-533-1468

ASBESTOS
Asbestos Victims of America   408-476-3646

ASTHMA
Asthmatic Children's Foundation   914-762-2110
National Jewish Center for Immunology
and Respiratory Medicine   800-222-LUNG

Parents of Asthmatic Kids   617-272-2866
American Lung Association   212-315-8700
                                                   212-599-8200

ATAXIA
National Ataxia Foundation   612-473-7666
Charcot-Marie-Tooth International   416-937-3851

AUTISM
Autism Services Center   304-525-8014
National Society for Children and Adults
  with Autism   202-685-3440

BALANCE DISORDERS
Dizziness and Balance Disorders Association 503-229-7705

BIRTH DEFECTS
Association of Birth Defect Children   305-859-1221
March of Dimes Birth Defects Foundation   914-428-7100
(Also See Individual Birth Defect Names)

BLINDNESS OR VISUAL IMPAIRMENT
American Council of the Blind   800-424-8666
American Foundation for the Blind   212-620-2000
Council of Citizens with Low Vision   616-381-9566
The National Association for Parents of the
  Visually Impaired   512-459-6651
National Association for Visually Handicapped 212-889-3141
National Federation of the Blind   301-659-9314
Parents and Cataract Kids   215-293-1917
Retinitis Pigmentosa (RP) Foundation   800-638-2300
                                                   or in Maryland
                                                   301-225-9400

BLOOD DISORDERS
National Rare Blood Club   212-243-8037
(Also See Leukemia, Cooley's Anemia, Hemochromatosis,
  Hemophilia, and Sickle Cell Anemia)

BRAIN TUMOR
Association for Brain Tumor Research   312-286-5571
Friends of Brain Tumor Research   415-563-0466

BREAST CANCER
ENCORE Program   212-614-2827
Y-ME Breast Cancer Support   800-221-2141
Self-Help and Rap Experience (SHARE)   212-877-0333

BURNS
National Burn Victim Foundation   201-731-3112
The Phoenix Society—The National Organization for
Burn Victims and Their Families   215-946-4788

CANCER
American Cancer Society   800-227-2345
National Cancer Information Service   800-4-CANCER
or in Colorado   800-525-3777
Cancer Counseling Hotline for Patients
and Families   800-352-7422
Cansurmount   303-758-2030
Make Today Count   314-348-1619
We Can Do!   818-357-7517
Candlelighters Childhood Cancer Foundation   202-659-5136
Cancer Care, Inc.   212-221-3300
Cancer Control Society (Alternative Therapies)213-663-7801
International Association of Cancer Victims
and Friends (Alternative Therapies)   213-822-5032
Leukemia Society of America   800-284-4271
National Leukemia Association   516-741-1190

CELIAC SPRUE (Gluten Intolerance and Other Digestive
Disorders)
American Celiac Society   201-432-2986
Gluten Intolerance Group of North America   206-325-6980
Celiac Sprue Association   515-270-9689
National Celiac Sprue Society   617-651-5230

CEREBRAL PALSY
United Cerebral Palsy   800-872-5827
                                           800-842-1266

CHRONIC FATIGUE/EPSTEIN-BARR VIRUS
National Chronic Epstein-Barr Virus Syndrome
  Association requests written correspondence only
PO Box 230108, Portland, OR 97223
Chronic Fatigue and Immune Dysfunction
  Syndrome Association   704-362-2343

CHRONIC PAIN
American Chronic Pain Association   412-856-9676
National Chronic Pain Outreach Association 301-652-4948

COCKAYNE SYNDROME
Share and Care   516-829-6768
                                           516-825-2284

COMA
Coma Recovery Association   516-228-9164

COOLEY'S ANEMIA
Cooley's Anemia Foundation   800-221-3571

CORNELIA DELANGE SYNDROME
Cornelia DeLange Syndrome Foundation   800-223-8355

CYSTIC FIBROSIS (CF)
Cystic Fibrosis Foundation   800-FIGHT-CF
International Cystic Fibrosis Association   216-271-1100

CYSTINOSIS
Cystinosis Foundation   415-834-7897

DEAFNESS AND HEARING IMPAIRMENT
National Association for Hearing and
  Speech Action Line   800-638-8255
Better Hearing Institute   800-EAR-WELL
Children of Deaf Adults   805-682-0997
Alexander Graham Bell Association for the
  Deaf—International Parents Organization 202-337-5220
National Hearing Aid Society   800-521-5247
American Society for Deaf Children   301-585-5400
National Information Center on Deafness 202-651-5109

DIABETES
American Diabetes Association   800-232-3472
                                         or in Virginia
                                          703-549-1500
Juvenile Diabetes Foundation International 800-223-1138
                                          800-JDF-CURE

DISABILITIES (GENERAL RESOURCES)
Pilot Parents Program   402-346-5220
Association for Persons with Severe Handicaps 206-523-8446
Clearinghouse on the Handicapped   202-732-1245
Disabled American Veterans   606-441-7300
Handicapped Organized Women   704-376-4735
International Center for the Disabled   212-679-0100
National Association of the Physically
  Handicapped   603-424-3676
National Easter Seal Society   312-243-8400
National Information Center for Handicapped
  Children and Youth   703-522-3332
National Organization on Disability   202-293-5960
Promote Real Independence for the Disabled
  and Elderly (PRIDE)   203-445-1448
Parentele   317-259-1654
Parents Helping Parents   408-272-4774
Siblings for Significant Change   212-420-0776
Sibling Information Network   203-486-4034
National Clearinghouse for Disabled Infants 800-922-9234

DOWN'S SYNDROME
National Association for Down's Syndrome	312-325-9112
National Down's Syndrome Congress	312-823-7550
National Down's Syndrome Society	800-221-4602
Association for Retarded Citizens	800-433-5255
Down's Syndrome International	913-299-0815

DRUG ABUSE
Cocaine Hot-Line	800-COCAINE
Drug-Anon Focus	718-361-2169
Families Anonymous	818-989-7841
Narconon	213-466-8413
Narcotics Anonymous	818-780-3951
National Parents' Resource Institute for Drug Education (PRIDE)	800-241-7946

DYSAUTONOMIA
The Dysautonomia Foundation	212-889-5222

DYSLEXIA
The Orton Dyslexia Society	800-ABCD-123
	301-296-0232

DYSMOTILITY
Chronic Dysmotility Support	609-829-0377

DYSTONIA
Dystonia Medical Research Foundation	213-272-9880

DYSTROPHIC EPIDERMOLYSIS BULLOSA
Dystrophic Epidermolysis Bullosa Research Association of America	718-774-8700

EATING DISORDERS
American Anorexia/Bulimia Association	201-836-1800
Bulima Anorexia Self-Help (BASH)	800-BASH-STL
	314-768-3838

National Anorexic Aid Society   614-436-1112
National Association of Anorexia Nervosa
      and Associated Disorders   312-831-3438
Overeaters Anonymous   213-320-7941

ECTODERMAL DYSPLASIAS
National Foundation for Ectodermal Dysplasias 616-566-2020

EHLERS DANLOS SYNDROME
Ehlers Danlos National Foundation   313-282-0180

EMPHYSEMA
Emphysema Anonymous   813-391-9977
Lung Line Information Service   800-222-LUNG
                                                       or in Colorado
                                                       303-355-LUNG

EPILEPSY
Epilepsy Concern Service Center   305-586-4805
Epilepsy Foundation of America   301-459-3700
Epilepsy Information Line   800-332-1000

FANCONI ANEMIA
Fanconi Anemia Support Group   503-686-7803

FRAGILE X SYNDROME
Fragile X Foundation   800-835-2246
                                                       Extension 58
National Fragile X Support Group   609-452-1375

FREEMAN-SHELDON SYNDROME
Freeman-Sheldon Parent Support Group   801-298-3149

FRIEDREICH'S ATAXIA
Friedreich's Ataxia Group in America   415-655-0833

GAUCHER'S DISEASE
Gaucher's Disease Registry   714-532-2212
National Gaucher Foundation   202-393-2777

GENETIC DISEASES (GENERAL GROUPS)
Alliance of Genetic Support Groups   202-625-7853
National Foundation for Jewish Genetic
  Diseases   212-682-5550
National Genetics Foundation   212-586-5800
National Maternal and Child Health
  Clearinghouse   202-625-8410

GLYCOGEN STORAGE DISEASE
The Association for Glycogen Storage Disease 319-785-6038

GUILLAIN-BARRE SYNDROME
Guillain-Barre Syndrome Support Group
  International   215-649-7837

HEADACHE
National Migraine Foundation   312-878-7715

HEAD INJURY
National Head Injury Foundation   617-879-7473

HEART DISEASE OR SURGERY
American Heart Association   214-750-5300
The Coronary Club, Inc.   216-292-7120
Heartlife, Inc.   800-241-6993
Heartmates Support Groups
  Written correspondence only.
  PO Box 16202, Minneapolis, MN 55416
The Mended Hearts, Inc. Visitor Program   214-750-5442
International Bundle Branch Block Association 213-670-9132
Intraventricular Hemorrhage Parents   305-232-0381

HEMOCHROMATOSIS
The Hemochromatosis Research Foundation 518-489-0972
Iron Overload Diseases Association 305-659-5616

HEMOPHILIA
The National Hemophilia Foundation 212-219-8180

HEREDITARY HEMORRHAGIC TELANGIECTASIA
Hereditary Hemorrhagic Telangiectasia
Foundation 413-259-1515

HERPES
Herpes Resource Center 800-227-8922

HIGH-RISK INFANTS
Parent Care 801-581-5323

HOSPICE REFERRAL NETWORKS
The National Hospice Organization 703-243-5900
Foundation for Hospice and Home Care 202-547-6586
National Institute for Jewish Hospice 800-446-4448
or in California
213-HOSPICE
Children's Hospice International 703-684-0330

HUNTINGTON'S DISEASE
Huntington's Disease Society of America 212-242-1968
800-345-HDSA

HYDROCEPHALUS
National Hydrocephalus Foundation 815-467-6548
Hydrocephalus Parent Support Group 619-726-0507
Guardians of Hydrocephalus Research
Foundation 718-743-GHRF

HYPERTENSION OR HIGH BLOOD PRESSURE
High Blood Pressure Information Center 301-496-1809

HYPOGLYCEMIA
National Hypoglycemia Association   201-670-1189
Adrena Metabolic Research Society   518-272-7154

HYSTERECTOMY
Hysterectomy Education Resources and Services
Foundation (HERS)   215-667-7757

ICHTHYOSIS
The National Ichthyosis Foundation   415-591-1653

ILEITIS AND COLITIS
Ileitis and Colitis Education Foundation   312-562-0424
National Foundation for Ileitis and Colitis 212-685-3440

IMMUNE DEFICIENCY DISEASES
Immune Deficiency Foundation   301-461-3127 East
                                         714-521-4979 West
                                         513-890-3400 Cent.
                                         918-438-4840 Sth.

INCONTINENCE (BLADDER CONTROL PROBLEMS)
Help for Incontinent People (HIP), Inc.   803-585-8789
The Simon Foundation   800-23SIMON
                                           312-864-3913

INTERSTITIAL CYSTITIS
The Interstitial Cystitis Foundation   213-820-4631

KIDNEY DISEASE
National Kidney Foundation   212-889-2210
The Kidney Transplant/Dialysis Association 617-267-3747
Polycystic Kidney Research Foundation   816-421-1869

LARYNGECTOMY
International Association of Laryngectomies 212-599-3600
                                           800-227-2345

LAURENCE-MOON-BIEDL SYNDROME
Laurence-Moon-Biedl (LMBS) Network   301-863-5658

LEUKEMIA (See Cancer)

LEUKODYSTROPHY
United Leukodystrophy Foundation   815-895-3211

LIFE-SUPPORT TECHNOLOGY, DEPENDENCE ON
Care for Life, Inc.   312-880-4630
Sick Kids Need Involved People (SKIP)   301-647-0164

LIFE-THREATENING ILLNESSES
Make Today Count, Inc.   314-348-1619
The Center for Attitudinal Healing   415-435-5022
Make-A-Wish Foundation of America   602-234-0960
Sunshine Foundation   215-335-2622

LIVER DISEASE
American Liver Foundation   201-857-2626
                                         800-223-0179
The Children's Liver Foundation   201-761-1111

LIVING WILLS AND ORGAN DONATION
Concern for Dying   212-246-6962
The Living Bank   713-528-2971
                                         800-528-2971

LOWE'S SYNDROME
Lowe's Syndrome Association   317-743-3634

LUNG CONDITIONS
American Lung Association   212-315-8700
Brown Lung Association   803-269-8048
The Lung Line Information Service   800-222-LUNG
                                         or in Colorado
                                         303-355-LUNG

LUPUS ERYTHEMATOSUS
The American Lupus Society 213-373-1335
The Lupus Foundation of America 800-558-0121
Lupus Erythematosus (LE) Support Club 803-886-6965
National Lupus Erythematosus Foundation 818-885-8787

LYMPHEDEMA AND PHLEBITIS
National Lymphatic and Venous Foundation 617-784-4104

MALIGNANT HYPERTHERMIA
Malignant Hyperthermia Association of
the U.S. 203-655-3007

MANIC DEPRESSION (See Mental Illness)

MAPLE SYRUP URINE DISEASE
(Maple Syrup Urine Disease Parent
Support Group 219-862-2992

MARFAN SYNDROME
National Marfan Syndrome 516-883-8712

MENKE'S SYNDROME
Corporation for Menke's Disease 219-436-0137

MENTAL ILLNESS
The National Alliance for the Mentally Ill 703-524-7600
National Sibling Network 612-822-1714
Reclamation, Inc. 512-824-8618
On Our Own, Inc. 301-488-4480
National Depressive and Manic Depressive
Association 312-446-9009
National Mental Health Association 703-684-7722
Depressives Anonymous 212-689-2600
Neurotics Anonymous International Liaison 202-232-0414

MOEBIUS SYNDROME
Association for Congenital Facial Paralysis 219-322-3389

MUCOPOLYSACCHARIDOSIS (MPS)
National MPS Society   516-931-6338
Children's Association for Research on MPS 914-425-0639

MULTIPLE SCLEROSIS (MS)
National Multiple Sclerosis Society   212-986-3240

MUSCULAR DYSTROPHY
Muscular Dystrophy Association   212-586-0808

MYASTHENIA GRAVIS
Myasthenia Gravis Foundation   914-328-1717

MYOCLONUS
Myoclonus Families United   718-252-2133
National Myoclonus Foundation   212-758-5656

NARCOLEPSY
American Narcolepsy Association   415-591-7979
Narcolepsy and Cataplexy Foundation
   of America   212-628-6315

NEUROFIBROMATOSIS
The National Neurofibromatosis Foundation 212-460-8980
                                              800-323-7938

ORGANIC ACIDEMIA
Organic Acidemia Association   913-422-7080

OSTEOGENESIS IMPERFECTA
Osteogenesis Imperfecta Foundation, Inc.   516-325-8992

OSTEOPOROSIS
National Osteoporosis Foundation   202-223-2226

OSTOMY
United Ostomy Association   213-413-5510

PAGET'S DISEASE
The Paget's Disease Foundation, Inc.   718-596-1043

PARALYSIS AND PARAPLEGIA
Paralyzed Veterans of America   202-USA-1300
Spinal Cord Injury Hotline   800-526-3456
Spinal Cord Society   218-739-5252
National Spinal Cord Injury Association   617-964-0521
                                            800-962-9629

PARKINSON'S DISEASE
American Parkinson's Disease Association 800-223-APDA
                                          or in New York
                                          212-732-9550
National Parkinson's Foundation   800-327-4545
                                          or in Florida
                                          800-433-7022
Parkinson's Disease Foundation   212-923-0470
Parkinson's Education Program   800-344-7872
                                          or in Calif.
                                          714-640-0218
Parkinson's Support Group of America   301-937-1545
United Parkinson Foundation   312-664-2344

PERTUSSIS VACCINE, (CHILDREN AFFECTED BY)
Dissatisfied Parents Together   703-938-DPT3

PHENYLKETONURIA (PKU)
PKU Parents   415-457-4632

PHLEBITIS (See Lymphedema)

POST-POLIO
International Polio Network 314-361-0475
United Post-Polio Survivors 312-784-6332
Post-Polio League for Information
and Outreach 703-273-8171

PRADER-WILLI SYNDROME
Prader-Willi Syndrome Association 612-933-0113

PROGERIA
Progeria International Registry 718-494-5230

PRUNE BELLY SYNDROME
Prune Belly Syndrome Network 602-838-9006

PSORIASIS
National Psoriasis Foundation 503-297-1545

RADIATION VICTIMS AND WEAPONS TESTING EXPOSURE
National Association of Radiation Survivors 415-654-0100

RARE DISORDERS
The National Organization for Rare Disorders 203-746-6518

REFLEX SYMPATHETIC DYSTROPHY (RSDS)
Reflex Sympathetic Dystrophy Syndrome
Association 609-428-6980

REHABILITATION SERVICES
National Rehabilitation Association 703-836-0850
Rehabilitation International USA 212-620-4040

RETARDATION
Association for Retarded Citizens 817-640-0204
800-433-5255
Mental Retardation Association of America 801-328-1575

Siblings of the Mentally Retarded (SIBS)   806-358-1681
Association for Children with Retarded
  Mental Development (ACRMD)   212-741-0100
People First International   503-362-0336
Special Olympics   202-331-1346

RETINITIS PIGMENTOSA (See Blindness and Visual Impairment)

RETT'S SYNDROME
  International Rett's Syndrome Association   301-248-7031

REYE'S SYNDROME
  National Reye's Syndrome Foundation   800-233-7393
                                         419-636-2679

RUBINSTEIN-TAYBI SYNDROME
  Rubinstein-Taybi Parent Contact Group   913-282-6237

SCHIZOPHRENIA (See Mental Illness)

SCLERODERMA
  United Scleroderma Foundation, Inc.   800-722-HOPE
                                         or in California
                                         408-728-2202

SCOLIOSIS
  The National Scoliosis Foundation   617-489-0888
  Scoliosis Association, Inc.   919-846-2639

SICKLE CELL DISEASE
  National Association for Sickle Cell Disease 213-936-7205
                                         800-421-8453
  Sickle Cell Self-Help Association   213-936-7205

SPINA BIFIDA
Spina Bifida Association of America   800-621-3141
301-770-7222

SPINAL CORD INJURIES
National Spinal Cord Injury Association   800-962-9629
617-964-0521
Spinal Cord Society   218-739-5252
Spinal Cord Injury Hotline   800-526-3456
Neurological Recovery Foundation   800-624-1698
Paralyzed Veterans of America   202-USA-1300

SPINAL MUSCULAR ATROPHY
Families of Spinal Muscular Atrophy   312-432-5551

STROKE
American Heart Association   214-373-6300
National Stroke Association   303-762-9922

TAY-SACHS DISEASE
National Tay-Sachs and Allied Diseases
Association   617-964-5508
Tay-Sachs Prevention Program   617-642-0175

THROMBOCYTOPENIA
Thrombocytopenia-Absent Radius (TAR)
Syndrome Association   609-927-0418

TINNITUS
American Tinnitus Association   800-547-9755
extension 5
503-248-9985
Hearing and Tinnitus Help Association   215-852-3475

TOURETTE SYNDROME
Tourette Syndrome Association   800-237-0717
718-224-2999

TOXOPLASMOSIS
Toxoplasmosis Foundation   617-632-7783

TRISOMY
Support Organization for Trisomy (SOFT)   801-569-1609

TUBEROUS SCLEROSIS
National Tuberous Sclerosis Association   312-668-0787
Tuberous Sclerosis Association of America 800-446-1211
     617-947-8893

TURNER SYNDROME
Turner Syndrome Society   416-736-5023

VENEREAL DISEASE
V.D. Hotline (Confidential Referrals)   800-227-8922

VETERANS (GENERAL RESOURCES)
Veteran's Administration   202-393-4120
Disabled American Veterans   606-441-7300
Paralyzed Veterans of America   202-USA-1300
National Veterans Outreach Programs   512-223-4088
Vietnam Veterans Agent Orange Victims 203-323-7478
National Association of Radiation Survivors 415-654-0100

WILLIAMS SYNDROME
Williams Syndrome Association   619-695-3139
     713-376-7072

WILSON'S DISEASE
Wilson's Disease Association   703-636-3014

These phone numbers were accurate as of the writing of this book. Thanks are given to the American Hospital Association and the Illinois Self-Help Center for their assistance in gathering much of this information. If you know of any additions or corrections, please write Dr. Felder at Box 451, Santa Monica, California 90406.

APPENDIX C

How to Locate or Start a Specialized Support Group

Most people think "Support Group" means "Intensive Therapy," but that's incorrect.

There are thousands of Support Groups for family members and friends of those who are ailing or disabled. At these weekly or monthly sessions, you might find:

- Expert speakers with the latest information on medications, treatment programs, rehabilitation strategies, or coping skills.
- Information exchanges where participants share their positive and negative assessments of various local resources and help you select the best facilities for helping a loved one.
- Success stories of people who have overcome the same hurdles you and your family are facing.
- Creative brainstorming for resolving the day-to-day challenges of helping an ailing or disabled loved one.
- Emotional support for you or for anyone you bring to the support group.

264

- Networking and connections so that you will always have greater access to the answers and resources you need to come through for your family member or friend.

Many people are reluctant to make that first phone call or attend that first support group meeting. Some are afraid to talk to strangers about something as private as the physical or mental illness of a loved one. Others are afraid they will be challenged or confronted. But this is *not* what support groups are about. Many individuals incorrectly believe that only people who are weak or who don't know how to help themselves look to a group for support.

I also was reluctant to attend my first support group and ask for assistance. As a health professional, I'm supposed to have answers but in fact I had mostly unanswered questions. It wasn't until I attended some meetings that I discovered many of the valuable resources and solutions that are available in my community. I began to see the decision to join a support group as a sign of strength, not of weakness.

If you are like most people, you probably have said to yourself, "I'm not the kind of person who goes to a support group. I like to handle things by myself."

While that kind of independence and self-reliance is appropriate in many areas of life, it can be dangerously short sighted when it comes to caring for a loved one with a complicated ailment. Unless you break out of your isolation and start connecting with people who can increase your effectiveness as a caregiver, you will be depriving your loved one of valuable information and resources that can help improve his or her quality of life.

Finding a Group Nearby

As I've begun to research this rapidly growing phenomenon of support groups, I've been amazed at how many there are and how many specialized local meetings have been initiated in the past few years. In addition to the thousands of local family support organizations, there are now a number of referral services and self-help clearinghouses that you can call immediately to find the group closest to you.

To find the local support group or organization that exists for patients and loved ones dealing with a specific ailment or group of ailments, here are some steps you can take:

1) Look in Apendix B. Find the organization that sounds closest to your loved one's illness or disability. Call them and ask for suggestions on where you can find a nearby group or a referral who might be able to help find one.

2) If your loved one has a rare illness, you can call the National Organization for Rare Disorders, located in Connecticut, at 1-203-746-6518. They have a networking program to help you find other families and groups that are dealing with the same disorder.

3) You can call a self-help clearinghouse to find out if they know of any existing groups that might have answers and support for many of your pressing issues. Here are the phone numbers of the national and local self-help clearinghouses:

The National Self-Help Clearinghouse
City University of New York
Room 1227
33 West 42nd Street
New York, NY 10036   (212) 840-1259

The National Self-Help Clearinghouse
New Jersey Office   (201) 625-7101

The National Self-Help Center
Illinois Office   If in Illinois, dial (800) 322-MASH
If calling from out of state, dial (312) 328-0470

The Self-Help Clearinghouse
California Office   If in California, dial (800)222-5465
If calling from out of state, dial (213) 825-1799

Self-Help Clearinghouses for Local States and Provinces:

	If calling from in that state:	If calling from out of state:
California	(800) 222-5465	(213) 825-1799
	(800) 445-8106	
Connecticut	(800) 842-1501	(203) 789-7645
Illinois	(800) 322-MASH	(312) 328-0470
Kansas	(316) 686-1205	(316) 686-1205
Massachusetts	(413) 545-2313	(413) 545-2313
Michigan	(800) 752-5858	(517) 484-7373
Minnesota	(612) 642-4060	(612) 642-4060
Missouri West	(816) 361-5007	(816) 361-5007
Missouri East	(314) 371-6500	(314) 371-6500
Nebraska	(402) 476-9668	(402) 476-9668
New Jersey	(800) FOR-MASH	(201) 625-9565
New York City	(212) 840-1259	(212) 840-1259
New York–Upstate	(518) 474-6293	(518) 474-6293
Ohio	(216) 762-7471	(216) 762-7471
Oregon and Washington	(503) 222-5555	(503) 222-5555
Pennsylvania	(609) 663-3422	(609) 663-3422
	(412) 247-5400	(412) 247-5400
	(717) 961-1234	(717) 961-1234
South Carolina	(803) 791-9227	(803) 791-9227
Tennessee	(615) 588-9747	(615) 588-9747
Texas	(214) 871-2420	(214) 871-2420
Vermont	(800) 554-5030	(800) 229-5724
Virginia and District of Columbia	(703) 536-4100	(703) 536-4100
Wisconsin	(414) 933-0428	(414) 933-0428
Alberta	(403) 262-1117	
British Columbia	(604) 721-8036	
Ontario	(416) 978-3270	
Quebec	(514) 731-8059	
Saskatchewan	(306) 652-7817	

If none of these clearinghouses can locate a support group, you have a few additional options to consider:

1) Call your local hospitals, health departments, and social service agencies to see if they know of any support groups that might not be listed with the regional or national clearinghouses.
2) Call and ask for a referral from the National Health Information Clearinghouse for the United States (1-800-336-4797) or the Canadian Network for Disease Information (1-416-937-3851).
3) Don't give up! If you are unable to find a support group in your area, or if you don't like the people or approach taken by the group that exists nearby, you can always start your own.

Most of the thousands of support groups that exist today were started not too long ago by someone like yourself who said, "There's got to be other people who are working on similar issues. I'm going to put together a group of family members and others who can pool their knowledge and contacts so we each can make progress caring for those we love."

Putting Together Your Own Group

If you decide to organize your own support group of people who can meet to discuss common issues and solutions, here are some suggestions that have worked for others:

1) Begin by contacting several local doctors, nurses, social workers and other professionals who've worked with people who have your loved one's ailment or disability. Ask them to publicize your meetings to patients, loved ones, colleagues, and local organizations.

2) Call the national Self-Help Clearinghouses and ask them for advice, contacts, and printed guidelines on starting a self-help group. Also, make sure they and your local state clearinghouse know of your new support group so they can refer people to your meetings.

3) At each meeting, make sure there is time alloted for both personal and emotional issues and for information and resource questions. While some group members prefer one or the other, providing *both* types of support means that everyone in attendance will benefit from each meeting.

Here are some ideas for conducting your meetings:

1) Set up ground rules for the group meetings that insure the following essentials:
   a) Respect for each other's diverse experiences, and an agreement that there is no one "right way."
   b) Good listening skills and a willingness to let each person have a chance to speak, either to the group as a whole or in one-on-one conversations.
   c) Patience for the fact that everyone moves through denial or discouragement at their own individual pace.
   d) An effort to allow each participant to have specific questions addressed, either in the structured meeting itself or in follow-up conversations.

2) Bring in outside speakers, experts, health-care professionals, and advocates for patients' rights, but make sure the focus of each group meeting is on participants' needs and concerns.

3) Spread the responsibilities for organizing group meetings to several individuals. This helps prevent you from burning out, and it makes the group stronger and more enduring when several individuals feel personally involved in leadership roles.

Some additional books and pamphlets that can help you start a new support group or improve an existing support group are:

"Guides for Caregiver Support Groups." This is a ten-page booklet that analyzes fifteen readily obtainable manuals and guides on how to start or improve a support group. Send $2.00 to The National Council on the Aging, 600 Maryland Avenue SW, West Wing 100, Washington, DC 20024. Ask for Order #2011.

Idea Book on Caregiver Support Groups, by Lorraine Lidoff and Patricia Harris. An excellent compilation of resources, networking, and practical suggestions for starting or improving a support group. Send $5.00 plus $1.50 postage and handling to The National Council on the Aging, 600 Maryland Avenue SW, West Wing 100, Washington, DC 20024. Ask for Order #2010.

"How to Organize a Self-Help Group." This is a guide for starting a successful group. Send $6.00 to the National Self-Help Clearinghouse, 33 West 42nd Street, New York, NY 10036.

Starting a Self-Help Group for Caregivers of the Elderly, by Louise Fradkin, Mirca Liberti, and Jacob Stone. A more detailed book on caregiving skills and support. Send $12.00 to The Children of Aging Parents, 2761 Trenton Road, Levittown, PA 19056.

Alzheimer's Family Support Groups: A Manual for Group Facilitators, by William Middleton. This is a detailed manual on how to set up a group, get referrals, understand the illness, conduct group sessions, and maintin group involvement. This manual was written for Alzheimer's support groups but could be used for other ailments as well. Send $10.00 to The Sun Coast Gerontology Center, University of South Florida Medical Center, 12901 North 30th Street, Box 50, Tampa, FL 33612.

"Family Seminars for Caregiving: A Facilitator's Guidebook." Published by The University of Washington Press, Seattle, WA.

"Leading Self-Help Groups," by Lucretia Mallory. A seventy-two-page booklet available from the Family Service Association of America, New York, NY.

Index

About the Author

Leonard Felder has a Ph.D. in psychology and counsels individuals and groups in West Los Angeles. His five books include A FRESH START (Signet) and the bestseller MAKING PEACE WITH YOUR PARENTS, which won the 1985 Book of the Year Award from *Medical Self-Care Magazine.* Dr. Felder's books have been translated into nine languages and have sold over 650,000 copies.

A frequent talk-show guest and keynote speaker nationwide, he has appeared on over 150 radio and television programs in the past five years. He also has written on family and health issues for *The Los Angeles Times Syndicate* and for 30 magazines, including *Redbook, Parents, New Woman, Glamour, Men's Health, The Rotarian, Golden Years, Mature Outlook, Success, Sylvia Porter's Personal Finance, Writer's Digest, Whole Life Monthly, The Aging Connection,* and *American Health.*

Originally from Detroit, Michigan, he lived in Ohio, Pennsylvania, and New York City before moving to Santa Monica, California, in 1978. Active in several nonprofit organizations, he recently received the Distinguished Merit Citation of the National Conference of Christians and Jews for his work on combatting racism, sexism, and religious prejudice.

He currently teaches at UCLA Extension in Los Angeles and conducts workshops on family coping skills nationwide.

Leonard Felder, Ph.D., is a widely-requested keynote speaker and seminar leader nationwide on:

- resolving family tensions
- preventing caregiver burnout
- what to say and how to listen to someone who's ill
- staying healthy during stressful times

For further information regarding personal appearances, please write to: Dr. Leonard Felder, Box 451, Santa Monica, CA 90406.